P9-DTA-325

Remediating Reading Disabilities

Simple Things That Work

Remediating Reading Disabilities

Simple Things That Work

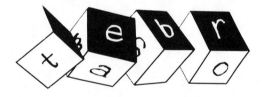

Jimmie E. Cook
Director of Clinical Services
Edinboro State College

and

Elsie C. Earlley
Professor Emeritus,
Special Education
Edinboro State College

Aspen Systems Corporation
Germantown, Maryland
London, England
1979

Library of Congress Cataloging in Publication Data

Cook, Jimmie.
Remediating reading disabilities.

Includes index.
1. Reading—Remedial teaching. 2. Reading disability.
I. Earlley, Elsie, joint author. II. Title.
LB1050.5.0663   428'.4'2   79-20412
ISBN 0-89443-154-4

Copyright © 1979 by Aspen Systems Corporation

All rights reserved. This book, or parts thereof, may not be
reproduced in any form or by any means, electronic or
mechanical, including photocopy, recording, or any
information storage and retrieval system now known or
to be invented, without written permission from the
publisher, except in the case of brief quotations embodied
in critical articles or reviews. For information, address
Aspen Systems Corporation, 20010 Century Boulevard,
Germantown, Maryland 20767

Library of Congress Catalog Card Number: 79-20412
ISBN: 0-89443-154-4

Printed in the United States of America
2 3 4 5

DEDICATION

To our children:

    Jason and Jordan Cook
    Laura Farnham
    Jack Culbertson
    Cathryn Snyder

*who have provided us with joy
and celebration.*

Contents

Contents

Preface

It has been our experience that teachers are given much advice on the theoretical aspects of teaching reading but offered little assistance on the practical applications of that theory. It seems that the practical side must appear as some divine revelation. To remedy this situation, the goals of this book are as follows:

1. To simplify the theoretical constructs.
2. To provide practical activities for the various learning modalities.
3. To serve as an inexhaustible source of activities.

We sincerely hope that we have met our goals and that you, and especially the children, benefit from our efforts.

The activities in this book have been used by us for more years than we care to count, and thousands of children through our teaching and the teaching of our students have helped us to refine and polish the materials herein. We hope these activities make your burden somewhat easier. Since both of us have been elementary and secondary classroom teachers, we know and understand the tremendous physical, intellectual, and emotional energy spent in teaching. To us, it has always seemed the most demanding, arduous, and important task of all.

Acknowledgements

We wish to acknowledge the many children and teachers who have made this book possible. The hours spent in proofreading by Mary Anne Hoffman Oaks and Laura Finamore are gratefully acknowledged, and their editorial comments greatly appreciated. We wish to express our gratitude to R. Curtis Whitesel, Acquisitions Editor for Aspen Systems Corporation, for his enthusiasm and encouragement. We thank Darlene Como, Editorial Assistant at Aspen Systems Corporation, for keeping the records straight and the monumental efforts of Margot Raphael, Production Editor, for her courtesy and friendly assistance. Finally, we express admiration and reverence for Laura Swift, our typist par excellence, for her good humor and dedication.

Much Ado about Something/Nothing?

1

There's nothing more you can do. Put him in a home. The day after that counsel, the mother . . . waited until her husband had left for work, took his pistol from the bedroom closet shelf, loaded it, and called her three young children into the living room. She lined them up in front of the fire-place . . . and prepared to kill each of them and then herself.[1]

The above is not fiction. It is one of the many true horror stories far more violent than anything seen on television. The child who was the cause of the desperate move by the mother was only six years old. The school had labeled the lad incorrigible, washed its hands of him, and recommended a reformatory. His parents were near divorce, and as is typical of families with learning disabled children, interpersonal relationships were in shambles.

The learning disabled child is often characterized as coming from a disorganized home. We believe that the disorganization is caused by the "different child" who does not fit in. Parents, not being teachers, simply do not know how to handle such disparate behavior. We further believe that this behavior is exacerbated by failure in the school setting. One of the most painful experiences for the learning disabled child is seeing everyone else read while he is ostracized for his reading failure.

We have seen the aberrant behavior and the confused home become things of the past when the child becomes successful in the school

---

1. Brutten, Richardson, and Mangel, p. 12.

setting—successful to the extent that the child is coping. And in our experience, the coping begins when the child begins to enjoy success in reading.

Learning disabled children and their parents can be helped, and the time to do it is in the early years. A team of physicians, psychologists, and educators can alleviate the suffering of families like the one described.

The medical profession is gaining knowledge daily about the problems of learning disabilities. Therefore, parents who suspect their child of being learning disabled should seek out a qualified pediatrician and demand a very thorough examination for the child. The information gathered by the physician should be shared with psychologists and educators so that a unique program can be developed for that child.

However, our clinical experience has been a lack of cooperation between the various professions and parents. Many of the learning disabled children with whom we have worked in clinical settings have made tremendous progress under our guidance. We have devised methods and materials that work very well with these children and we want to share this information with the schools so that assistance can be continued. We have determined learning modalities and particular kinds of materials that appeal to the child, and have determined the kinds of situations within which the child can function, but to no avail. There has been resistance by parents. Although on the surface it appears strange that a parent would not permit us to share our knowledge with the school, persistent questioning has brought incredible insights.

Simply stated, the parents hold the schools responsible for their children's failures and are somehow afraid that now that the child is succeeding in our clinic, the school will become angry at its lack of success with the child and use the new information to punish the child in some fashion.

The authors know this is not true. There might be isolated incidents where this would occur, but most schools would welcome the assistance. However, realizing that many parents feel this way will aid capable administrators in overcoming this serious problem.

MUCH ADO—THE CHALLENGE

The Administrator's Role

Administrators must accept as their own responsibility any stigma that attaches to their school. Although most schools are publicly owned and financed, most of us have heard principals state, "This is my school."

Such a possessive attitude is commendable in many ways. A principal can bask in the reflected glow of any success that the school achieves. Any failure must be borne by the principal, too.

The authors suggest that learning disabilities is an area in which most administrators are failing. There are some things that can be done. A few suggestions follow.

DEVELOP A SCHOOL PHILOSOPHY. Does your school have a philosophy that includes the learning disabled? If not, then develop one. A philosophy must state that the school is concerned about the learning disabled and that plans are being implemented to assist them. PTA meetings allow you the opportunity to say, "We care."

INTERPRET THE PROGRAM FOR TEACHERS AND PARENTS. This is the most important step to be taken initially. Either the principal must do this or arrangements must be made with outside professionals to spend some time with parents and teachers explaining the problems of working with the learning disabled. Universities and colleges, local mental health units, and local chapters of the Association for Children with Learning Disabilities can provide this expertise. Further, the school district must provide in-service time for the teachers to become aware of the depth and breadth of the problems.

DETERMINE THE SCHOOL'S PHYSICAL NEEDS. Is the school's physical plant adequate? What kind of classrooms are available? Is environmental control an absolute necessity? B. P. Gearheart in his book, *Learning Disabilities: Educational Strategies* (St. Louis, Mo.: C. V. Mosby Company, 1973), presents an articulate discussion of physical plants in Chapter 10.

DELINEATE THE NATURE AND SCOPE OF THE PROGRAM. The principal will have to determine if the school staff is up to the demanding task of working with the learning disabled. Using information about the staff's strengths and weaknesses, the principal can effectively expand or limit the extent of the school's participation, and determine the gaps that must be filled by outside assistance.

PROVIDE FOR EARLY DETECTION. The administrator must take an active part in all testing done on preschoolers about to enter the school. Many of the readiness tests administered by staff can prewarn of learning failures not related to real abilities. By sagacious interpretation of test results, many learning disabled children can be isolated at the beginning and have their special needs attended to immediately.

CAREFULLY SELECT PERSONNEL. No task is more important than personnel selection. If the school is to be provided with a special staff to work with learning disabled children, what person can best fill the role? Too often a school puts a sign over a room, declaring it to be the learning disabilities classroom (which is a mistake in itself for obvious reasons) and places a teacher in charge who has no special training. Or, the school might select a teacher trained to work with the mentally retarded. We must remember that the learning disabled are not mentally retarded. Granted, many of the techniques used with the mentally retarded can be applied successfully to the learning disabled as long as the teacher realizes that the children are not retarded mentally.

Because reading is the most difficult obstacle for the learning disabled, the reading specialist and the experienced classroom teacher with clinical experience with the learning disabled are best qualified to work with these children in the beginning.

SELECT AND EVALUATE MATERIALS. The learning disabled are known for their high distractibility. Therefore, material selection assumes a most important role. Many of the teacher-made products described in the following chapters are very useful, and more items can be created by teachers alert to the needs of the learning disabled. Administrators should encourage teachers to try these materials with their children and make the teachers understand that if something does not work after a reasonable time, then other approaches must be considered. The stigma of failure must not be attached to a teacher or student who does not succeed, especially in the first few outings.

EVALUATE STUDENTS PERIODICALLY. The administrator must conduct evaluations of progress of each of these special students. Each month, the principal and faculty should sit down and share experiences, both failure and success, in a mature, productive way. The administrator must establish a rapport with the staff that will enable them to share their failures without fear of recrimination.

The Teacher's Role

The classroom teacher of the learning disabled must, because of position, bear the largest burden. The teacher's failures will far outnumber the successes. That unique person—the teacher of the learning disabled—must be mentally and emotionally able to withstand all the "slings and arrows" of which Shakespeare spoke, plus additional barbs from an uninformed public and fellow teachers.

The teacher must remain abreast of developments in dealing with learning disabilities, as well as keep long, anecdotal records on each of the children in the classroom. Every failure, as well as the few successes, must be noted. In essence, the teacher must be an open individual who is willing to place the record of failure and success before the general school public. Although that takes an incredibly strong individual, many such teachers do exist.

MUCH ADO—THE CHALLENGE CONTINUED

The Right To Be Recognized

Many learning disabled children are simply not recognized as such, and the problem is one of ignorance. Let us go back to the boy whose mother was at the point of murder.

> The boy's supercharged behavior was destroying his family. His parents were on the verge of separation. His school . . . was threatening to have him committed—at the age of six—to a reformatory, for incorrigibility.[2]

Obviously this child's behavior was extremely unusual. How could it have gone unnoticed for such a long time? Naturally, his "badness" was noticed. Did not a physician recommend incarceration? Was not the school considering a reformatory? What about his quiet moments? Did he have any? He obviously knew much of the world around him. How did he learn? Had anyone bothered to find out? Probably not. It was easier to consider "putting him away."

It is a simple fact that most children of six have not been exposed to civilization long enough to develop psychotic tendencies. Yet, without hesitation, we label psychotic, children who are different. It is an easy way out. In this way, teachers, parents, and others do not have to admit to ignorance about learning disabilities.

The Association for Children with Learning Disabilities is fighting an uphill battle to have learning disabled children recognized. Often they run into the problem of "not enough money" to study the issue, or the argument that there is no such thing as learning disabilities. This is an argument without substance. Learning disabilities do exist and will always be with us. We who work with these children have seen them grow where before they floundered.

The argument of "not enough money" deprives these children of their rights. It has been estimated that as much as nine percent of our students are learning disabled (Stewart and Olds, 1973, p. 26). That is approximately eight million of our children today—eight million who are not receiving equal treatment under the laws of this country. If there is money for public education of the overall population, then there is money for these children. Parents and teachers of the learning disabled must demand of their local, state, and national governments a fair share for their special children.

This country recognizes drug-related problems, mental retardation, corruption in politics, murder, robbery, emotional disturbance, and various other social and educational problems and attempts to deal with them. We must do no less for the very precious learning disabled children. The rewards of helping them can be put on a monetary basis if need

---

2. Brutten, Richardson, and Mangel, p. 13.

be. If they succeed, they pay more taxes. If they fail, we pay to incarcerate them. The journals are fast becoming filled with articles noting the high incidence of juvenile delinquency and learning disabilities.

Some children are able to overcome their problems without serious assistance, but, regrettably, most cannot without competent guidance and leadership. We can help these children to overcome their problems and become contributing members of our society. It is criminal not to do so, because the children have a right to be recognized.

MUCH ADO—THE CHALLENGE CONTINUED AGAIN

Characteristics of the Learning Disabled

McCarthy and McCarthy (1969, p. 8) list ten of the "most frequently cited characteristics of learning disabled children", in order of frequency cited, as follows:

1. Hyperactivity
2. Perceptual-motor impairments
3. Emotional liability
4. General orientation defects
5. Disorders of attention
6. Impulsivity
7. Disorders of memory and thinking
8. Specific learning disabilities in reading, arithmetic, writing, and spelling
9. Disorders of speech and hearing
10. Equivocal neurological signs and electroencephalographic irregularities

At one time or another, most of us have been subject to these disorders, but the experiences have been short-lived and no great damage has been done. But imagine, if you can, living with this syndrome every day, all day. The children who suffer from learning disabilities are perceptive enough to see that they are different from their classmates, yet little is done to make them understand that they are not responsible for that difference. This is where we fail these children so dramatically.

Hyperactive children cannot sit still. They are constantly jumping from their seats, pushing others, striking out, and in general creating havoc. They are almost always in trouble. Their parents and teachers long for medication that will quiet them down so that they themselves can rest.

Children with perceptual-motor impairments cannot do the things that other children their age can do. They are awkward in games that require physical prowess. They cannot play pick-up-sticks without becoming frustrated and angry. They always make the first error in any game. They cannot even erase the board for the teacher in a smooth, effortless way.

The emotional stability of the learning disabled is obviously strained. How could any of us fail constantly and not develop a poor self-concept? That the children expect they are going to fail insures failure. The pressures of everyday life manage to bring all of us to emotional peaks from time to time, yet we can reason them away and know that the pressure will ease. Not so the learning disabled. They know from day to day that life is going to be one failure after another. We would be emotionally depressed, too.

Yet, look for the moments of emotional peace. They do occur, although rarely. When the teacher sees that quietness, a teachable moment is at hand and should not be wasted. But be ever so careful—make sure that success is assured.

Learning disabled children have trouble with the concepts of time and space. Time can be lost, and walking down an aisle can produce instant confusion. The teacher must understand that timed assignments, for example, are disasters for the learning disabled. General and constant orientation defects are a part of the learning disabled child. They must be understood and accepted.

The attention span of the learning disabled runs from nil to short. Anyone who has worked with learning disabled children knows that they are unable to attend for long periods of time in the beginning. The teacher must understand this and plan lessons accordingly. Success comes in very short leaps and over long periods of time. In our clinical situations we may cover six to ten activities in an hour, with liberal breaks between each lesson, and consider ourselves quite successful for having done so. In essence, the child determines his progress and pace. The alert teacher quickly determines the uniqueness of each child and plans accordingly.

The impulsivity of the learning disabled is one of the most difficult problems. Many teachers have simply thrown up their collective hands when faced with this most disturbing aspect. It seems that the children react "out of the clear blue sky," and for no apparent reason. Quite often, there is no regret for the disturbance either. It is a serious problem, but instant punishment, corporal or otherwise, will not solve the problem, but only delay the next occurrence for a moment, or perhaps even a day. The children must learn to control their own impulsive actions, and the teacher must constantly counsel them on this.

Disorders of memory and thinking are exhibited on both the auditory and the visual planes. These children cannot recall a word or sound that was just pronounced for them. They are unable to recall even the most basic of auditory utterances. The teacher can present one visual stimulus after another, none of which are remembered by the learning disabled. Even when the slowest intellectual performer in the class manages to recall visually the performance, the learning disabled can-

7

not. This explains their inability to do auditory or visual thinking. If they cannot retain the auditory and visual stimuli, they cannot have the base so necessary for creative thinking.

In the academic areas, problems in reading, arithmetic, spelling, and writing are the obvious results of learning disabilities. These are the areas we begin to stress so early in school and in which failures predictably occur. With so many other things working against them, the learning disabled are preordained to fail initially in academics and will continue to fail unless they are identified and given special assistance.

Disorders of speech and hearing are areas that we have rarely encountered in our clinical settings. It is possible, however, that the learning disabled could have excellent auditory acuity and still not be able to hear and speak in a normal way. An audiometric test should be ordered immediately if these signs are exhibited, and a speech teacher should be consulted without hesitation.

Irregularities of electroencephalograms are rare in the learning disabled. One test after another will show normal brain waves, and therein lies the difficulty of diagnosis. These children seem normal in every way but they and others know they are not like others.

MUCH ADO—VICTORY?

It is a simple task to harangue teachers and administrators about their inabilities to work with children with reading disabilities but a bit more difficult to offer meaningful assistance without appearing pontifical. We hope to accomplish the difficult immediately.

The purpose of this book is to offer alternative approaches to teaching reading at every grade level—alternatives to traditional basal approaches. In Chapter 2 we will argue for more informal assessment of children's problems after the initial formal screening. In Chapter 3 we will advise you about the materials required and the importance of sequencing skills. In Chapters 4–9 we will deal with alternative approaches for children who are in grades kindergarten through six and who have been unsuccessful in reading. In fact, we are certain that the activities would augur well for children who are learning to read with ease. In Chapters 5, 10, and 11 we will offer numerous activities that have at one time or another sparked the reading interests of older children and adults.

We are not assuring you of victory in this difficult encounter. But we are sincere in our belief that the teacher has to be a "risk taker" when traditional approaches fail. We believe the activities in this book will be of great value to the classroom teacher or specialist in their difficult, frustrating encounter with children and their reading disabilities.

As you can see, this chapter has been neither unduly long nor difficult to understand. The remaining chapters will be more detailed, but just as easy to understand.

Before you start flipping pages to find out what the mother did to the children in the incident mentioned at the beginning of this book, we are going to tell you. We do not want you to skip one page of the chapters to follow. The mother could not go through with it—at that time. We do not know what happened later but we surmise that the child found a teacher like you who cares and went on to great success.

BIBLIOGRAPHY

BRUTTEN, MILTON; RICHARDSON, SYLVIA O.; AND MANGEL, CHARLES. *Something's Wrong with My Child.* New York: Harcourt, Brace, Jovanovich, 1973.

McCARTHY, JAMES J. AND McCARTHY, JEAN F. *Learning Disabilities.* Boston, Mass.: Allyn and Bacon, 1969.

STEWART, MARK A. AND OLDS, SALLY WENDKOS. *Raising a Hyperactive Child.* New York: Harper and Row, 1973.

2 | The Rationale

The Informal Reading Inventory (IRI), an excellent tool for informal assessment of reading strengths and weaknesses is defined by Kennedy (1974, p. 106) as follows:

> The term "informal inventory" . . . . refers to a technique for finding a student's status in all phases of reading by observing his performance on selections in basal reading texts or specially prepared paragraphs and recording the *types of errors he makes.*

THE WHEREWITHAL

By using an IRI, a teacher can be reasonably accurate in making informal assessments on children's reading strengths and weaknesses. An IRI is a relatively simple thing to prepare. Before preparing one, you should understand that you are seeking an instructional level for the child. In finding an instructional level, you will also establish an independent and a frustration level. For purposes of information, the levels are defined as follows:

Instructional Level—The level where the child misses five out of one hundred running words or his comprehension falls below 75 percent. The important aspect here is comprehension. Even though the child may miss more than 5 words in a 100-word selection, his comprehension may be total. As a rule of thumb, if the child continues to understand above the 75 percent level in spite of missing more than 5 words, you would be better off to accept as his instructional level that point where comprehension falls below 75 percent. Often errors in oral

10

reading do not interfere with understanding, and it is far better to have a child reading at a level that matches his maturity and interests in spite of a few word-calling errors.

Independent Level—The level where the child reads with complete understanding and relative ease.

Frustration Level—The level where the child makes numerous word-calling errors and understands very little of what is read. Do not try to maintain a child on this level too long. It is painful and embarrassing, and teachers must not make reading unpleasant.

In constructing an IRI, the teacher should select from the basal series that is being used within the school system. Basal readers produced by different publishers have varying levels of readability (the level of reading difficulty within a given book or chapter). Even though books from two companies have "Level Four" printed on the book, one book is invariably more difficult than the other. Therefore, if we expect a child to perform in a given book, his reading placement based on the IRI should be from the book in which he must work.

A suggested procedure for preparing an IRI is as follows:

1. If, for example, you are a fourth-grade teacher, your selections should come from basals two grades below your level, on your level, and two grades above the fourth grade. Therefore, you would prepare selections from grades 2–6. It is a good idea to make your selections from the beginning, middle, and end of a book since stories in graded books are not constant in their readability levels.

2. Type the selection of approximately 100 words on 8½ × 11 paper using a primary typewriter if possible. Double-space between each line and make certain the type is clear and distinct (see Exhibit 1). You will have questions on each selection, but they shall not appear on the child's copy.

EXHIBIT 1

Informal Reading Inventory

Student's Copy

Bobby was very upset. His mother was preparing to leave for the hospital to have a serious operation. He did not know what kind of operation she was to have but he knew it was bad because he had seen his mother cry, and father seemed very worried also.

"Why don't they tell me what's wrong," he said aloud. "I'm a big boy. I'm eight years old." He started crying, very softly at first, then his wailing became a shrill scream.

His mother rushed into his room, expecting to find the worst, but saw Bobby standing in the middle of the room, his body shaking with fear. She hugged him until he became quiet and then asked what was bothering him. He looked at her through tear-stained eyes and said, "Mommie, why do you grown-ups treat us kids like babies? I want to know what's wrong with you. Kids worry, too."

---

3. Establish a base level by giving the child a selection to read where in your best estimate the child will read without error. If an error is made, simply go lower until one is read perfectly. That is your base level. At that point, you will have the child read higher levels until the instructional level is established.

4. Tape-record the entire reading. You can then go back and mark the errors in private. Marking errors while the child is reading may be very distracting to the child and for that reason alone is not a good idea. Use of tape recordings also leaves you free to observe the child in the reading act and to make mental notes on faulty reading habits.

5. Prior to marking the teacher's copy for errors, it is a good thing to fix in your mind a consistent marking pattern and use it on every IRI you do. The following is a generally accepted marking code.

   a. / to indicate pauses or hesitations.

      The / boy / cried.

   b. ∧ for inserted word.

      little
      The ∧ boy cried.

   c. ◯ around all words pronounced for reader.

      The ⦅boy⦆ cried.

   d. X on all words or punctuation omitted.

      The boy cri̸e̸d.

   e. ‾ above all words repeated.

      The boy c̅r̅i̅e̅d̅.

   f. Phonetically reproduce the student's incorrect pronunciation of a given word.

      crid
      The boy cried.

   g. Write substituted word over correct word.

      dog
      The boy cried.

   h. If a child mispronounces a word, then corrects it, write above the word mispronounced and place a "C" above it.

      C
      dog
      The boy cried.

12

Once you have administered the IRI, it should look something like the one in Exhibit 2.

EXHIBIT 2

Informal Reading Inventory

READABILITY *5th grade*   NAME OF STUDENT ___Jim___   GRADE __5__

Teacher's Copy

Bobby was very upset. His mother was preparing to leave for the hospital to have a serious (operation.) He did not know what kind of operation she was to have but he knew it was bad because he had seen his mother cry, and father seemed very worried also.

[handwritten annotations: "bad" above "serious"; "operation" circled; "that" above "what"; "real" above "very"; "too" above "also"]

"Why don't they tell me what's wrong," he said aloud. "I'm a big boy. I'm eight years old." He started crying very softly/at first, then his wailing became a shrill scream.

[handwritten annotations: "aloud" with X mark; "wailing" above "crying"; X mark after "crying"]

His mother rushed into his room, expecting to find the worst, but saw Bobby standing in the middle of the room, his body shaking with fear. She hugged him until he became quiet and then asked what was bothering him. He looked at her through tear-stained eyes and said, "Mommie, why do you grown-ups treat us kids like babies? I want to know what's wrong with you. Kids worry, too."

[handwritten annotations: "the" above "his room"; "right" above "standing"; "now" above "to know", with "c" above]

Q. What would make a good title for this story?
A. Mother goes to the hospital.

Q. What was the boy's name?
A. Bobby

Q. Why was he upset?
A. His mother was having a bad operation.

Q. How old was Bobby?
A. Eight.

Q. Do you think parents should discuss problems with their children?
A. Yes (or no).

Q. Why?
A. Kids sometimes get afraid when something is wrong with their parents. Telling us would help us to understand.

13

ANALYZING THE RESULTS OF THE IRI

Even though Exhibit 2 shows a number of errors, there is really very little to be concerned about with this reader. There was only one repetition, and only one word was pronounced for him, which he immediately pronounced a few words later. His substitutions throughout were semantically and syntactically correct with one exception, and for the most part, no meaning change occurred. The omission of the word *aloud* did not

---

EXHIBIT 3

[*saw*] Bobby was very [X] upset. His mother was [*saw*] preparing [*ed*] to leave for the (hospital) to [*live*] have a [*has*] (serious) (operation.) He did not know what kind of (operation) she was to have but he knew [*saw*] [*as*] [*Knowed*] it was bad b[*see*]cause he had seen his mother cry, and father [*Dad*] seemed very [*see*] worried also.

"Why don't they tell me what's [*She*] wrong," [*that*] [*wring*] he said aloud [*alone*]. "I'm a big boy. I'm eight [*eighty*] years old." He started [*start*] crying [*cry*], very softly [*Soft*] at first, then his (wailing) became [*came*] a (shrill) (scream.)

His mother rushed [*rush*] into [*in*] his room, (expecting) to find the (worst) but saw [*was*] Bobby standing [*stay*] in the m[X]ddle [*of*] the room, his body shaking [*shake*] with fear [*fever*]. She hugged [*hug*] him [X]until he [X]became [*quit*] quiet and then asked what w[X]as [*ast*] bothering [*bother*] him. He looked [*look*] at her (through) tear-(stained) eyes [*eye*] and said [*sez*] [*Mom*], "Mommie, why do y[X]ou grown-ups treat us [X]kids [*people*] like babies? I want to know what's wrong with you. [X]Kids [*I'm*] worry, t[X]oo."

Q. What would make a good title for this story?
A. Question repeated three times) Bobby and his Mom has a fight.

  (Since he names the child, the following question was submitted.)

Q. Why do you think they had a fight?
A. He was crying.

Q. Why was Bobby upset?
A. Because of the fight.

Q. How old was Bobby?
A. I don't know.

Q. Do you think parents should discuss problems with their children?
A. I don't know.

Q. (*Above question repeated.*)
A. I told you I don't know.

---

substantially change meaning, and omitting the comma after *crying* probably explains the hesitation after *softly*. The child realized he had missed something and was trying to editorially correct the omission. He corrected the improper *now* to *know* immediately. Finally, his comprehension was excellent. Traditional thinkers in remediation might assume a reading problem here because of the substitutions. Reading is a meaning-seeking process and the child obtained understanding. Chances are that if a remedial program was initiated for the child, he would live up to your expectations and become a disabled reader.

Exhibit 3 presents another problem. Although the selection was obviously too difficult and testing should have been terminated after the first paragraph of the story, there is much to be gained by a thorough analysis of the IRI.

One of the more obvious problems is the reversal of *was* and *saw*. Since this was a fifth-level selection, and assuming the boy was ten years old, simple reversals like this can bode serious visual perception problems. Some of the Kindergarten–Three activities in Chapter 4 would be most beneficial and would serve for further screening to decide whether referral to a specialist is necessary.

The constant dropping of suffixes could indicate a carelessness on the part of the child in that he looks at only part of the word, or it could be indicative of a cultural difference. Again, the activities in Chapter 4 would be helpful.

There is a serious vocabulary deficit indicated by the numerous words that were pronounced for him. The activities in Chapter 11 are remarkable ways to build vocabulary and much of it would be interesting to a boy, especially the part dealing with "Stinky and the Thermos Bottle" and "Words That Talk."

The omissions are probably the result of a combination of carelessness (lack of attention to detail) and quite possibly an attempt to edit in such a way that it makes sense for him. Echo Impress and Neurological Impress as explained in Chapter 10 would be a natural for this problem.

The child was unable to respond to any of the questions in a meaningful way. Much of this is due to unknown words and the inability to use the context for assistance. The many activities in Chapter 9 are sequentially presented in order to develop comprehension skills in a systematic way from the simple to the complex.

Now that the analysis of the IRI is complete, it would be advisable to develop a checklist that could be used for all children who are administered an IRI. Exhibit 4 is a suggested form.

If an IRI is used in conjunction with the checklist and the normally good intuition of the teacher is brought to bear on the situation, there is no good reason why the material in this book will not be profitable when applied to any person with a reading disability. Torgesen (p. 75) "suggests that reading disabled children can use encoding strategies effectively if they are instructed and supported in their use." One thing is certain, however. If you do not bring your best thinking to the problem, we seriously doubt any stratagems will work.

EXHIBIT 4

IRI Checklist

NAME OF STUDENT _____

GRADE _____

DATE IRI ADMINISTERED _____

EXAMINER _____

		Yes	Sometimes	No
1.	Was the child a word by word reader?	_____	_____	_____
2.	Was phrasing faulty?	_____	_____	_____
3.	Were initial consonants a problem?	_____	_____	_____
4.	Were blends a problem?	_____	_____	_____
5.	Were short vowels understood?	_____	_____	_____
6.	Were long vowels understood?	_____	_____	_____
7.	Were digraphs understood?	_____	_____	_____
8.	Were diphthongs understood?	_____	_____	_____
9.	Were words inserted?	_____	_____	_____
10.	Were words omitted?	_____	_____	_____
11.	Were there mispronunciations?	_____	_____	_____
12.	Were words repeated?	_____	_____	_____
13.	Was punctuation ignored?	_____	_____	_____
14.	Did child recognize sight words?	_____	_____	_____
15.	Were polysyllabic words a problem?	_____	_____	_____
16.	Did child understand the reading?	_____	_____	_____
17.	Is the child capable of critical reading?	_____	_____	_____

Chapters 4–8 address the problems found in checklist questions 1–14. Chapters 9–11 provide varied activities for questions 15–17.

BIBLIOGRAPHY

KENNEDY, EDDIE C. *Methods in Teaching Developmental Reading.* Itasca, Ill., F. E. Peacock Publishers, 1974.

TORGESEN, JOSEPH K. "Performance of Reading Disabled Children on Serial Memory Tasks: A Selective Review of Recent Research." *Reading Research Quarterly.* 14(1): 1978–1979.

3 Material Preparation and Record Keeping

Since reading disabled children have failed to perform in typical school reading programs that utilize basal readers, it is important that teachers provide alternative approaches that give the children experience with success.

In preparing materials, teachers always must keep in mind the special needs of the learning disabled. Commercial kits have many advantages and are certainly time savers, but in order to have activities to suit each child, teachers will find it necessary to produce some materials of their own. They can take the commercial kits that often move too fast and add the needed graduated, intermediate steps. They also can use materials on hand. Almost every classroom storage cupboard contains copies of old workbooks, textbooks, parts of games, and manipulative materials that can be organized into job folders and put to practical use. To be effective, such materials must be structured, simple, and carefully sequenced. Each task must be brief enough to be accomplished in a reasonably short time to insure task completion for the highly distractable child with limited attention span and concentration ability. In addition, teachers should minimize clutter and "cuteness" when preparing materials for the highly distractable child. Tasks that are properly sequenced in small increments help the reading disabled child progress successfully, preventing undue frustration and discouragement. Manipulatives and materials relevant to the particular child are interesting for the child to work with and involve more than one sense.

Time spent preparing quality material is time well spent since the materials can be used over and over. Even though each reading disabled child is different and has different needs, each one requires the basic learning skills at some time.

To aid the child in getting the correct response in most of the activities, materials should be constructed so that he is required to recognize the correct response from a number of responses displayed than to recall from his memory bank. When remediating reading disabilities, teachers also must be sure that the task is not made too complex by requiring skills in addition to the skill being taught. Even requiring handwritten answers instead of verbal responses may prove to be a stumbling block for the child with poor fine motor coordination.

Very often, one modality—visual or auditory—has met with failure, so a different channel may need extra emphasis and practice. Whatever the mode used—visual, auditory, or a combination of both—be sure that the child understands what he is required to do. Do not let him fail because of the mechanics of the task. For instance, if he is to make the selection of a picture from an array of pictures for matching to a word, be sure that he is able to identify the pictures.

Letter-size manila file folders provide a suitable medium for learning tasks. They are easily stored, fit on a small table or desk, and provide a boundary for the child's work area. These folders fit well in 10 × 13-inch kraft envelopes and can be color-coded and numbered for easy access. Write complete directions for the use of the folder on the outside so that the materials can be utilized by a paraprofessional under the teacher's direction. Keeping an index of all materials and having the material clearly marked for task and level make for easy access and return. Colors, letters, numbers, or other symbols can be used to aid in recognition; for example, A-1, A-2, etc., for the auditory first level; V-1, V-2, etc., for the visual first level; and so on.

In preparing folders, you will save time if you use some standard sizes of materials. Cardboard templates 1, 2, and 3 inches wide and 16 inches long will save you much time in marking off spaces on folders. You can paste pictures on 2-inch squares of four- or six-ply railroad board, which is available at stationery stores and comes in many bright colors. The colors will add interest and variety to the folders, since you are going to keep the technique rather rigid. Keep a supply of precut squares to save time when you need to add a new step to the sequence of activities. Strips of the same material measuring 1 inch × 3 inches are suitable for words and phrases. Indelible fine-point markers are best for lettering on these strips. Permanent and water-soluble felt-tip markers, although useful in certain circumstances, are not good for this purpose. The permanent may bleed through the folder, and the soluble will rub off or smear when handled by children's perspiring hands.

Activity folders that are going to be handled a great deal or on which the children are to make marks should be covered with clear, pressure-sensitive paper or laminated. The children can then write with crayons, grease pencils, or watercolor felt-tip markers, and the answers can be wiped off when finished. If the plastic becomes ingrained with the color or soiled, it can be renewed by spraying with a household cleaner and then wiped dry.

Placing pictures or more interesting components of a lesson on the squares to be handled by the children may help to hold interest while words, letters, or parts that are apt to be less attractive are put on the folder.

Many of the materials made for use with the reading disabled child employ pictures, colors, or special symbols instead of letters or words because some learning disabled children have not yet learned, nor are they ready to learn, the alphabet. These children may be ready for such basic skills as directionality, auditory, and visual discrimination, but may be unable to deal with such abstractions as letters at the same time. Other children have been confronted with letters and words, have met failure, and therefore have negative feelings about anything that seems to be connected with reading. So, by using shapes, colors, and symbols, you can help these children master basic skills through matching and manipulating operations.

The vocabulary used in the materials should be relevant and extremely simple. For example, the word *load* should be kept within the range of success for each child so that positive reinforcement can be given. By using a few nouns already within the child's speaking vocabulary, adding appropriate verbs to make simple phrases, and then adding inflected endings, combining them with color and number words, you can develop a large number of phrases. The child may then be able to achieve success. Ten or 12 items in a folder usually will be as much as can be handled at one sitting.

Keep a supply of 2-inch colored squares, 1 × 3-inch and 1 × 4-inch strips, and pictures. Using your 1- or 2-inch templates, you can quickly line a folder and construct tasks. (See Exhibit 1, which illustrates a typical activity folder with 2-inch spaces and cards for matching.)

When a folder is completed, take time to:

1. Make a key.
2. Number all of the component parts to match the number of the folder and envelope.
3. Write the complete directions on the folder as well as the skill being taught.
4. Place all small parts in a self-closing plastic bag. Put the folder and the bag in a manila envelope.
5. Color-code different skills if you are making materials for several skills (optional).
6. Provide some means of record keeping for each series (suggestions follow).

RECORD KEEPING FOR THE TEACHER

Prepare a duplicating master for each skill area with the activities included listed down the left-hand side, followed by three columns, headed *Completed, Completed with Difficulty,* and *Too Difficult.* Using a sheet

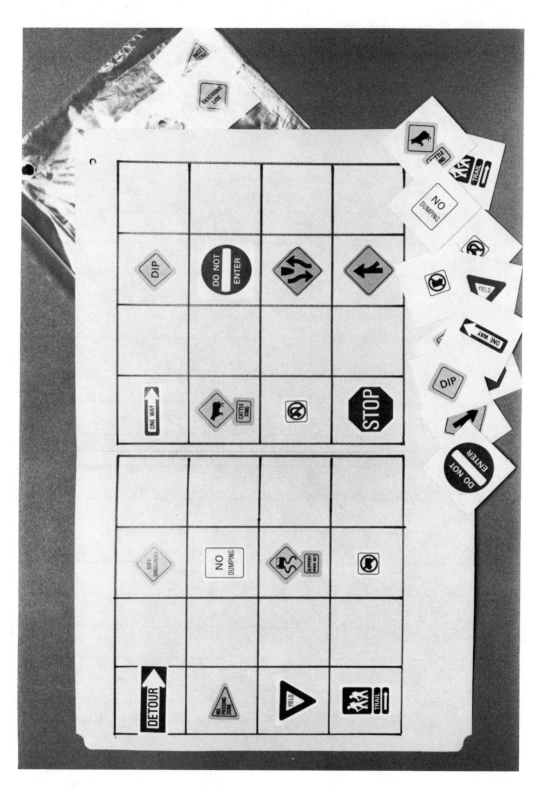

EXHIBIT 1

21

EXHIBIT 2

NAME _____

SKILL _____

Activity	Date Completed	Completed With Difficulty	Too Difficult
1. _____			
2. _____			
3. _____			
4. _____			
5. _____			
6. _____			
7. _____			
8. _____			
9. _____			
10. _____			
11. _____			
12. _____			
13. _____			
14. _____			
15. _____			
16. _____			
17. _____			
18. _____			
19. _____			
20. _____			

for each child, put the date the task was attempted in the appropriate column. This sheet will serve as an instant reminder of the task that should be attempted next and can be used by the teacher or a paraprofessional. (See Exhibit 2.)

RECORD KEEPING FOR THE CHILD

It is a source of satisfaction for a child to have a record of what he has accomplished. His achievements are not a secret that the teacher alone is privy to. Using a 3 × 5 file card, prepare a card for the child similar to those used by a newspaper carrier—a 2 × 3 card with numbers around the sides representing each pay period. This card is kept in a safe place by the child. When a task is completed satisfactorily, punch out the corresponding numeral with a metal punch. (See Exhibit 3.)

EXHIBIT 3

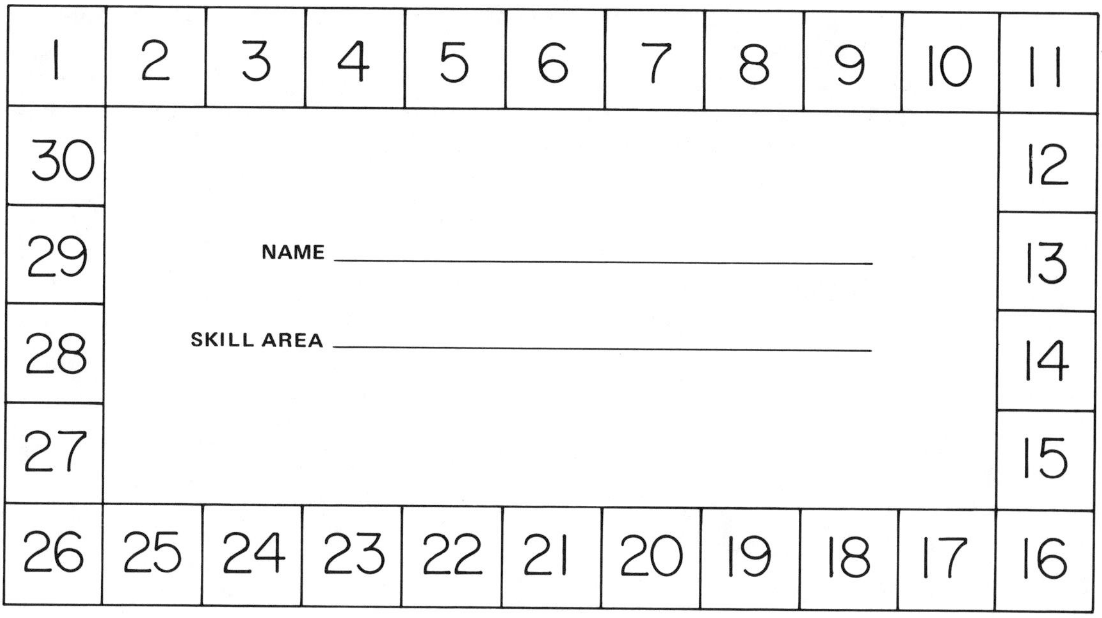

1	2	3	4	5	6	7	8	9	10	11
30										12
29		NAME _____								13
28		SKILL AREA _____								14
27										15
26	25	24	23	22	21	20	19	18	17	16

SOURCES OF MATERIALS AND SUPPLIES

1. *Pictures*
    Old workbooks, advertising brochures, book-club miniatures, magazine miniatures, to be found any number of places.

Rubber stamps—animals, common objects, letters, and numerals from:
> Didax Stamps
> Box 2258
> Peabody, Mass. 01960

Shapes and beads from:
> Fingerprint Press
> 20A Hilltop Road
> San Mateo, Calif. 94402

Shapes, clocks, and coins from:
> Developmental Learning Materials
> 7440 Natchez Avenue
> Niles, Ill. 60648

Gummed and pressure-sensitive seals of animals, birds, flowers, airplanes, dinosaurs, sports, etc., are available in card shops, stationery stores, and gift shops.

2. *Wooden Cubes for Game Markers*
   #3601 plain wooden cubes are available from school supply houses.

3. *Cards for Card Games*
   #63 round-corner cards, used for printing tickets for various functions, are available from print shops and paper wholesalers.

4. *Railroad Board*
   Four- or six-ply—colored on both sides—used for 2-inch squares, quad domino, and sentence strips, are available from school supply houses, paper companies, and variety stores.

Visual Activities

4

Visual perception is defined by Gilliland (1974, p. 254) as "the ability to see a thing and perceive it as it is." In his usual manner, Gilliland removes much of the chaff from the problem and deals with the germ. Granted, the concepts of Visual Form Discrimination, Visual Figure-Ground Differentiation, Visual Memory, and Visual Sequencing can be awesome to define, let alone teach, but the ability to see things as they are requires you to understand clearly these terms and to be able to develop this very important aspect of learning, because through one's eyes comes the world.

The following definitions are offered:

- *Visual Form Discrimination*—The ability to differentiate visually the forms and symbols in one's environment. Child can match identical pictures and symbols, such as abstract designs, letters, numbers, and words.
- *Visual Figure-Ground Differentiation*—The ability to perceive objects in foreground and background and to separate them meaningfully. Pupil can differentiate objects in "front" and "back" part of pictures; can differentiate his name from others on chalkboard; can perceive simple forms and words embedded in others.
- *Visual Memory*—The ability to recall accurately prior visual experiences. Pupil can recall from visual cues where he stopped in book; can match or verbally recall objects removed or changed in the environment; can match briefly exposed symbols.

- *Visual Motor Memory (Sequencing)*—The ability to reproduce by motor movements prior visual experiences. Pupil can draw designs and symbols following brief exposure; can reproduce letters, numbers, simple words on demand; can portray prior objects or events through gestures or drawings; can reproduce varied patterns and identify hidden materials (Valett, 1968).

The following activities are designed to develop the preceding skills. They are simple to make and require minimal time on your part, but the understanding they can bring to a child is endless.

ACTIVITIES TO DEVELOP VISUAL SKILLS

Since so much of the child's ultimate success in reading seems to depend on his ability to discriminate visually and to understand the meaning of the many visual cues in reading material, you must be sure that the learning disabled child has a sound foundation in these areas, and you must build on this foundation sequentially until the child produces at his expectancy level or as near this level as possible.

Before you can start at a level that will insure initial success in an area, say reading, you must first find this baseline for the child. Then, you must decide what increments to use to build up the skill step by step. For example, assuming a child from a background of little familiarity with printed material, start the activities at a very low level of visual discrimination. Supply as many steps as needed until the child is able to discriminate visually minimal interior differences, such as the difference between reading the words *conversation* and *conservation*. It is the responsibility of the teacher to ascertain the beginning level for each child and to proceed from that point.

Following are lists of activities that can be assembled in folder form and organized sequentially for individual use with children.

Visual Discrimination

Activities   1. Real Objects—Through examining and matching like objects such as fruits and vegetables, the child learns that objects can be identified through more than one attribute. Color, shape, and size must be included in object discrimination. Two objects may be similar on one or more attributes. For instance, tomatoes and apples may both be round and red. Therefore, a third attribute (at least) must be used for accurate discrimination—in this case, perhaps size. Likewise, leaves from trees may all be green, but shape helps decide from which tree they came.

Of course, if the child has real objects to examine, he can also discriminate on the basis of touch, smell, and taste. Unfortunately, however, you cannot always provide the child with real objects to examine, so you must rely on the use of symbols to represent objects.

2. Realia—Matching Three-Dimensional Replications—

   a. Using plastic fruits and vegetables or toys such as cowboys and astronauts, have the child match objects that are the same by length, width, and depth.

   b. Using the same three-dimensional plastic objects, have the child disregard the variety of attributes and match together by color all of the green, red, or yellow objects.

3. Realia—Learning that Three-Dimensional Objects Can Be Represented by Two Dimensions—

   a. Have the child match the plastic fruits or vegetables used in Activities 1 and 2 to colored pictures of fruits and vegetables mounted in a folder. The colors will cue the child in his selection. (See Exhibit 1.)

      The same type of folder, reinforcing the same skill, could be made with toys instead of fruits. Have the child match a car, a ball, a balloon, etc., to a picture of the same color.

   b. The concept of classes of objects can be included at this point by another folder containing pictures to which the child matches three-dimensional objects. In this task, he cannot depend upon color as a cue because he must match a picture of a red inflated balloon to a real yellow balloon not inflated, a yellow plastic flower to a picture of a pink flower, a little U.S. flag to a picture of a different flag. This is an optional step and should not be included if the child does not seem to be ready.

4. Realia—Visual Discrimination by Color, Size, or Shape Using Identical Materials but with Differing Cues—Using construction paper of the six primary colors, cut from each color circles, squares, triangles, and rectangles in two sizes—3 inches and 1½ inches. Prepare three folders for each attribute—color, shape, and size.

   Color—Divide each folder into six columns. (See Exhibit 2.) Folder 1—Make a band of each color at the top of the column. Folder 2—Letter the six color names in color. Folder 3—Letter the six color names in black. The first two folders check on knowledge of color concepts, and, for the child who is ready, the last one checks ability to read the color words.

   Shape—Divide each folder into four columns. Folder 1—Put replica of the four shapes in black at the top of the

EXHIBIT 1

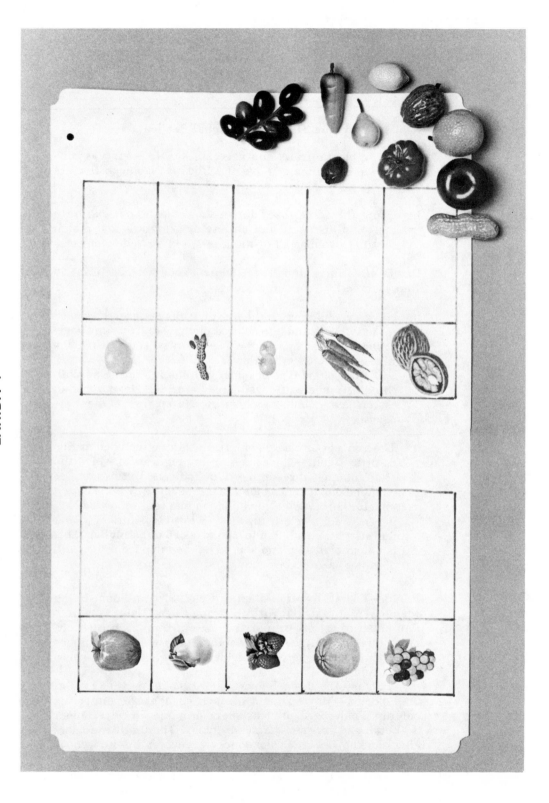

Color — Folder 1

Folder 2

YELLOW	BLUE	RED	PURPLE	GREEN	ORANGE

Folder 3

GREEN	ORANGE	YELLOW	BLUE	RED	PURPLE

EXHIBIT 2

29

Shapes — Folder 1

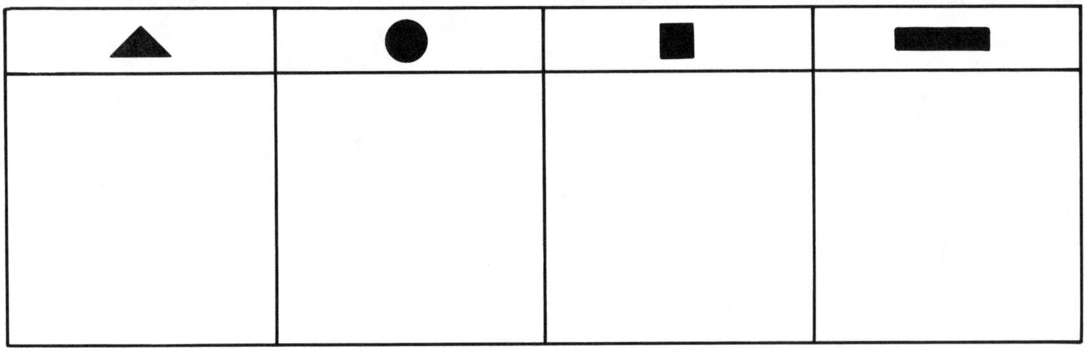

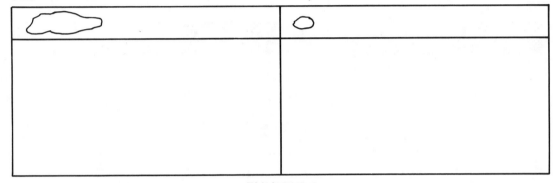

EXHIBIT 3

Size — Folder 1

EXHIBIT 4

columns. (See Exhibit 3.) Folder 2—Put the shapes and the shape words at the head of the columns. Folder 3—Put shape words only at the head of the columns.

Size—Folder 1—Divide each folder in half and put a large irregular form at the top of one side and a small form at the top of the other. (See Exhibit 4.) Folder 2—Divide folders as with Folder 1 and add words *large* and *small*. Folder 3—Use words *large* and *small* only.

If you cut several sets of the colored shapes and keep each set in a separate plastic bag, more than one child can be involved with these folders at the same time.

5. Matching Pictures with Exterior Differences—Prepare folders for 12–16 pictures with a space beside each for the child to place the card of the matching picture.

    a. Strong Color and Shape Cues—fruit or flower seals.

    b. Less-Predominant Color Cues—farm or forest animals, shades of brown.

    c. Some children with well-developed concepts of animals will match these by class rather than visually discriminate the outlines, so add a set using pictures of one animal in different positions, or of different colors.

6. Matching Pictures with Fine Interior Differences—Prepare folders for 12–16 pictures and spaces. Use the following.

   a. Flags of the world.

   b. Faces with different expressions.

   c. Postage stamps. (A whole series with degrees of difficulty can be made from a bag of collector's stamps, found in most variety stores.)

7. Matching Pictures or Diagrams without Using Color Cues—

   a. Using a rubber clockface stamp, make a folder with ten clockfaces in the 2-inch spaces and on the 2-inch cards. With a fine-point, black marker, put hands on the clocks to indicate certain times. This task can be made easy by using just the hours and half-hours, or it can be made more difficult by using intervals of a quarter of an hour or less.

      An exact match for each clockface on the folder is to be made on the small cards.

   b. Using rubber coin stamps, make a folder with the six U.S. coins on the left side and combinations of two coins on the right side. Stamp the identical coin combinations on the small squares for matching.

      This activity includes work with laterality since the child must be certain that the order of the two coins on the card matches the order of the coins in the folder.

8. Matching Letters—Prepare a folder using horizontal spaces. (See Exhibit 5.) Print or write the same letters on the 2-inch squares.

      Have the child match letter to letter.

9. Matching Words—Prepare folders as in Activity 7, except that the spaces and cards should be 2 × 4 inches.

   a. Put simple words with different configurations on the folder and the cards for matching. Use words such as:

   cat   pig   boy
   dog   goat
   girl   me

b		f			r		
a		g			s		
c		n			t		
g		p			b		
h		o			d		

    b. Words that are easily confused, such as:

was	tap	no
saw	bat	on
ton	tap	
not	tab	

    c. Words with the same beginning letter:

can	cat	cop	cub
car	caw	cob	
cow	cap	cog	
coo	cup	cad	
cot	cod	cab	

    d. Difficult sight words:

these	their	though
them	there	through
those	then	thorough
this	throw	three
that	threw	

10. Matching Phrases—Prepare a folder like that shown in Exhibit 5. Match phrases such as:

over the house	on the road
up the road	over the road
on the car	in the house
over the car	in the car
on the house	

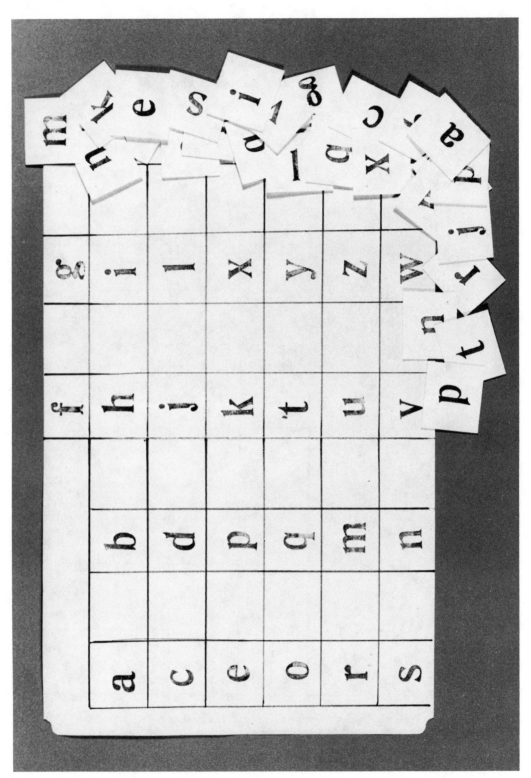

EXHIBIT 5

33

EXHIBIT 6

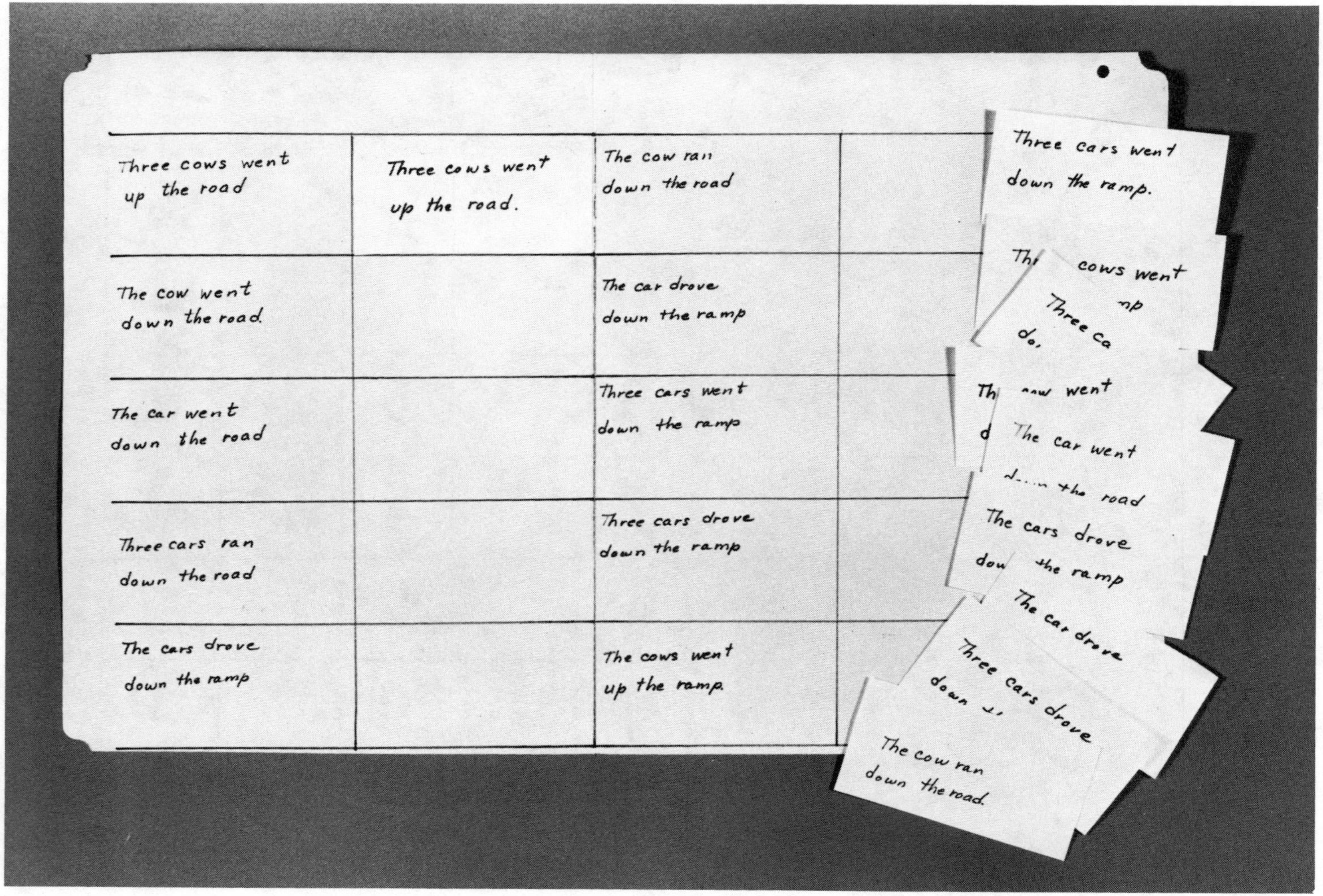

11. Matching Sentences—Use the same format as in Activity 9. (See Exhibit 6.) Match sentences such as:

> The car went down the road.
> The cow went down the road.
> The car went up the road.
> The crow flew over the road.
> Three cars went down the road.
> The cars went up the road.
> A crow walked over the ramp.
> A car drove on the ramp.
> Three cars drove down the ramp.

These folders also can be used for oral reading when appropriate.

Each child, starting on a step in the preceding sequence of activities where he can succeed, and following through the steps in order, should gain a high level of competence in visual discrimination. For older children having difficulty with this skill, refer to Chapter 5.

Position in Space

The sequence that follows was prepared for children who have difficulty with Activity 7 in the preceding sequence. They have difficulty in matching letters or in recognizing them in different positions in words. Such children may reverse or invert certain letters when they write them. The sequence starts with the use of colored squares to be arranged, and proceeds to lined squares, lines, shapes, and letters.

Activities

1. Patterns with Squares—

   a. (See Exhibit 7.) Child arranges squares to make a pattern on a folder. Boundaries for each square are provided.

   b. (See Exhibit 8.) Child arranges squares to make a pattern on a folder. No boundaries given.

2. Patterns with Vertical and Horizontal Lines—

   (See Exhibit 9.) Child arranges squares to make the given pattern.

3. Patterns with Diagonal Lines—(See Exhibit 10.) Child arranges squares to make the given pattern.

4. Patterns with Irregular Shapes in Changed Positions—(See Exhibit 11.)

5. Patterns with Lines and Circles in Changed Positions—(See Exhibit 12.)

EXHIBIT 7

EXHIBIT 8

37

EXHIBIT 9

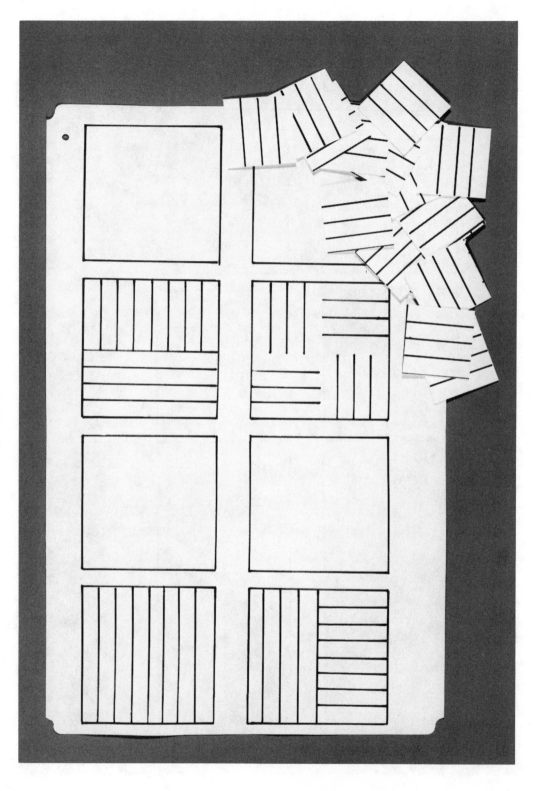

EXHIBIT 10

39

EXHIBIT 11

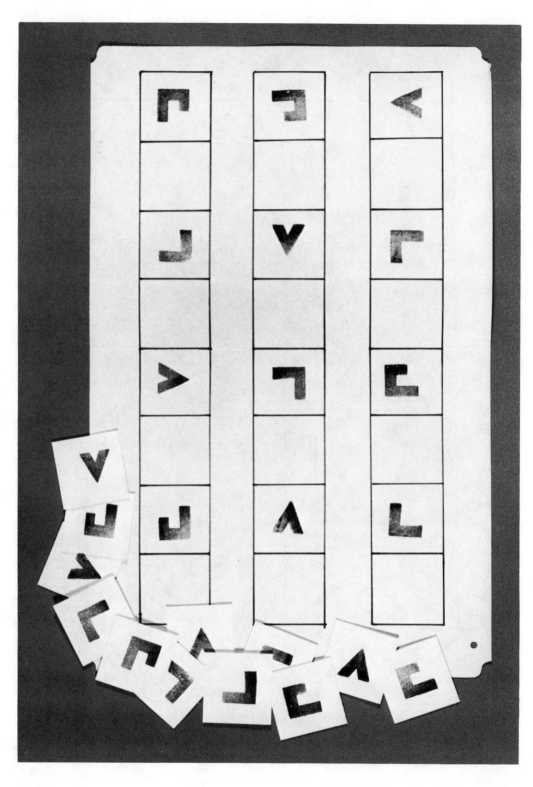

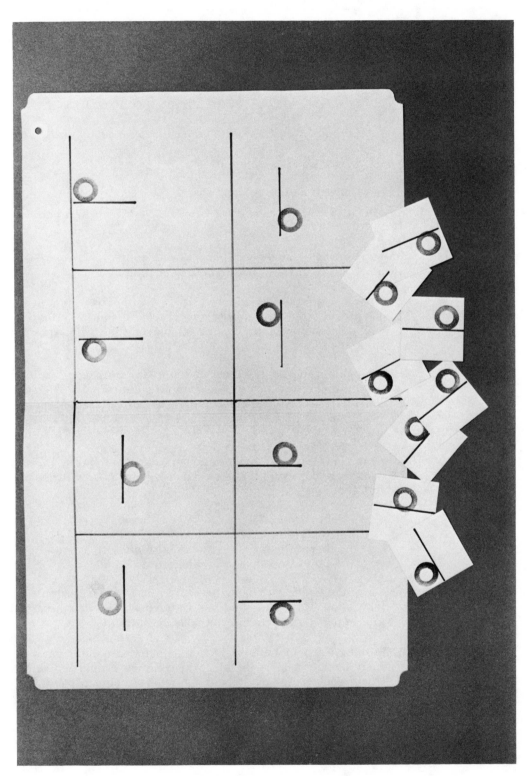

EXHIBIT 12

6. Letters—

   a. Straight-Line Letters—*A, E, F, H, I, K, L, M, N, T, V, W, X, Y, Z.*

   b. Curved-Line Letters—*B, C, D, G, J, O, P, Q, R, S, U.*

   c. Letters Often Confused—*b, d, g, q, p, n, u.*

   d. Lower Case to Capitals.

   e. Capitals to Lower Case.

Missing Parts

Activities From magazines such as *Sports Illustrated* or *National Geographic,* cut pictures of sports figures or animals.

1. Sports Figures—Cut the feet from each player. Mount the players on a folder, and the cut-off feet on squares. Have the child match the correct feet to each player. Cues will be position and type of shoes. (See Exhibit 13.)

2. Animals—Cut the tail portion (or head) from each animal. Mount the animals on a folder, and the cut-off tails (or heads) on squares. Have the child match the correct missing part to each picture. Pictures of endangered species are fairly easy to find.

3. Common Objects—Divide a folder into eight parts. In each section, make a simple sketch of a common object with one part missing, such as:

cat—no tail	door—no knob
table—three legs	vest with buttons—
hen—one leg	no buttonholes
face—one ear	pitcher—no handle

   Cover the folder with clear, pressure-sensitive plastic or have it laminated. Have the child use watercolor, felt-tip markers or grease pencils to draw in the missing parts.

4. Missing Parts of Letters—Divide a folder into eight parts. In each section, glue a picture of a common animal or object. Under each picture, letter the name of the object, leaving off one part of a letter; for example:

   do ⌐(dog), I all (ball), c ir (car)
   I ike (bike), I e I (bed), ⌐ig (pig),
   I ool (book)

EXHIBIT 13

Cover the folder with plastic or have it laminated.
Have the child use a watercolor marker or grease pencil to add the missing parts of the letters.

Figure-Ground

The child who has a difficulty with figure-ground may be unable to sort out individual words or to focus on one area long enough to decode the meaning. He may not be able to shift focus from word to word as he attempts to read a line of print. The following activities should help him.

Activities 1. Make patterns on a folder or sheet of tagboard. Cover the patterns with clear plastic film or laminate them. Have the child use a grease pencil or watercolor marker to trace patterns or identify figures according to directions.

a. Draw three large, overlapping shapes.

Have the child trace any one figure without breaking the line of tracing.

b. Trace around common objects, overlapping them. Use objects such as a pair of scissors, eyeglasses, a ruler, and a pencil. Have the child trace one object as directed.

c. Trace around the outline of one object such as a star or diamond several times, overlapping the images.
Have the child trace any one of the stars or diamonds without hesitation. (See Exhibit 14.)

d. Make large (about 4-inch) capital letters, overlapping them. Have the child trace any letter as directed. Have him trace each letter.

2. Use hidden-picture puzzles from children's magazines or puzzlebooks. Have the child trace the hidden pictures as he finds them.

3. From a sheet of letters written in random order, direct the child to find and touch a given letter.

4. In an arithmetic problem, instruct the child to underline all of the numerals (1, 2, 3, etc.).

EXHIBIT 14

45

5. On file cards, type sentences or brief paragraphs containing a number word, a color word, a date, the name of a city, etc. Instruct the child to touch a number word, a color word, etc.

These activities can be developed further into skimming and scanning.

Visual Memory

Activities   The child who cannot remember words to which he has been introduced needs to learn the technique of looking at words with the purpose of noting distinguishing characteristics so that he will recognize the words later. To aid the child in mastering this technique, prepare folders as follows.

Rule five 2-inch horizontal spaces across the folder. On the left of each side of the folder, make a 2-inch space vertically. Make a flap to cover each of these ten spaces by putting a hinge of strapping tape across a 2-inch square to cover each of these spaces.

Under the flap, make a shape or symbol following the sequence that follows. At the right of the flap, repeat the symbol along with two other symbols in random order.

Provide the child with a 2 × 6-inch strip to be used to cover these three symbols at the right of the flap. Teach the child the routine that follows, watch to see that he does it correctly, then give him the folder and a strip and instruct him to practice until he has mastered this activity.

Routine—Have the child:

1. Cover the three symbols at the right of the flap.

2. Lift the flap in the first line, exposing the symbol briefly.

3. Lift the cover strip and select the symbol just seen under the flap.

4. Lift the flap and check for accuracy.

When the child is able to cover, expose, select, and check without help, he is ready to work on the technique by himself. (See Exhibit 15.)

Levels for folders:

1. Solid shapes   ▲ ● ⬤ ▬ ■

2. Shape outlines   △ ○ ⬭ ▭ ▢

3. Open shapes   ∠ C ⊏ ⊓ ⅃⊏

4. Open letters (*L, M, N, V, W*, etc.)

5. Round letters (*P, B, R, S, O, D*, etc.)

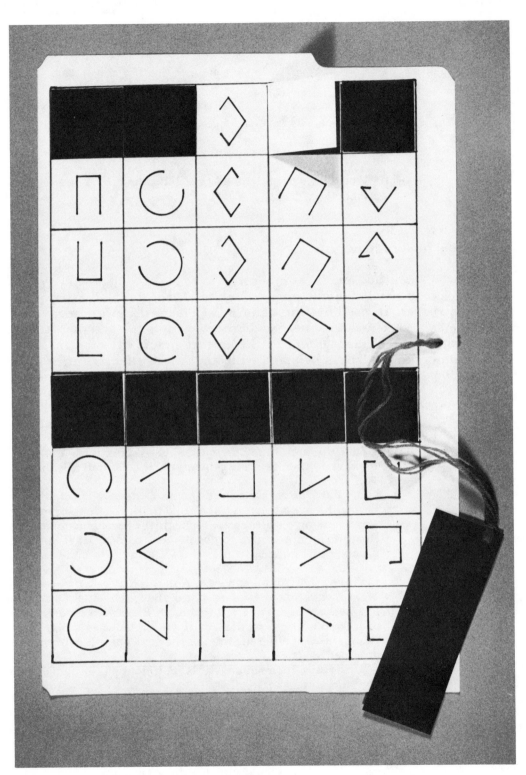

EXHIBIT · 15

47

6. Lower case letters (*a, b, g, d, c,* etc.)

7. Two-letter words

8. Three-letter words

9. Words easily reversed (*saw, was, not, ton,* etc.)

10. Words with same beginning letter (*blue, bow, brown,* etc.)

11. Words hard to remember (*this, that, then, than, there, those,* etc.)

Visual Motor Memory

Now we can add another dimension to visual memory and practice developing visual motor memory. The child needs this skill to become an able speller. In spelling, the child must choose from the array of 26 letters the specific letters needed for the word at hand, and then he must arrange the selected letters in the correct order. In some instances, auditory skills will be of help, but with other words such as *knife, cough,* and *bough,* he must rely on visual motor memory.

Activities
1. Divide each side of a folder into quarters using one horizontal and one vertical line. Make a flap over the two left-hand quarters on each side of the folder using strapping tape as a hinge. Under the flap, make the outline of a knife, fork, and spoon, making a different arrangement under each flap. (See Exhibit 16.)

   Place an array of plastic picnic cutlery on the child's desk beside the folder. Instruct the child to lift the flap, observe the arrangement, close the flap, replicate the arrangement as seen, then lift the flap again to check for accuracy. Have the child practice this until he can do the folder quickly and correctly.

2. Make five horizontal spaces across the folder, 2 inches apart. Make a vertical line on each side of the folder 4 inches from the left side. Make a flap 2 × 4 inches with a strapping-tape hinge over each of these sections on the left. Under each flap, place two pictures of different animals, flowers, or birds using colored gummed seals.

   On two-inch-square cards, put identical gummed seals, one to a card.

   Place this array of squares on the child's desk beside the folder. The child is to lift the flap, observe the arrangement, close the flap, select from the array the two animals seen, and then place them in the correct order in the space to the right of the closed flap. He then lifts the flap again to check for accuracy. The child should practice this procedure with this folder until he can do the whole folder correctly.

EXHIBIT 16

49

Further steps in this sequence using the same procedure as in Activity 2 would be:

a. Three Pictures under Each Flap—Identical pictures on 2-inch cards.

b. Three Abstract Shapes (No Color)—Identical pictures on 2-inch cards.

c. Arrangements of Three Coins—The child's reproduction must be in correct order left to right. If rubber coin stamps are not available, use black-and-white sketches or pictures from workbooks.

d. Letters—Make two lower case letters under the flap and place identical letters singly on the 2-inch squares for selecting and arranging.

e. Words—Put three-letter words under the flaps. Put the component letters singly on the 2-inch squares for selecting and arranging in correct order.

f. Eye-Hand Coordination—Prepare a folder with five 2 × 4-inch spaces with flaps on the left of each side of a folder; instead of continuing the lines across the folder, glue one-half of a commercial magic slate to each side of the folder at the right of the flaps. Under the flaps, print or write (depending on the level of the child's handwriting) two-letter words.

Have the child raise the flap, observe the word, close the flap, use a stylus on the slate to write the word, and lift the flap to check for accuracy. If the child has written the correct word, he proceeds to the next word, but if he has made a mistake, he lifts the film on the slate and gets rid of his error. He continues practicing until he can write the word correctly. No one needs to tell him to write each word a given number of times. He simply practices until he has written a word correctly to be proud of. At this point, it may be a good idea for him to show his success to you so that you can give added positive reinforcement.

Make folders with three-letter words, four-letter words, etc., giving as much practice with this skill as seems necessary.

Configuration

The shape of a word is a clue to recognition. For the child who is visually minded and has difficulty with sounding, it may be a very important cue. For the recognition of some sight words, it is vital.

Activities 1. On paper with lines ½ inch apart, print the following three-letter words in two columns 2 inches apart using three full spaces, the upper one to accommodate the ascenders and the lower one for the descenders. Leave one space between the words.

age	add
may	yes
pat	lot
was	sky
ton	try
ate	and

All these words have different configurations. Using ½-inch quadrille paper as a guide, cut the shape of each word from construction paper or card stock.

Have the child place the shape on each word so that no printing shows. If he does them correctly, he will be able to place all of the shapes.

2. Line a folder with three 3-inch spaces across the folder horizontally and three 6-inch spaces across vertically. In the left portion of each space, make the shape of each of the following words using the units noted. (See Exhibit 17.)

pot	tin	toy
bit	met	age
pup	ate	gum

letter without ascender or descender—1 inch
letter with ascender—2 inches
letter with descender—2 inches

Cut pieces of tagboard 1 inch × 1 inch and 1 inch × 2 inches. On these pieces, print the letters needed for the nine words:

2 *a*'s	2 *u*'s	1 *b*
3 *e*'s	3 *p*'s	2 *m*'s
2 *i*'s	6 *t*'s	1 *y*
2 *o*'s	2 *g*'s	1 *n*

At the top of the folder, letter the nine words.

Instruct the child to use the letters he has been given and, in each shape on the folder, to arrange the letter pieces to form each of the nine words given at the top. If he does the task correctly, all of the letters will fit perfectly in the shapes you have drawn.

3. On 2-inch-square cards, print the following words. Allow ½ inch for ascenders and ½ inch for descenders.

its	ape	you
use	say	all
sat	but	get
why	for	buy

EXHIBIT 17

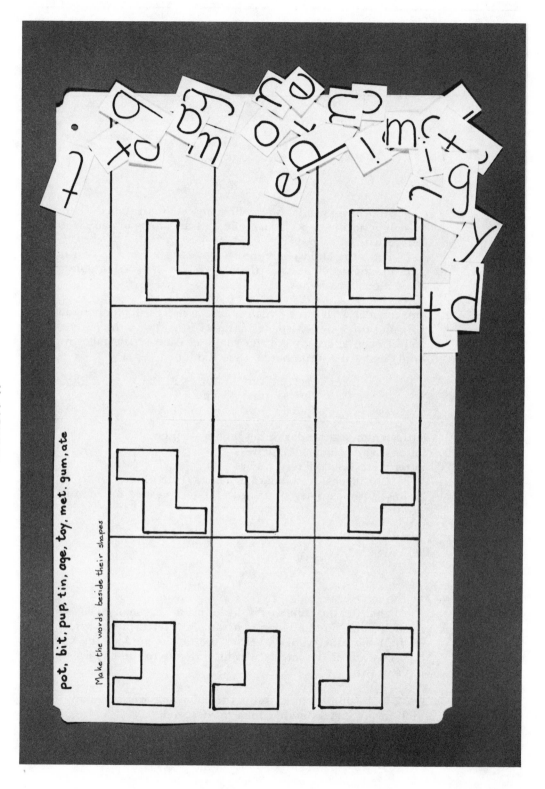

pot, bit, pup, tin, age, toy, met, gum, ate

Make the words beside their shapes

Have the child match the word on a card to the word on the paper that has the exact configuration.

4. On a folder, make six vertical columns (each about 2½ inches wide). Letter the following four-letter words at the top of the columns:

this   said   down   look   step   tell

Using the same-size lettering, print the following words on 2-inch cards:

than	must	here	beat	ship	both
then	want	four	hurt	clay	hold
flew	wash	have	book	slap	kill
blue	work	from	fish	shag	full

Have the child place the cards in the columns with words that have the same configuration.

Sight Words

There are many words in the English language that cannot be sounded out no matter how good a person is at auditory skills. Words such as *said, was,* and *once* must be recognized by visual skills and memorized. In addition, there are many words that are used so frequently that they should be recognized instantly. These sight words, as they are frequently called, give the poor reader real problems since they do not have distinctive configurations and are often rather abstract in meaning. Lists of these words (those by Dolch, Johnson, and others) usually have 200–300 entries. Incessant drill on these words using flash cards becomes like the dentist's drill—extremely boring (excuse the pun). To improve on this situation, we propose practice with a variety of interesting activities to hold the child's interest and to provide motivation for learning the words.

To teach these words, the lists are broken into small bite-size bits, giving the child a reasonable amount to learn at one time in order to insure success. The child will also be more likely to remain interested if he has a means of record keeping so that he can see the future goal and know that he is gaining on it. A simple record-keeping device is a wallet-sized card with numbers, colors, or symbols around the edge to be punched out as tasks are mastered. (See Exhibit 18.)

Activities 1. New-Word Bingo—Rule a 6 × 8-inch card into twelve 2-inch squares. In each square, print one of the new words. On twelve 2-inch squares, print the same words.

    a. Have the child match the words on the small cards to those on the large cards. This is a pure visual-discrimination task.

53

EXHIBIT 18

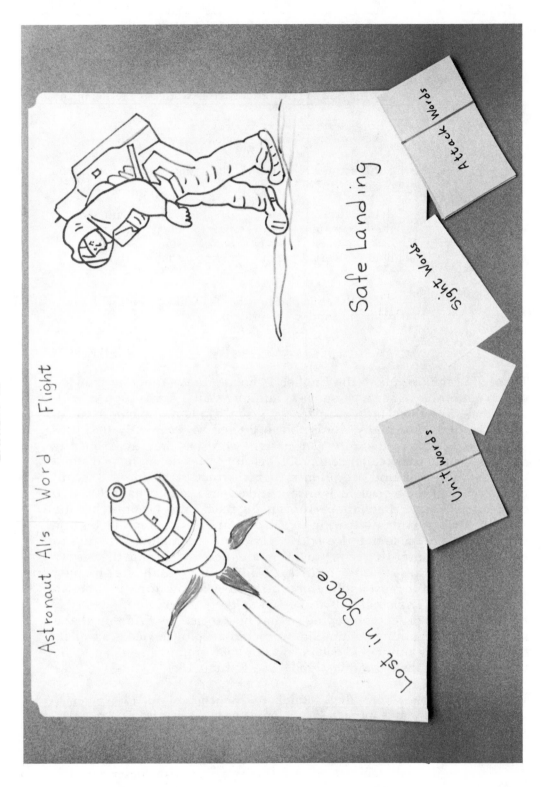

b. Lay the small cards face up on the desk beside the large cards. Call a word. The child is to pick up that word and place it on the large card. The child recognizes the word when he receives an auditory cue.

c. Lay the small cards face down beside the large card. Have the child pick up the cards one by one, read them aloud, then place them on the large card.

d. Using several bingo cards with the same words in different positions on the cards, let small groups of children play bingo, each child taking a turn at being the caller.

Some reading plans such as the Wisconsin Design (1972) have the Dolch words arranged in order of difficulty. It may be well to use one of these lists to arrange the words on the cards. Since there are approximately 200 words, you will need at least 18 different bingo cards. These can be coded into levels by number, using 1–18 on the child's punch card; by color, making each level of difficulty a different color; or by symbols, using squares, circles, hearts, stars, etc., to designate levels of achievement.

2. Personalized word folders—Using a legal-size file folder, fold up 3 inches at the bottom, making a pocket to hold word cards. Secure the ends with masking tape and put a drop of glue in the center fold to make two separate pockets. Decorate the top portions of the folders according to the child's interest by cutting pictures from magazines, tracings from coloring books, or by using the child's own drawings. Some suggestions follow.

a. *Cowboy Charlie's* Word Corral—On the left side, make or paste a picture of a wild bronco or steer with the word *Wild* on the pocket. On the right side, put a picture of a cowboy lassoing an animal, and on the pocket, the word *Tamed.* (See Exhibit 19.)

b. _____' Space Shot—On the left, picture of rocket with words *Lost in Space;* on the right, picture of moon landing with phrase *Safe Landing.*

c. Cartoon Characters—Snoopy's Charlie Brown, Snoopy's Word Folder—On left, Snoopy in dejected pose, with words *Snoopy Needs Help;* on right, Snoopy dancing with phrase *Snoopy Knows His Words.*

d. Car Racing—_____'s Word Pit—Pictures of racing cars on both sides. *Losers* on left; *Winners* on right.

e. The child may have an idea for his own folder. By all means, encourage him to make and decorate his own if he wishes.

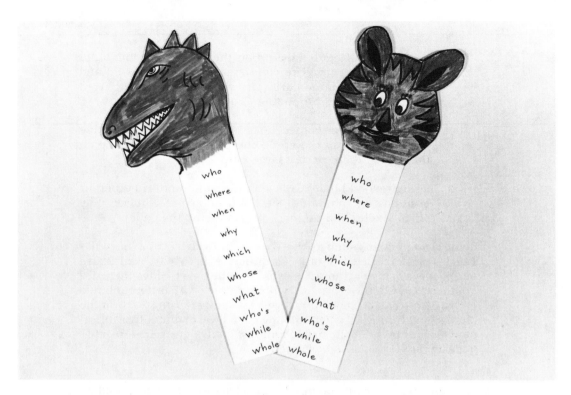

FOR VOCABULARY WORDS, CUT SLOT IN PLASTIC TOP
OF POTATO CHIP CAN.

EXHIBIT 19

Using numbers, colors, symbols, or whatever means of grouping words, make 2 × 4-inch flash cards to fit in the pockets. Introduce the cards in small groups such as those on the bingo cards. The folder becomes a permanent record of the child's achievement in learning his sight words. When a word is learned, it moves over to the right, or winner's side. When these words are reviewed, the ones that the child has forgotten move back to the left, or loser's side. The folder content is flexible and constantly changing. The teacher can direct an aide or another child to work with the child on this folder at any time without spending time to find the child's achievement level. The folder is always ready—words to be learned on the left, words known at one time on the right. If the teacher directs review, the helper knows to work with the words on the right. Attack words requiring phonic skills, words from a new unit, and needed words from a subject-matter area can also be kept in this folder if suitably marked or color-coded.

3. Puppet Strips and Potato Chips—On a 4 × 14-inch strip of tagboard, make vocabulary strips to be used in the cylindrical potato chip cans. (See Exhibit 20.) The metal cans that tennis balls come in can also be used. Cover the exterior of the cans with adhesive plastic covering. Avoid busy designs for use with highly distractable children. Using your, or the child's, imagination, make series of heads for the strips from a cartoon (use the characters from *Peanuts, Star Wars, Sesame Street, Spider-Man*, etc.). Using the series gives the child a means of keeping a record of his achievement. For instance, he must master Ernie and Bert to get Grover, and then complete the Count, etc., to get to Big Bird.

Make the head of the strip about 4 × 4 inches. Then, cut the remainder of the strip to about 2¼ inches wide to slip into a slot cut in the plastic lid of the can. When inserted, only the head will show.

Letter words about ¾ of an inch apart on the strip, allowing 12–15 words per strip.

Raise (or have a helper raise) the strip out of the slot one word at a time. If the child responds correctly, the next word is exposed; if not, the strip is released and falls back into the can. When the child successfully completes one strip, he is allowed to try the next one.

This technique is also good to use with mathematical facts. The answers can be lettered on the back of the strip so that children can work with each other.

Laminating the puppet strips or covering them with clear, pressure-sensitive plastic will make them more durable. If you wish your word lists to be permanent, letter them on the strips before covering. If you want to be able to change the lists, cover the strips first, then write the words with water-soluble markers or grease pencils so that they can be erased.

4. Dominoes—For particularly troublesome words, such as the *th* words (*three, that, there, they, this, them, then, think, thank,*

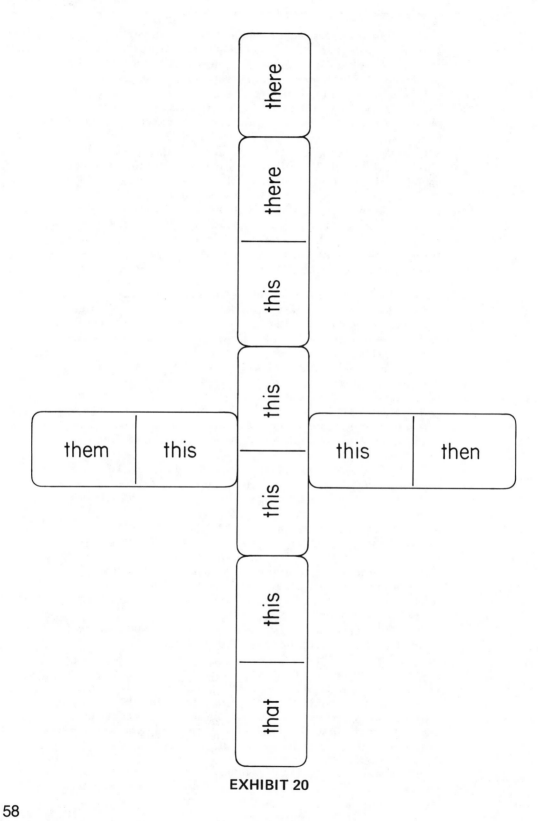

EXHIBIT 20

their, these, those, etc.), make a domino game. Select seven or eight words to be used. Make a line across each card, dividing it in half so that it resembles a domino. On each end, letter one of the words. Make a double for each word plus all of the possible combinations. For eight words, you will need 36 dominoes.

Two or more children play the game exactly like dominoes, each drawing five cards, leaving the rest face down in the boneyard. One child plays, preferably a double, saying the word on his card. In order to play, the next child must match words and read the words on both ends of his card. If he cannot read the words, he loses his turn. If he doesn't have a match, he may draw up to three cards from the boneyard. Play continues until one player uses all of his dominoes. A double may be played on from all the sides. (See Exhibit 21.)

5. Snap—This card game is good for two, three, or four players. Select 10 or 12 words that need practice. Letter the words on 3 × 5 file cards or #63 round-corner blank cards. Letter each word twice on a card so that it can be read from left to right from either side. Make four cards for each word.

Shuffle the deck and divide the cards evenly among the players, who place them face down in a pile. Players take turns exposing a card and laying it face up in front of their pile. When two cards with the same word are exposed, the first child to say the word correctly gets all of the cards that are face up. He places these face down under his pile. Play continues until one player has all of the cards. Players who have lost all of their cards may get back into the game by being first to call a matched pair.

6. Everybody Show Cards—Each child has an identical set of twelve to twenty 2-inch-square word cards, which he places face up in rows on his desk. Face the children and call out words. As a word is called, each child selects that word from his array and holds it up so that it is visible to you. All children with correct responses place their card face down on the desk. Those with incorrect responses turn it face up. When all of the words have been called, the children with all cards face down are winners. Those with cards face up can continue playing until all are winners, or those cards missed can be used in other techniques for further practice.

7. Tactile Recognition of Sight Words—On cards at least 5 × 8 inches, letter lightly in pencil troublesome words using letters 1–2 inches high. Trace each letter with liquid white glue, using a pencil to tease the glue into a fairly uniform line. As you finish each letter, sprinkle the card with dry gelatin powder, shaking the card until all of the glue is covered and as much gelatin powder as possible adheres to the letters. Shake off the unused powder to use again. Do all of your words in this way. Allow the cards to dry thoroughly before stacking. The result will be raised letters in color that even smell pleasant.

Show the cards to the child or group. Using a simple Halloween half-mask with the eyes covered, each child traces the letters with his fingers, seeing how many of the words he can recognize by touch.

Depending on the level of the child, these cards can be made with manuscript or cursive writing.

8. Board Games with Variations—Board games can be very elegant affairs. They can be made in file folders—simple to make and store.

    a. Make a 2-inch-wide trail around a file folder, spiraling in snail fashion to a winner's circle in the center. (See Exhibit 21.) Mark off steps 2 inches apart around the trail.

        i. Permanent Words—Letter the words to be learned in the squares around the board. Children take turns rolling a 1-inch wooden cube with the numerals 1, 2, 3, 1, 2, 3 on its sides. They advance a marker or button the number shown on the cube and must read the word on which they land or retreat word by word until they can read a word. Make the game more interesting by putting a hazard or reward square every ten or fifteen spaces. A hazard space (*Collision, Dam Breaks*, etc.) causes them to retreat a space or two, and a reward space (*Found Some Money, Read a Book*, etc.) allows them to go ahead a space or two.

        ii. Changeable Words—On the squares, put the numerals 1–6, repeating them over and over. Divide the sight cards into six groups according to difficulty, or at random if you prefer. Put the six piles on a sheet or board face down in spaces labeled *One, Two, Three, Four, Five, Six*.

            The children take turns rolling a die and then selecting a card from the pile indicated by the number of dots showing on the die. If a player reads the word correctly, he moves his marker to the next space on the game. If not, he remains on the same space. In either case, the card gets returned to the bottom of its pile.

            If you want to arrange the words by difficulty, you can color-code the cards so that they can be easily sorted by the children.

            To make the game more interesting, allow a one-space advance for words from Piles 1 or 2, a two-space advance for Piles 3 and 4, and a three-space advance for Piles 5 and 6.

    b. Commercial Boards—A Parcheesi board is easily adapted for an interesting word game. The board will accommodate 70 words and provide lots of practice. For older children, make two trails around the board by lettering two words in

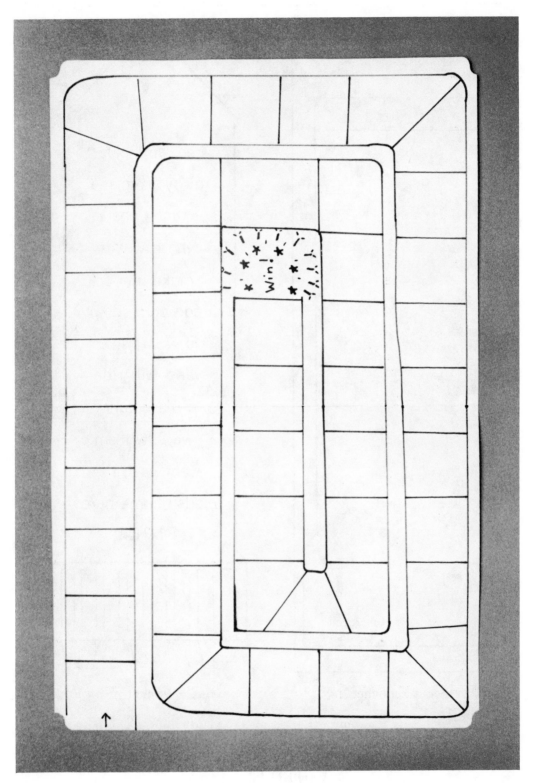

EXHIBIT 21

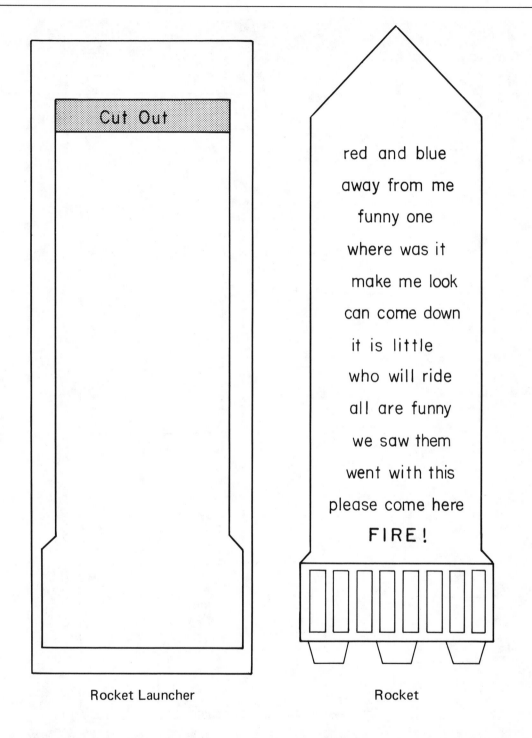

Rocket Launcher
Rocket

red and blue
away from me
funny one
where was it
make me look
can come down
it is little
who will ride
all are funny
we saw them
went with this
please come here
FIRE!

Cut Out

EXHIBIT 22

each space, making [diagram] an inside and an outside trail, or by lettering one word in the space blue and the other red, making a red and a blue trail around the board. This more complicated format requires a player to bring home two men in order to win and gives practice with 140 words.

On the first few spaces after each player's entry point, letter some of the easiest words so that the player will be apt to meet with success initially.

On the home paths for all players, put identical words so that each player gets practice with the same words.

Each player has one to four men to bring home depending on your rules. Follow the rules for the commercial game except that the player must read a word to stay on the space, and to prevent discouragement, delete the rules about players sending other players' men home by landing on their space.

If you can't locate a Parcheesi board that has been discarded as a game, you can simulate a board on a piece of poster board.

9. Sight Word in Context—Rocket Launch—Make a tachistoscopic device for flashing phrases that resembles a rocket launcher. Use a piece of tagboard 8 × 11 inches. Cut an opening near the top where the phrases will appear. (See Exhibit 22.)

Fold the tagboard lengthwise, leaving 3½ inches for the front. Secure the back with masking tape, making a flat pocket. Draw lines to simulate a rocket.

Make rockets to fit inside the launcher. Letter the phrases to be read on the rocket far enough apart that they will show singly in the cut-out space. Letter the bottom word, *Fire!*, in red.

Insert the rocket into the tube. Pull out from the top as the child correctly reads the phrases. If he reads them all and the word *Fire!* appears, he has successfully "launched" that rocket and may go on to another.

This rocket-launcher device is so simple to make that it may be profitable to send one with the child to be used at home. Different rockets can then be sent home for practice with words or phrases.

BIBLIOGRAPHY

GILLILAND, HAP. *A Practical Guide to Remedial Reading.* Columbus, Ohio: Charles E. Merrill Publishing Co., 1974.
VALETT, ROBERT E. *A Psychoeducational Inventory of Basic Learning Abilities.* Belmont, Calif.: Fearon Publishers, 1968.

Visual Activities for Older Students

According to Frostig (1963), the visual modality is essential to the development of reading and writing skills, and just because a child is now older, we do not stop the training of this important learning sense. As a matter of fact, all of us realize the importance of the visual in our everyday learning. Most of us are sight readers as adults (if we are successful readers). How often do you stop to "sound out" a word? Probably not very often. To help a person reach this level of competency, the visual modality must be refined continuously throughout the important years of elementary education. Proceed and teach well.

The definitions in Chapter 4 of Visual Discrimination, Visual Memory, and Visual Sequencing apply here as well. The activities in this chapter will help polish these skills. We do not deal with the other aspects of the visual modality here because the activities in Chapter 4 designed to teach these skills apply to older children as well as to younger ones.

The older child who is having trouble with reading probably suffers from the same deficiencies as the young child. However, in order to hold the older student's interest and not to appear condescending, more mature activities are required. Since all of the following activities are purely visual discrimination tasks, do not be concerned that the student cannot read the words. You are merely calling his attention to minimal interior differences.

Activities   1. Road Maps—Using the 2-inch format in Chapter 4, you can create at least three levels of difficulty using road maps. Prepare the folder with four horizontal spaces 2 inches wide and eight vertical shapes. (See Exhibit 1.)

Using map sections as directed in the following, glue one set on the folder in alternate squares and the second set on 2-inch squares for matching.

    a. From two identical road maps, cut sixteen 2-inch squares with cities as the focal points. This selection makes for easy visual discrimination since the city name makes for quick identification.

    b. From the same maps, cut sixteen 2-inch squares from rural areas. These squares are much harder to match since the student must depend on route numbers and towns in smaller print.

    c. Procure a different map covering the same area as the maps in (a) and (b). Cut a third set of 2-inch sections from one of the maps used in (a) and (b), but for matching, cut a set of squares of the identical area from the new map. This set will be much more difficult to match since the colors and symbols will be different, and the student must rely entirely on route numbers, natural topography, and the names of small towns.

  2. Fingerprints—Draw a horizontal line down the middle of a 3 × 5 or larger file card. Have the student make his fingerprints, his left prints on the left half, his right prints on the right half. Use an inkpad of wet tempera paint on a piece of flannel for the ink. Have the child roll each finger on the card to make sure of getting a complete print.

Instruct the child to classify each fingerprint according to the eight basic fingerprint patterns used by the FBI. (See Exhibit 2.)

If more than one student does this activity, have them compare prints to see if any are identical. This activity is good for self-image since it shows that each person is different and special.

  3. Visual Discrimination Bingo—Prepare bingo cards on 8 × 8-inch tagboard by dividing the cards into 16 2-inch squares. Using words from the following list of words that are easily confused, letter words in the squares, making sure that no two cards are the same (that is, omit a different set of four words from each card). Letter all of the words from the list on 2-inch squares.

board	conservation	cavalry	picture	matched
broad	conversation	calvary	pitcher	marched
dairy	scared	scheduled	stripped	contest
diary	sacred	secluded	striped	context

EXHIBIT 1

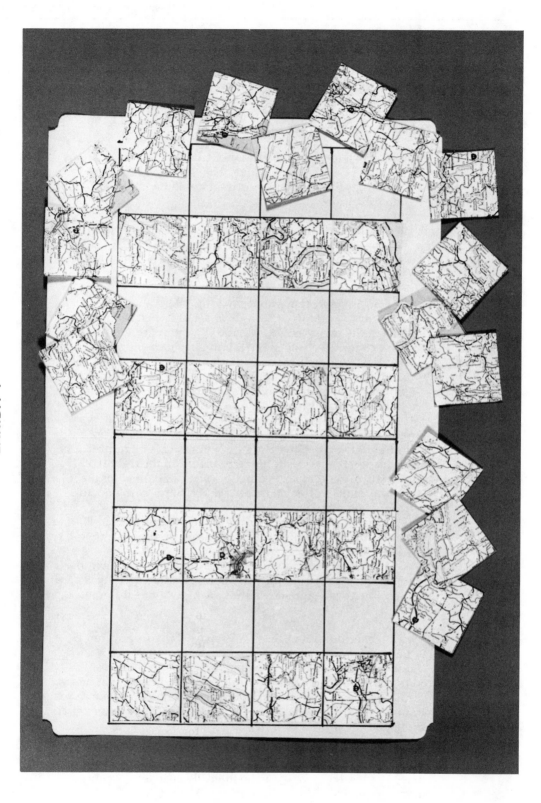

Fingerprint Patterns

There are only eight basic fingerprint patterns. The eight patterns are shown below. The FBI uses these patterns to classify and file fingerprints.

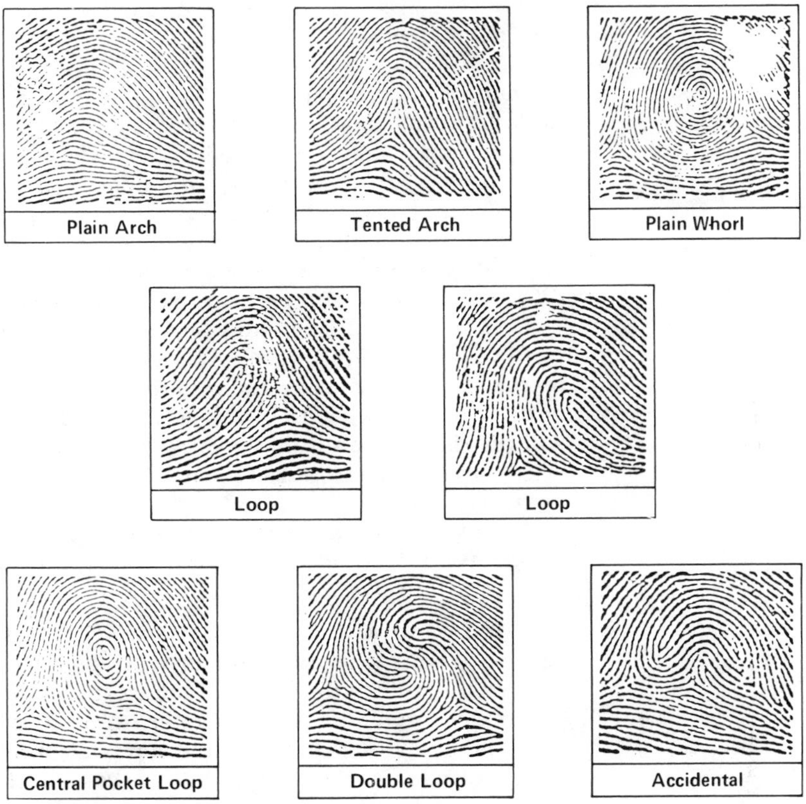

Plain Arch	Tented Arch	Plain Whorl

Loop	Loop

Central Pocket Loop	Double Loop	Accidental

EXHIBIT 2

Play like bingo, except that no auditory clue is given. Simply hold up a card. The students put a marker on the same word on their cards if they have it. They play until someone has a full card.

If a child has difficulty with this activity, have him take the small cards and play solitaire, matching the words to his bingo card.

4. Concentration—This task is designed for two or more students. Using the words in Activity 2 or similar words, prepare a Concentration game on 3 × 5 file cards or #63 round-corner cards. Using all 20 words, the deck will comprise 40 cards. Put them face down in four rows of 5 cards each.

67

5. Matching Covers—Prepare folders using the 2-inch format in Activity 1. For matching, use miniature magazine covers, record jackets, or book covers (these are used in various promotional materials). A student is not going to think it's a childish activity if asked to match *Playboy* covers.

6. Figure-Ground—Use the figure-ground activities from Chapter 4. More advanced activities follow.

   a. Hidden-Word Puzzles—(See Exhibit 3.) Use ½-inch quadrille paper or make your own grid on a duplicating master. Letter words on the squared paper, always from left to right, and with more advanced students, from top to bottom. Putting words in reverse order or diagonally makes this task unsuitable for the student who already has a problem with reversals. Leave spaces between the words, then fill in the spaces with random letters.

   The student finds and boxes in the words. Suitable words include sight words, names of professional sports teams, days of the week and months of the year, presidents of the United States, and names of the states. Such words will provide concomitant learning by familiarizing the student with important words he may be experiencing in other learning areas.

   If you laminate each puzzle and have the students use grease pencils or watercolor markers, the puzzle can be used over and over.

   b. Figure-Ground with Comprehension—This task is suitable for two players. Prepare a folder with five rows of 4 words each on one side of the folder. Each word should represent a different category of words. Letter these 20 words on the left. Then, invert the folder and letter 20 different words representing the same categories as those on the first side, making the folder so that students facing each other will each have a playing board in front of them. (See Exhibit 4.) The following are suggested categories and words:

Category	Side 1	Side 2
Color	blue	brown
Number	ten	eight
Month	December	April
Day of week	Thursday	Tuesday
Bird	robin	wren
Flower	rose	daisy
Car	Ford	Buick
Sport	football	tennis
Tool	hammer	saw
Jewel	opal	diamond
Tree	oak	elm
Country	England	France
State	Georgia	Maine
River	Mississippi	Missouri

W	M	O	N	T	H	Z	J	A	T	B	J	U	N	E
E	O	T	O	U	T	O	U	C	U	M	A	N	O	S
D	N	O	V	E	M	B	E	R	E	P	N	R	V	O
N	D	D	E	S	D	E	N	F	S	T	U	A	R	T
S	A	T	U	R	D	A	Y	G	D	X	A	Y	M	H
D	Y	R	B	E	R	H	M	J	A	N	R	A	R	U
A	P	R	E	L	S	Y	A	C	Y	B	Y	F	C	R
Y	F	E	B	R	U	A	R	Y	T	H	U	R	D	S
D	E	C	E	M	N	E	C	R	I	M	A	I	A	D
E	B	T	J	E	D	S	H	I	M	A	R	D	Y	A
C	W	U	U	A	A	U	M	W	A	P	R	I	L	Y
E	A	S	L	I	Y	N	O	E	Y	R	A	S	E	D
M	R	E	Y	P	M	O	N	D	E	Y	C	E	M	B
B	Y	D	M	R	I	Y	D	N	U	L	T	P	R	I
E	F	A	I	J	U	B	A	E	S	A	E	T	H	U
R	L	Y	L	A	U	G	U	S	T	O	M	E	B	E
C	O	M	D	N	D	A	Y	D	U	C	B	M	A	I
O	C	T	O	B	E	R	U	A	E	T	E	B	U	R
A	T	O	F	R	I	D	A	Y	S	A	R	E	Y	I
C	E	D	R	Y	O	Y	S	E	P	P	E	R	U	L

EXHIBIT 3

EXHIBIT 4

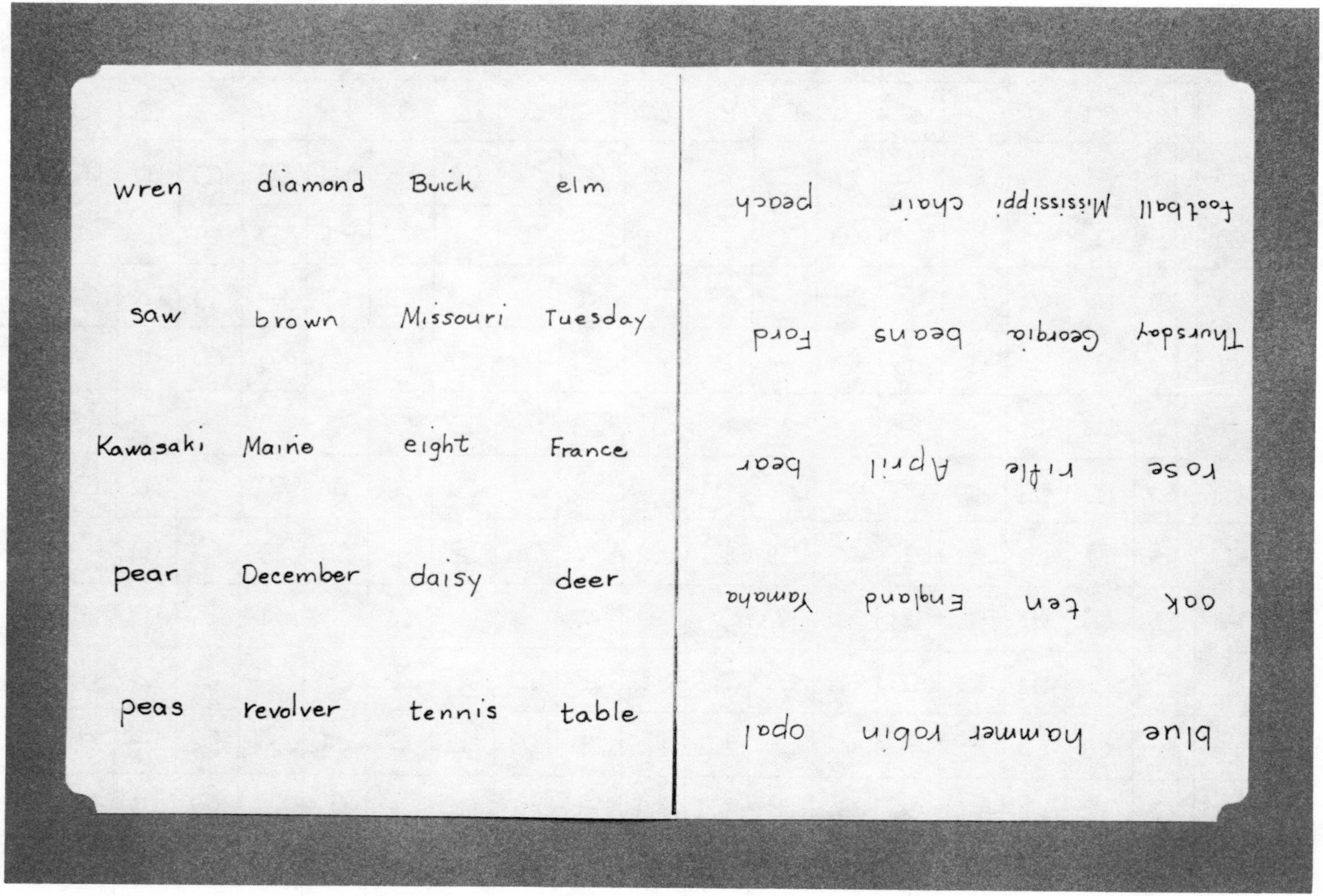

blue hammer robin Opal

oak ten England Yamaha

rose rifle April bear

Thursday Georgia beans Ford

football Mississippi chair peach

table tennis revolver peas

deer December Pear

daisy

France eight Kawasaki Maine

Missouri Tuesday brown S008

elm Buick diamond Wren

Category	Side 1	Side 2
Motorcycle	Yamaha	Kawasaki
Gun	rifle	revolver
Animal	bear	deer
Vegetable	beans	peas
Furniture	chair	table
Fruit	peach	pear

A caller names a category. Each player must scan his side of the board for the word that fits the category and touch it with his finger. The player who succeeds first gets a point.

c. The same technique used in (b) can be used with sight words from a prepared list correlating with the categories used on the cards.

d. Figure-Ground Using Maps—This task can be a small-group or class activity. Select a map from a social studies book or use road maps from your state's tourist bureau. Each student has a copy of the map to look at. One student writes a name from the map on the blackboard, and the rest of the group sees who can find it on the map first. The person who succeeds becomes the writer. Names that spread across an area, such as *Rocky Mountains*, are the most difficult to find, and a city printed in bold type is the easiest.

VISUAL MEMORY

Activities Use the same technique with the flaps on the folder as described on page 26 in Chapter 4, with the following variations.

1. Use words with the same beginning letter or digraph.

2. Use words with the same configuration.

3. Use words from a subject-matter area, such as mathematics (*subtrahend, subtract, multiplier, multiplicand,* etc.).

4. Use road signs. The student is on a limited-access highway and briefly sees a sign. He comes to the exit and must remember which sign he saw. (See Exhibit 5.)

5. Letter two difficult sight words under a 4-inch flap. Letter the same words plus one more to the right of the flap. The student exposes, closes, then puts a marker on the word that was not under the flap. Start this activity with words easy enough to insure success, then proceed to more challenging words.

EXHIBIT 5

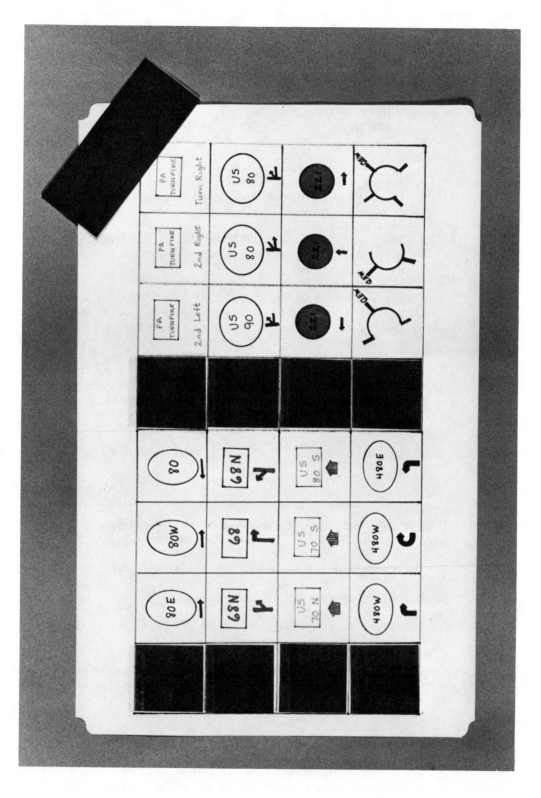

6. Concentration—Make a Concentration deck consisting of 2 cards for each of 20 difficult sight words. Use words such as:

through	neighbor	laugh	ghost
though	height	laughter	ghostly
thorough	weight	cough	gnome
pneumonia	ptomaine	thought	phlegm
			phylum

First, have the student play Concentration with the deck requiring only that he pick up two matching cards; then, require that he say the word in order to keep the pair.

VISUAL MOTOR MEMORY

Activities Use the magic slate for spelling words as described in Activity 2(f), on page 50 in Chapter 4.

1. Configuration Bingo—Make bingo cards with 25 squares. In each square, put a four-letter word with a different configuration. On 5 × 8-inch cards, make the configuration for each word. Sample words and their configurations are shown in Exhibit 6.

   The caller holds up a 5 × 8-inch card, and the players put a marker on their word with that configuration.

Configurations — 4 Letters

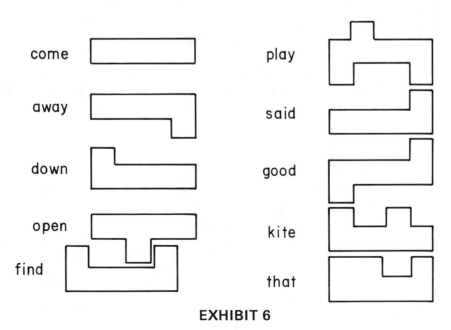

come

away

down

open

find

play

said

good

kite

that

EXHIBIT 6

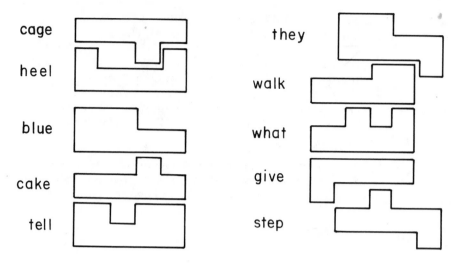

cage

heel

blue

cake

tell

they

walk

what

give

step

EXHIBIT 6 (continued)

2. Configuration Quad Dominoes—This activity may be used as a puzzle for one student or as a domino game for two or more. Make sixteen 3 × 3-inch cards. Make an X on each, dividing the card into four parts. On alternate sides of these dominoes, make the same configurations as those in Activity 1, but use different words. (See Exhibit 7.)

Each player gets five quad dominoes. The rest are placed face down for the boneyard. A player with a corner card or a border card starts. All sides must match. The player using all of his quad dominoes first wins. Play continues until the complete square has been formed.

BIBLIOGRAPHY

FROSTIG, M., et al. *The Marianne Frostig Developmental Test of Visual Perception.* Palo Alto, Calif.: Consulting Psychology Press, 1963 standardization.

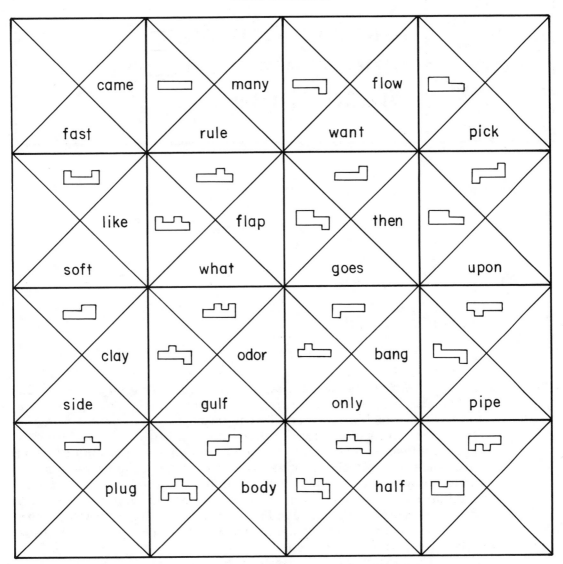

EXHIBIT 7

6 | Auditory Activities, Kindergarten through Grade Three

The auditory modality is exceptionally important in beginning reading. Much of the emphasis in early reading programs dwells on phonic analysis, which requires keen powers of auditory decoding inasmuch as initial consonant sounds like *b, p, t,* and *d* can be awfully confusing to a young mind encountering them for the first time. All of the activities in this chapter are teacher tested and are effective when proper attention is paid to sequence. Many teachers make the mistake of jumping too quickly from the simple to the complex. For example, it is more complicated than one might expect to move from successfully discriminating between *b* and *p* to discriminating between *br* and *pr*. This is especially true with reading disabled children. In essence, it is far better to overteach these children than underteach them.

The following are definitions of the categories to be used in this chapter.

- *Auditory Discrimination*—The ability to understand sounds or spoken words. Pupil can follow simple verbal instructions; can indicate by gesture or words the meaning or purpose of auditory stimuli such as animal sounds, nouns, or verbs.
- *Auditory Memory*—The ability to retain and recall general auditory information. Pupil can verbally relate yesterday's experience.
- *Auditory Sequencing*—The ability to recall in correct sequence and detail prior auditory information. Pupil can imitate specific sound patterns; can follow exactly a complex series of directions; can repeat digit and letter series. (Valett, 1968.)

AUDITORY SKILLS

A child who appears to have problems in the auditory area should be checked first for auditory acuity. Once physiological problems are ruled out, you can work with techniques to help him learn to interpret sounds. He must learn to classify sounds, associate them with particular meanings, and respond to the meanings.

If you cannot develop in a child the ability to interpret sounds, you will have to rely on his visual capabilities. First, however, you must exhaust all of your resources in an attempt to help him build learnings in the auditory area.

You already have developed in the child visual recognition of letter forms. In this chapter, you will give sounds and combinations of sounds to letters and letter groups.

Auditory Decoding

Activities 1. Identification of Common Sounds—Using a cassette tape, record common sounds heard around the house such as telephone ringing, door slamming, vacuum cleaner, door-bell chimes, hammering, and sawing. Leave several seconds of blank tape between sounds to allow time for the child to turn off the recorder or to accomplish the task. This tape can be used three ways.

a. Oral Identification—Have the student identify the sound orally.

b. Identification Using Pictures—Prepare a folder with numbered 2- or 3-inch squares. Use as many numbers as you have sounds on the tape. On 2- or 3-inch squares of railroad board, place pictures to represent the sounds on the tape. (Take pictures from old science books, primary workbooks, catalogs, paperback picture dictionaries, etc.)

Tape or read directions to the child as follows: Open the folder and spread your pictures on the desk in front of you. Turn on the tape. On this tape, you will hear some sounds. When you have decided which object is making the sound you hear, pick up the picture of that object and place it in the numbered square. Ready for sound number 1. (*sound of door slamming*) What did you hear? Pick up the picture of that object and place it in the numbered square. (*five-second pause*) Continue through the sounds on the tape in this manner; then turn off the tape.

You should make yourself available to check the child's answers immediately upon completion. If the child has errors, rewind the tape and go through it slowly with the child, helping him to analyze the sounds.

c. Identification Using Words—Use the folder format from (b), but instead of pictures on the cards, put the word that identifies the object.

77

2. Identification of Animal Sounds—For a second series of sounds to be used as in Activity 1, make a tape of animal sounds. These are available on many sound-effects recordings.

3. Auditory Decoding—Comprehension of Simple Statements— Prepare a folder with *Yes* lettered at the top of the left side and *No* lettered on the right. Give the child a supply of numbered markers.

   Read numbered statements aloud. After the child hears the statement, he picks up the corresponding number and places it on the appropriate side of the folder indicating whether the statement is true or not. Sample statements are:

   > Cars can go.
   > Books eat food.
   > Golf is a game.
   > We see with our ears.
   > Robins are green.

   Adjust the vocabulary and difficulty of the statement to the ability of the child, but keep in mind that this is not a test of scientific knowledge but a check on the child's understanding of statements heard.

4. Auditory Decoding with Picture Interpretation and Response— Instead of using yes and no statements alone, pictures are added, making this a two-step activity.

   Collect a set of 12 pictures of common objects or activities, glue them on cards, and number them 1–12. Use the folder format in Activity 1(b). Give the following instructions:
   Put the open folder in front of you and spread out the numbered picture cards. Take picture Number 1. (*picture of football player*) This is a football player. If the statement is true, place the picture under *Yes*. If the statement is not true, place the picture under *No*.
   Samples are as follows:

Picture	*Statement*
yellow banana	The banana is purple.
boy sitting	The boy is running.

5. Auditory Decoding—Classification of Sounds—Objects, like letters, may make a variety of sounds. In this activity, using a recorded tape, the child classifies the sounds by their sources.

   Suggested sounds to be taped are listed in indiscriminate order. Allow five seconds between sounds to give the child time to place a marker on his folder.

   > clock—ticking, striking, alarm ringing
   > water—dripping, running, waterfall
   > horse—walking, galloping, neighing
   > car—motor starting, revving, horn blowing
   > dog—whining, barking, growling, scratching
   >   at door

Prepare a folder with as many columns as you have sources of sounds (three or four in the preceding list).

Give the child numbered markers to be placed on the folder as the sound is heard. Check for accuracy immediately after completion. If the child has difficulty comprehending the sources, play the tape again, stopping it between sounds, re-playing a troublesome sound, and helping the child with iden-tifying characteristics of that sound.

6. Auditory Decoding—Identification and Interpretation of Sounds—Prepare a tape with sounds of a bell ringing and a table-tennis ball bouncing. Each time the particular sound is made, it should be made a different number of times. Example:

> Sound number 1—Ball, three bounces
> Sound number 2—Bell, four rings

In preparing the tape, be sure to hold the clapper of the bell between rings to insure distinct, separate rings. Leave five seconds between each group of sounds.

Prepare a folder with ten spaces numbered 1–10 to ac-commodate responses to ten sound groups. Give the child 12 2-inch squares. Six squares will have an outline of a bell and the numerals 1–5 plus a repeat of one of the numerals. Six will have the outline of a ball numbered in the same manner.

As the child plays the tape, he must decide which object he has heard and how many sounds the object has made. Allow him to stop the cassette between sound groups if he needs more time to select and place the appropriate card on the numbered space.

This activity can be done without a tape. You may simply make the sounds from behind a cardboard shield.

7. Auditory Decoding—Recognizing Like Sounds in the Beginning of Names of Objects—Collect a number of common objects or small toys with duplicate beginning sounds, such as:

cork	fork	zipper
candle	fish	zebra
bulb	gum	
battery	gun	

   a. The child must recognize the object, name it, and then re-late it to another object whose name has the same begin-ning sound. These objects are placed together in a muffin pan or in separate spaces on a folder.
   b. Put letter labels on the spaces so that the child must not only recognize like sounds but be aware of the letter that produces that sound.
   c. Make the same activity using pictures of objects instead of the objects themselves.

8. Auditory Decoding—Recognizing Like Sounds of Letters—You produce two sounds, and the student tells orally if they are like or different. If you are doing this activity with a group, give

each child a folder with one side marked *L* for *Like*, and the other *D* for *Different*. Each child has numbered markers which he places on the correct side of the folder as he hears the sounds.

a. Letters—Say pairs of letters such as:

> *m m,*   *s b,*   *t f,*   *p p,*   *d d,*   *z s,*   etc.

pausing between each group of two to allow the child to respond.

b. Letters as Beginning Sounds—Say pairs of words such as:

> bat boy,   man sun,   take win,   top dot,   etc.

c. Letters as Ending Sounds—Say words such as:

> bad bag,   run fun,   take cake,   dip sit,   tub tug,   etc.

Auditory Memory and Sequencing

Activities

1. Remembering Sounds in Order—
    a. Say two numerals and have child repeat them in the correct order. Continue the activity with three, four, five, or more numerals, stopping when the child has reached his level of frustration. Each time this task is used, go back and end with a level where the child is successful so that he will remember it as a positive experience. Use this activity regularly to extend the child's ability in this area.
    b. Numerals in Reverse—Have the child repeat the numerals heard in reverse order.
    c. Letters—
    d. Letters in Reverse Order—
    e. Letters and Numerals Mixed—2 *a b* 4 *c* etc.
    f. Sound Patterns—Beat a pattern on a coffee can or tom-tom. The child repeats the pattern.

2. Remembering Words in Order—
    a. Say related words, which the child is to repeat in correct order. Use groupings of words such as *red, blue, green, purple; dog, cat, cow, horse; dime, nickel, penny, quarter.*
    b. Play games such as I'm Going on a Trip and I'm Taking Some Money. The child repeats what you have said and adds one item, you repeat what the child has said and add another item, etc., as long as successful.
    c. Repeat Couplets (Two-Line Jingles)—
    d. Repeat tongue twisters—Simple at first, then more difficult.

AUDITORY SKILLS APPLIED TO READING

In all devices for developing auditory skills, oral response is important. Be sure to have the child check his answers by reading them aloud to you so that he hears the sound as well as sees the letter.

Activities
1. Beginning Consonants—Start with two letters that are not easily confused such as *m* and *s*.
   a. Prepare a folder with the letter *m* along with a picture of an easily identifiable picture of an object whose name begins with *m* (e.g., mitten or monkey) on one side of the folder and an *s* with a picture on the other side. Paste small pictures of objects beginning with these sounds on 2-inch circles or squares.

   Have the child place the pictures on the correct side of the folder according to the beginning sound.
   b. Prepare a folder as in (a), but omit the picture as a cue. The child must depend on the letter only. Continue this activity through several folders with different sets of consonants. After teaching four, make a review folder. After teaching eight, make a review folder. Omit *x* as a beginning consonant since it usually has a *z* sound in this position.
   c. Mobiles—Cut out a piece of construction paper 4 × 8 inches for each consonant. Print the consonant to be learned on both sides. Make a hole in the center of this strip and slip it over the hook of a coat hanger, fastening it together at the bottom.

   Have the children cut from magazines or catalogs pictures of objects beginning with that letter. Paste these on various shapes of construction paper and hang them from the bottom wire with black thread.

   Have the children "read the mobile" by naming all of the objects that begin with that letter. Repeat for all consonants.
   d. Wizard—Self-correcting practice with beginning sounds. Use ½-pint plastic fruit-drink bottles or plastic bleach bottles with fairly large openings. Cut a ¼-inch slot halfway through the bottle at the center of the bottle. (See Exhibit 1.) If you make eyes on each side of the opening and a curly tail at the end opposite the opening using a permanent magic marker, this device becomes a pig.

   On ten or more 3 × 5 or smaller cards for the ½-pint bottle, paste small pictures of objects top center.

81

EXHIBIT 1

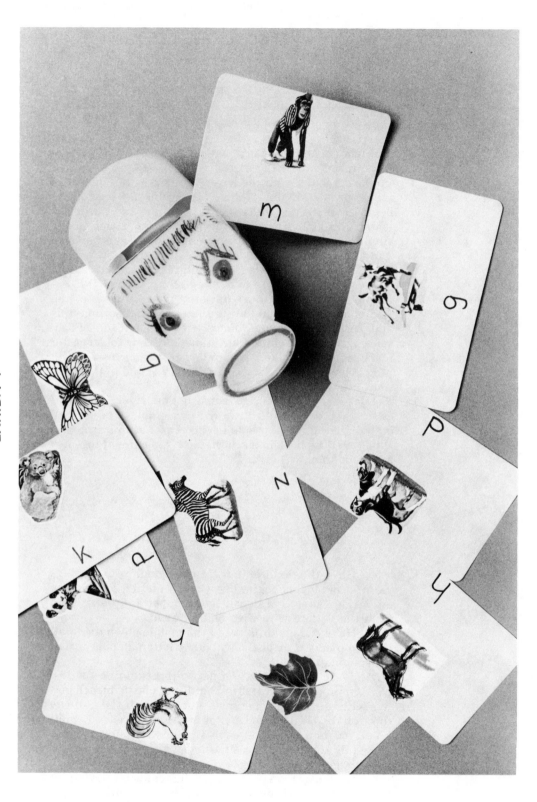

Put the beginning letter bottom center. Put the whole set of cards in the slot with the picture showing and the letter concealed in the bottle.

Have the child look at the picture, say its beginning sound, then look in the open end of the bottle where he can see the letter to check his answer for accuracy. With success, he then should move the front card to the back and go on to the next picture.

The Wizard works well for any set of facts to be learned (contractions, abbreviations, plurals, math facts, etc.).

e. Shoelace Sounds—Paste pictures of objects with various beginning sounds on pieces of 3 × 3-inch tagboard. Put each letter to be used on a similar piece of tagboard. Punch two holes in the top of each piece of board.

Give each child a letter card and a shoelace with a large knot in one end. Spread the pictures on the table in front of the group. Have each child find the pictures that begin with his letter and string them on his shoelace. (See Exhibit 2.)

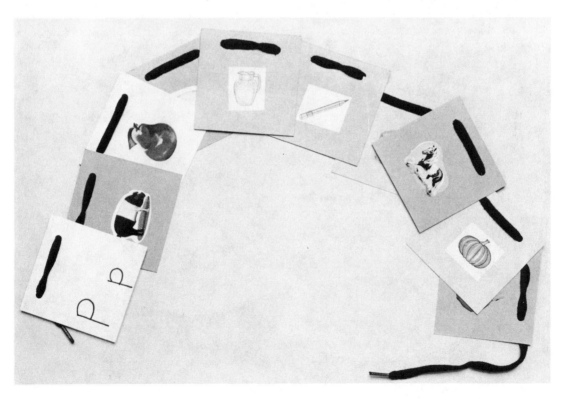

EXHIBIT 2

f. Clothespin Sounds—On a stiff piece of cardboard (tablet back or corrugated board) with dimensions of about 3 × 12 inches, paste small pictures of objects with various beginning sounds. Print the letters to be used on the ends of spring clothespins using a permanent fine-point marker. Be sure to print them so that they will be right side up when clipped on the board.

   The child clips each beginning letter to the picture of the object.

g. Beginning Consonant Substitution—Take two inexpensive, plain-white paper plates. From one plate, cut a 1½-inch section from the edge. (See Exhibit 3.) Directly in from the notch, letter an ending such as *an*. Around the edge of the other plate, at least ¾ of an inch apart, make the letters *b, c, d, f, m, n, p, r, t, v*. Put the two plates together and fasten with a paper fastener in the exact center.

   Have the child move the top plate around and pronounce each word as it appears. This device can be used with many endings such as *old, ill, in, all*, etc. You may

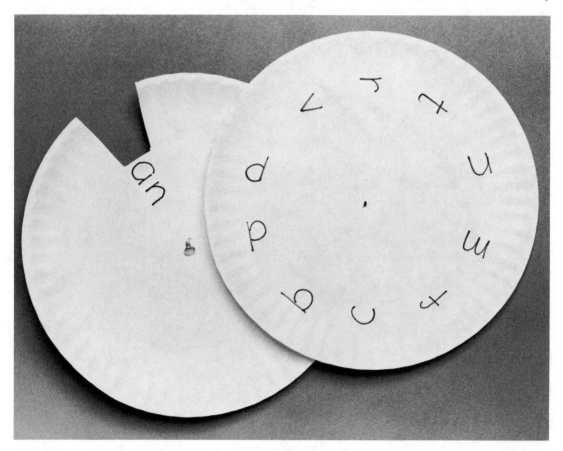

EXHIBIT 3

limit your beginning letters on each to those that make words, or you may include nonsense words if you wish.

h. Beginning-Sound Domino Word Chain—Draw a line across the center of twenty 3×5 file cards, making $3 \times 2\frac{1}{2}$-inch rectangles. On the right end of each card, letter a consonant, omitting x. On the left end of each domino, paste or draw a picture of an object beginning with the next consonant in the alphabet. On the left end of the b card, paste a picture of an object beginning with z.

The child starts with any card and places the matching picture or word on both ends. If he turns a corner to the right after each five pictures, he will have a completed square.

These same cards may be used by two or more children to play a game of dominoes. Each child is dealt five dominoes, one domino is placed face up in the center of the table for a starting place, and the remainder are placed face down for the boneyard. (See Exhibit 4.)

2. Ending Consonants—
   a. Prepare a folder with five vertical columns. Place one of the letters b, m, t, s, l (these are not easily confused) at the top of each column. Put pictures of objects whose names end with these consonants on 2-inch squares for the child to classify according to ending sounds. Make a similar folder using the ending letters d, x, g, n, p, r, k.
   b. Make a separate folder for any letters that the child confuses, such as b, d, t. Be sure to have the child read his responses orally so that his pronunciation can be checked.
   c. Ending Consonant Review—Big Art Show—Prepare a folder with empty 2×2-inch frames, each with a line to represent a wire hanging from a nail. Under each nail, make an ending letter.

      On 2×2-inch colored railroad board, paste pictures of objects whose names have ending letters to match those below the nails.

      The child puts all of these pictures in the correct frames by matching final sounds. (See Exhibit 5.)

3. Rhyming Words—Prepare a folder with 2×4-inch horizontal spaces.
   a. Match Picture to Picture—Put one set of pictures on the folder. Place the second set of pictures on small cards. The name of each object in the second set rhymes with the name of an object in the first set. Use pictures of a bell and a shell, a car and a star, a house and a mouse, etc.
   b. Match Pictures to Words—Put words in spaces on the folder, allowing a 2-inch space beside each for the child to place a matching picture card.
   c. Concentration—On each end of 3×5 file cards, stamp or paste pictures of objects whose names rhyme, such as cork and fork, cat and hat, lamp and stamp, etc. Make about eight or ten sets.

Beginning Sound Word Chain Dominoes

(Words in Circles Indicate Pictures)

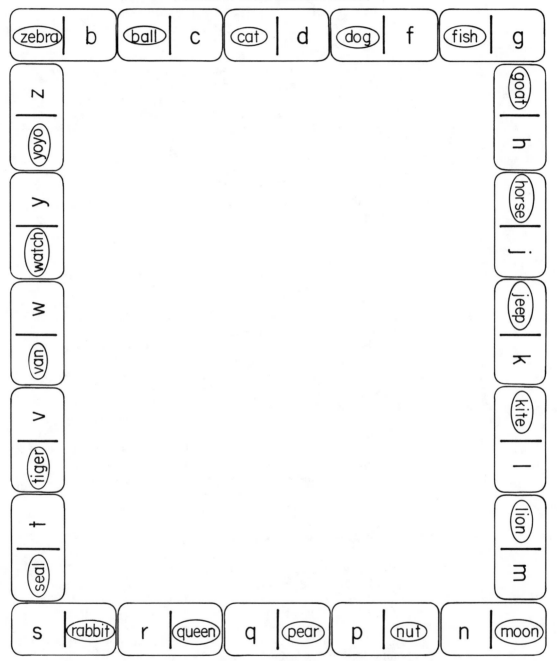

EXHIBIT 4

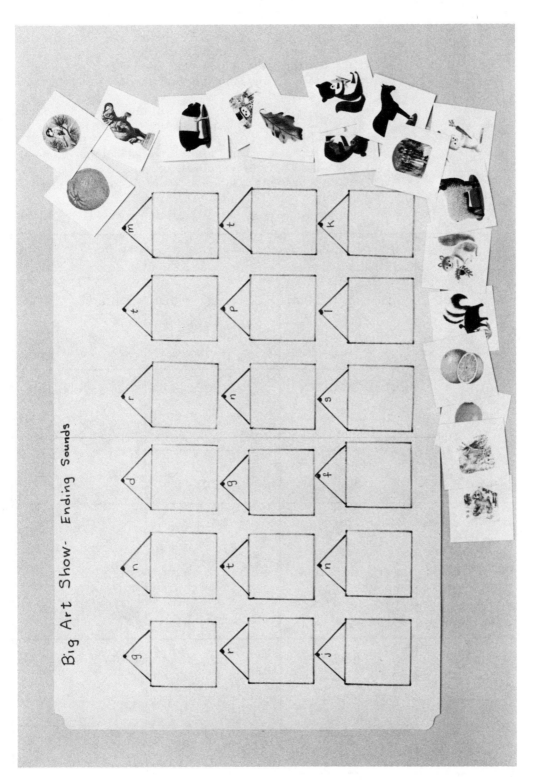

EXHIBIT 5

87

i. Have the child name the objects on each card so that he hears the rhyming sounds of the words.

ii. Cut the cards in half, separating the pictures. Shuffle the cards and have the child match the ends by rhyming sounds.

iii. Place the cards face down in rows and play Concentration. See who can get the most rhyming picture cards.

d. Cut 16 3-inch cards. Make a quad domino game for rhyming words as explained on page 74 in Chapter 5 ("Configurations"). Sixteen cards require 24 different matches. (See Exhibit 6.)

Rhyming Words

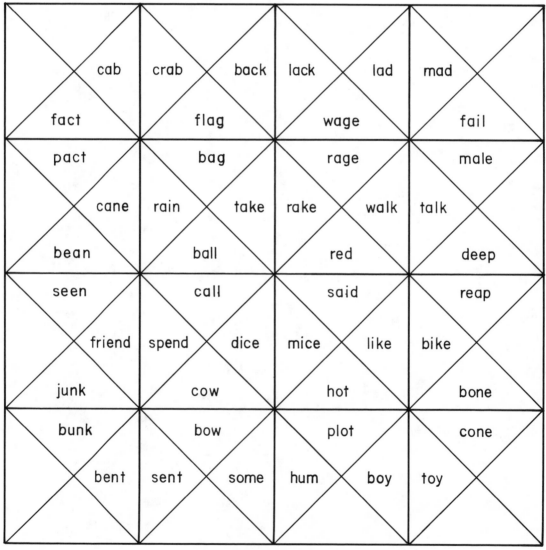

EXHIBIT 6

4. Medial Consonants—Prepare a folder with six vertical columns. Paste at the head of each column a picture of an object whose name has one of the following letters for its medial sound:

p (zipper)   *n* (penny)
l (ballroom) *t* (mitten)
b (rabbit)   *d* (ladder)

Put the following words on 1 × 3-inch sentence strips:

habit	pillow	pattern
table	sailor	hotel
cabbage	tulip	lettuce
robin	ruler	sweater
planet	radish	slipper
miner	spider	paper
pony	model	stupid
canal	pudding	pepper

The child places each strip under the picture with the same medial sound.

5. Position of Consonant Sounds—Prepare a folder with 4 vertical columns. (See Exhibit 7.) Draw horizontal lines 2½ inches apart, making 16 spaces. At the center top of each space, fasten with a paper fastener a 1½-inch-long cardboard arrow. At the bottom of each space, make three short horizontal lines, one at the left side, one in the center directly under the paper fastener, and one to the right. These lines represent beginning, middle, and end.
   a. Visual Concept of Position of Sound—Tell the student to watch for the consonant *m*. Hold up a picture of a camel. Tell the student to show with the arrow where to find the *m* in *camel*. Proceed down Column 1 with other pictures whose names contain *m*, such as mitten, drum, comic. Check to see if he has moved his arrows to the correct position for each word.
   b. Auditory Comprehension of Positions of Sound—Use Column 2. Announce the letter to be listened for. Pronounce four words containing the letter. Have the student move the arrow to show the position of the letter in the words. Check for accuracy.
   c. Silent Application of the Concept—Use Columns 3 and 4. Give the student two strips of tagboard measuring 4 × 12 inches. At the top of each, place a letter, and under each, place four pictures of objects whose names contain that letter in some position. Have the student look at the picture and move the arrow to show the position of the designated consonant.

6. Consonant Blends and Digraphs—Some series treat these as two separate groups, whereas others classify them all as consonant blends. Follow whatever plan your series uses.

EXHIBIT 7

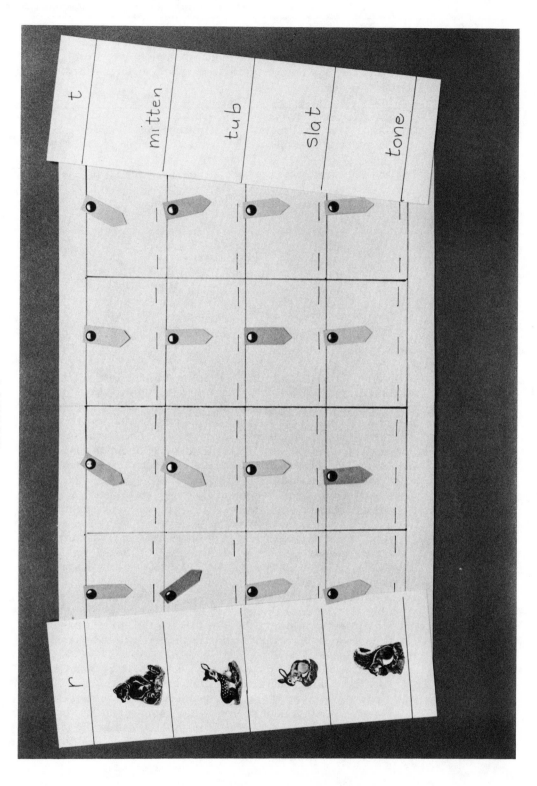

a. The *l* Blends—Prepare a folder with six columns headed, respectively, *bl, cl, fl, gl, pl, sl*. On small cards, paste or print pictures of objects whose names start with these blends (block, clown, flower, glass, plate, sled). Make as many cards as you can find pictures. Have the student put the cards in the correct column.

b. The *r* Blends—Prepare a folder as in (a) with seven columns headed *br, cr, dr, fr, gr, pr, tr*. Make picture cards using such pictures as brick, crown, drum, frog, grape, propeller, tree.

c. Blends Beginning with *s*—Prepare a folder with ten sections. Head each with one of the following blends: *sc, sk, sm, sn, sp, st, sw, scr, spr, str*. Make cards with such pictures as scarecrow, skunk, smoke, snail, spool, stamp, swing, screw, spring, strawberry.

d. Common Digraphs—Prepare a folder with four horizontal sections. At the beginning of each, print one of these digraphs: *ch, th, wh, sh*. Give the student picture cards to classify using such pictures as:

cherry	thumb	wheel	sheep
chair	thimble	whale	shelf
church	thermos	whistle	shower

e. Blend and Digraph Bingo—Divide 10 × 10-inch tagboard cards into 25 sections by making 5 2-inch spaces horizontally and vertically. Write selected blends and digraphs in each of the sections, making each card different.

Provide the caller with a list of words utilizing all of the sounds used on your cards. Have several words for each sound. As the caller pronounces words from the lists, the players put a marker on the appropriate blend (or digraph) on their card. Play until a child has filled x number of rows, or his entire card. Be sure to have the caller mark the words called for checking. To make this easier, put the words for calling on separate cards instead of utilizing the list.

7. Long and Short Vowel Sounds—

a. Make a folder for each vowel. At the top of each, put a picture of an object whose name has the short vowel sound on the left side and one with the long vowel sound on the right. Beside each picture, make the vowel with the diacritical marking. Paste or stamp pictures to represent the long and short vowel sounds on small cards.

Have the student work with one folder at a time, placing the pictures on the side of the folder with the same vowel sound. Have the student say the names of the pictures as he places them if he is doing it with you. If he is doing the folder by himself, have him name the pictures when the folder is checked. Having him say and hear as well as "think" the sounds is an important reinforcement step.

91

b. After the student has mastered two vowels, prepare a folder with four sections, each labeled with letters and pictures to depict the long and short sounds of two vowels. Give the student the four sets of pictures to classify.

c. Make the same folder for two more vowels, etc., until the child has mastered the ten sounds.

d. Whose House Is That?—Prepare a folder with a horizontal line 2 inches down from the top. Divide each side of the folder into five vertical sections. At the top of each section, make the outline of a house.

In the houses across the folder, put the five vowels, making the symbol for the short vowels on one side and the long vowels on the other. (See Exhibit 8.)

Give the student a collection of pictures on cards to be classified under the correct house. For the more able child, prepare cards with words to be classified in the same way. Make a Key Card for self-checking.

e. Vowel Table Tennis—May be played by one or two children. Prepare a table-tennis tabletop on a folder by making a simulated net on a strip of green construction paper 1½ × 10 inches. Fasten this at the crease in the folder by putting cellophane tape hinges on both sides. When the folder is put flat on the table, the net stands upright. Label one side of the folder *Short*, and the other *Long*.

Cut or have the student(s) cut a number of 2-inch circles from construction paper. On these balls, write words with long and short vowel sounds. Put the balls in a pile face down beside the court.

If played by two, one player takes a ball and puts it on the correct court according to vowel sound. If he is correct, he scores a point and keeps the ball. If he is incorrect, the ball is still in play, and the other player gets it.

If on some balls you put words that have neither long nor short vowel sounds, the game is more challenging. These balls are fouls. If they are correctly called, they go out of play (discard pile), and the player selects the next card. Make a Key Card with correct answers to be available for checking disputed calls.

f. Blending Cubes—Use four 1-inch-square wooden beads or have holes drilled in cubes to make beads. Using a bobby pin, pull a rubber band through the holes, making the ends secure on each end with a plastic-bag tie. (See Exhibit 9.)

On the first and third beads, print consonants; on the second, vowels (omit *e*); and on the fourth bead, leave two sides blank, put *e* on one side, and *s* on the other.

First, positioning the fourth bead so that it is blank, have the student say all of the sound combinations possible by rotating the first bead; second, by rotating the third bead; third, change the vowel and repeat the first two steps.

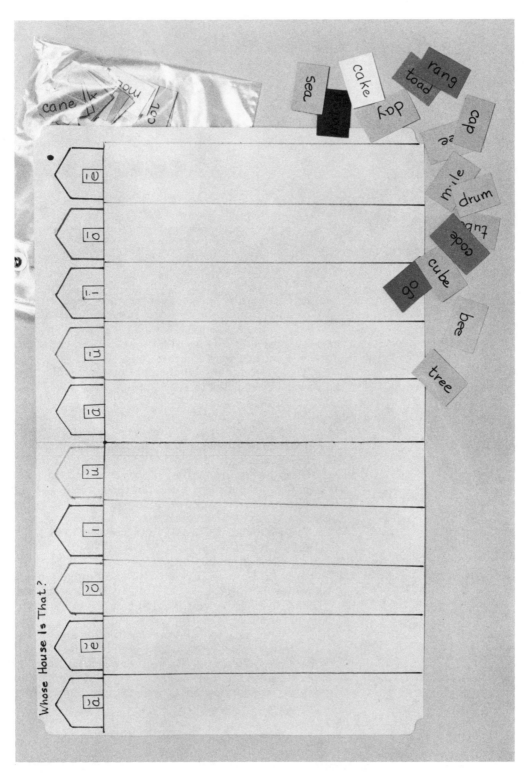

EXHIBIT 8

EXHIBIT 9

After all of the possible consonant-vowel-consonant (CVC) combinations have been practiced, change the final bead to the *e* position. Now, have the student repeat the first three steps using the final *e*, which will change the vowel sounds from short to long.

Then, change the last bead to *s*, which will change the vowel sounds back to short sounds. The words will be in plural form.

g. Bagging Vowel Sounds—Use ½- or 1-pound, square-bottom, brown kraft bags (penny-candy bags). Fold inside the top 2 or more inches of the bag to make it shorter and to reinforce the top edge.

Glue the square bottom of the bag to a folder. Fold the bag. On the sides facing out, put the ten long and short vowels. (See Exhibit 10.) The open bag serves as a three-dimensional device for sorting vowel sounds.

The following are items that can be sorted:
i. Small Objects (clip, nail, pen, etc.)—pin.
ii. Pictures Pasted on Cards
iii. Words on Cards—This activity can be made on several levels: First, use CVC and CVC + *e* words only. Then, use harder vowel clusters and sounds such as found in *chief, breathe, aisle,* etc.

This activity, like most of the folder activities, can be made self-checking by preparing Key Cards on 5 × 8-inch file cards. Be sure to code the Key Cards the same as the folder. When the child completes the folder, he gets the Key Card and checks his work for accuracy.

8. Vowel Variants—
a. Controlled by *r*—The letter *r* is very powerful. When it follows a vowel, it controls the vowel's ability to make

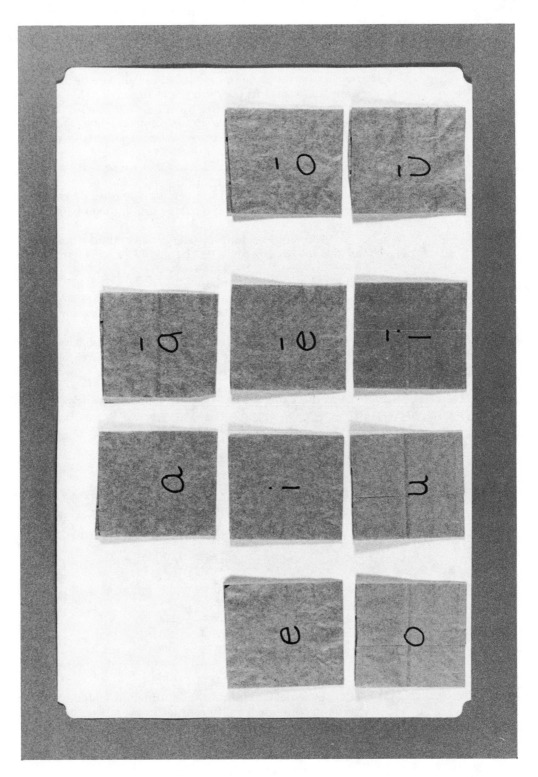

EXHIBIT 10

either its long or short sound and reduces the sound to a grunt. The common sound (Wilson and Hall, 1968, p. 24) for *ar* is as it is heard in *car*, for *or* as it is heard in *for*, and the *er, ir, ur* combinations usually make the identical sound, as heard in *bird, her*, and *turn*.

Make a folder with three sections for classifying these three sounds. Put a picture of an object at the beginning of each to demonstrate the three sounds (e.g., star, bird, fork).

Have the student classify picture or word cards in the three sections according to vowel sound.

    b. Sounds of *oo*—Prepare a folder with two sections. Put a picture of a book (o͝o) on one side and a moon (o͞o) on the other.

Have the student classify picture, then word, cards on the folder according to the sound of *oo* heard in the word.

    c. Diphthongs and Digraphs—

        1. Sounds of *ou* or *ow*—Prepare a folder with two sides. Put a picture of a cow on one side and a crow on the other.

First, have the students classify pictures as to the sound of *ou* or *ow* heard. Use pictures of snow, bow, window, pillow, owl, plow, flower, clown, etc.

Second, give the student word cards to classify on the same folder. Use the following words:

now	blow	foul
howl	show	soul
brown	grow	south
growl	out	loud
flow		

        ii. Sounds of *ea*—Prepare a folder with three sections. At the top of each, write one of the following:

ea (ĕ)   ea (ā)   ea (ē)

        iii. Put the following words on cards for classification:

bread	steak	bead
deaf	break	steam
thread	great	feast
health		meal
spread		deal

    d. There is almost no limit to the number of folder activities that can be made for different letter-sound combinations. Make classification activities for the ones needed, such as:

> hard and soft *c*
> hard and soft *g*
> sounds of the letter *s* (*s, z, sh*)
> voiced and unvoiced *th*

e. Missing vowels—This is a self-checking exercise. Mark a folder into five 2-inch horizontal sections. On the extreme left of each side of the folder, put a picture of an object to depict a long or short vowel sound. On the extreme right of each side of the folder, put a 2-inch hinged flap in each of the five sections. Between the picture and the flap, letter the word with the vowel omitted. (See Exhibit 11.) Under the flap, write the missing letter.

Give the student an array of 2-inch cards, each imprinted with a vowel. He looks at the picture, selects the card with the missing vowel, and puts it in the vowel space. He then lifts the flap to check the answer. It should not be a concern if he lifts the flap first since this is a teaching, not a testing, activity. However, he should practice the folder until he is able to do it without looking for the answer.

This technique works equally well for consonants, blends, etc.

9. Quad Dominoes for Vowel Sounds—(See Exhibit 12.)

10. Other Techniques for Practicing Letter Sounds—Using the food-ad pages of the newspaper—Give each child a full-page food ad from the newspaper. These can be all alike or all different. These pages are easy to accumulate and can be used for many different skills. Fresh pages can be used each time.
   a. Classifying Letters and Numerals—Give the child two different colored markers or crayons. Have him mark each word with one color and each numeral with the other.
   b. Letter Recognition—Give each child a colored marker or crayon. Have him mark whatever letter is being presented as many times as it appears on his page. If the child has learned counting, have him count and record the number on the paper. Have the children check each other's pages for accuracy.

   If you are presenting every letter of the alphabet, keep a record of the number of times different letters appear to ascertain which letters are used most frequently.
   c. Blends—Have each child mark each consonant blend found on his page. Have him list the blends, and then put them in alphabetical order.
   d. Vowel Sounds—Give each child two different colored markers or crayons. Have him mark all of the short vowel sound words with one color and the long vowel sound words with the other.

11. Vegetable Soup—This activity uses a bag of large, dried lima beans. On one side of 26 beans, print the letters of the alphabet using a fine-point permanent marker. On the other side, print just the vowels, repeating them until all 26 beans have letters on each side. Make several sets of these, at least as many as you have children in your group. Mix all of the beans together. Give each child a one-ounce medicine measuring cup or coffee

EXHIBIT 11

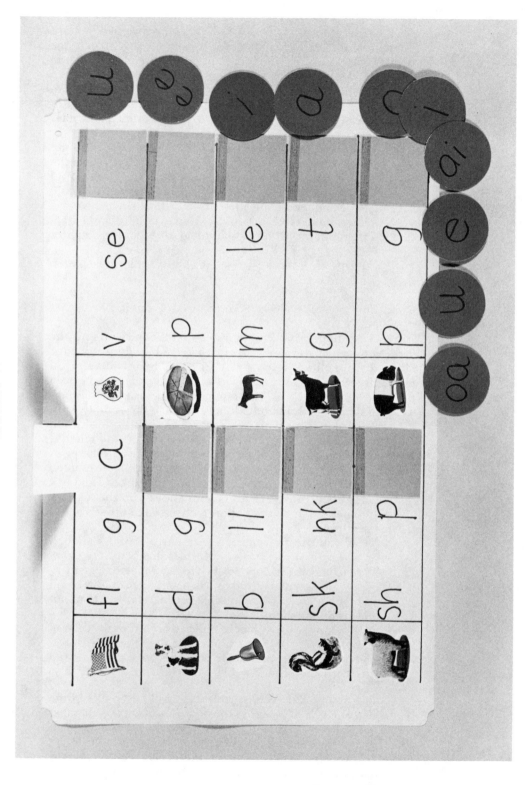

cone	groan	bed	red	cup	run

(Grid of words:)

cone   groan   bed   red   cup   run
rain   bead   pie   tube
pane   seed   high   cube
        toy   boil   glad   ran   dear   fear
grow   fur   dead   ball
though   bird   said   stall
        for   core   pear   bear   book   cook
come   out   car   is
from   cow   star   grit
        learn earth moon   stool doll   frog

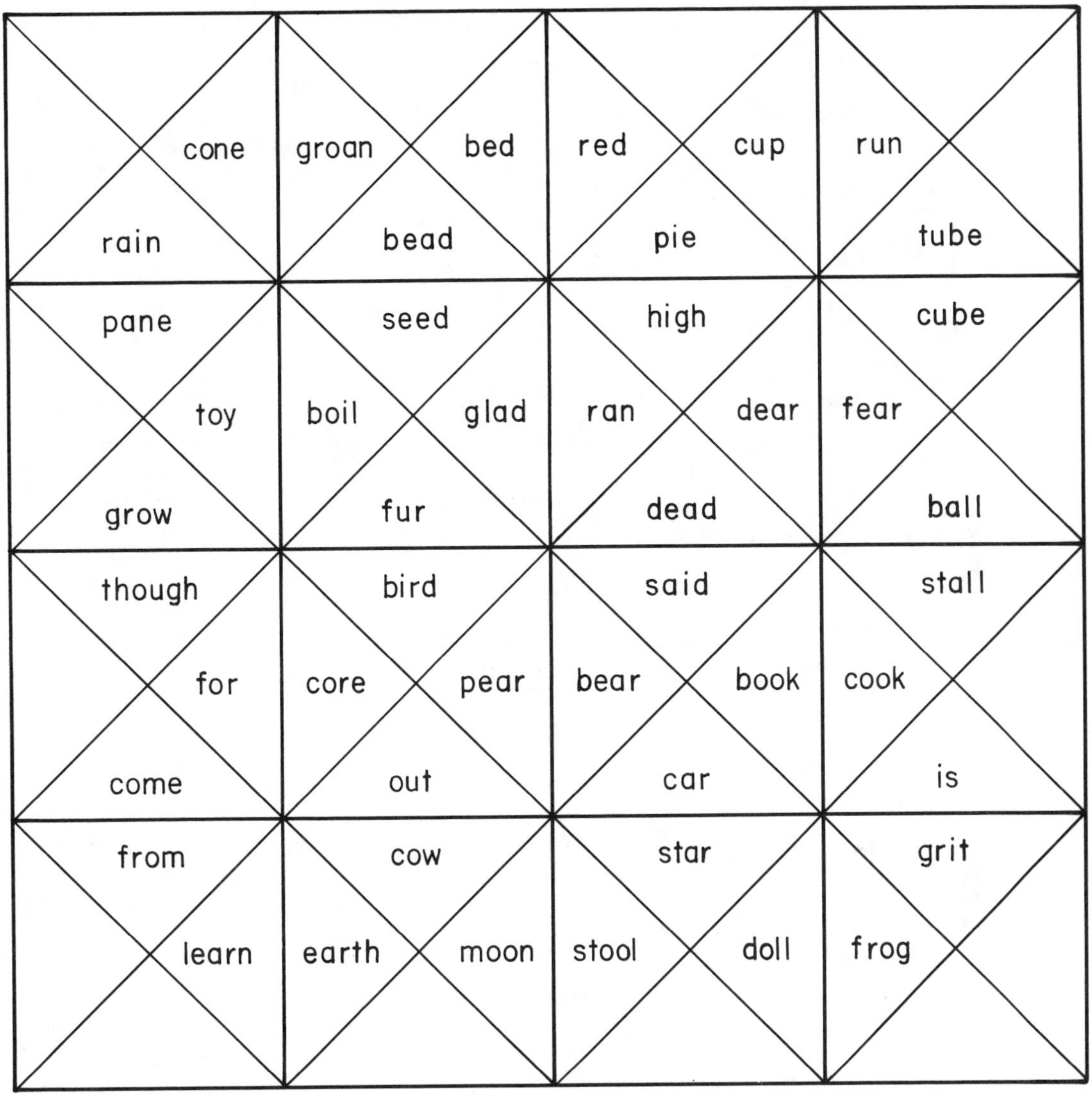

EXHIBIT 12

measuring cup of beans. This size cup usually holds 26–27 beans. (See Exhibit 13.)

a. See how many words can be made with the beans.
b. See if all the beans can be used in words.
c. Give number scores, such as one point for a two-letter word, two points for a three-letter word, etc., to encourage longer words.
d. Make this a timed activity. Use a three-minute egg timer. See how many words can be formed in three minutes.

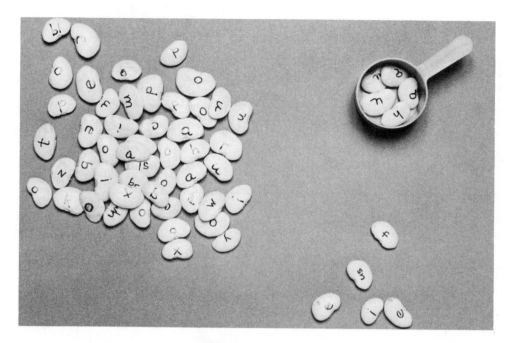

EXHIBIT 13

As new word-attack skills are learned, add more beans to the "soup." For instance, when consonant blends and consonant digraphs are learned, add beans at the ratio of one set of blended digraphs for each set (26 beans) you have made. Later, add vowel digraphs, diphthongs, etc., forcing these letter combinations to be used in the formation of words.

As you add many different clusters, you may want to use a ¼-cup measuring cup to give out portions to each child.

To make this activity more challenging, have the child write the words he was able to make, put them in alphabetical order, etc.

12. Alphabetical Order—
 a. The Letters in Order—Prepare three folders, each having 26 2-inch spaces. On 26 2-inch squares, print the letters of the alphabet.

 On the first folder, start with *a*, leave a space blank, then make a *c*, and continue through the alphabet. On the second folder, leave a space blank, make a *b*, then continue through the alphabet. Leave all spaces blank on the third folder.

 The child works through the three folders, putting in the missing letters. If he needs it, give him a chart containing the letters in order until he is able to do the folders without it.

 b. Words in Order, All Letters—Mother Hubbard's Cupboard—Put a picture of a woman in the upper left corner of a folder. Make "shelves" across the folder 2 inches apart. (See Exhibit 14.)

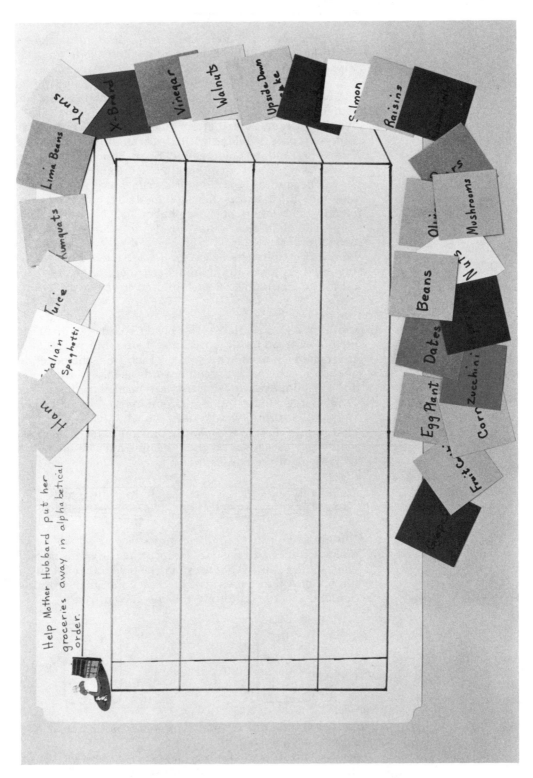

EXHIBIT 14

101

On colored 2-inch squares to simulate packages, print the names of foods beginning with each letter of the alphabet (use *X Brand* for *x*).

Make other sets of food packages requiring alphabetizing by second, third, and fourth letters as the skill is needed.

c. Words in Order, Some Letters Missing—Put Towels on the Line—Prepare a folder with three slightly curved lines across to simulate a clothesline. Every 3 inches, make two marks to represent a clothespin. (See Exhibit 15.)

On squares or rectangles, write words utilizing second and third letters for alphabetizing, omitting completely some letters of the alphabet.

The child places the "towels" left to right in alphabetical order.

d. Names in Alphabetical Order, Last Names First—Have the children make an alphabetized room directory using all of the last names of the children in the room.

13. Contractions—

a. Clothespin Contractions—Use poster board or cardboard 6 inches wide and 12 inches long. Letter the words to be contracted down the two sides, 1 inch from the edge and about an inch apart. Use such words as *I am, we are, you did,* including whatever words are needed at this level.

Using a fine-point permanent marker, letter the contractions for the words used on the ends of spring clothespins. Letter the contraction on each side of the clothespin as shown so that the pin may be clipped to either side of the cardboard.

b. Old Ain't—Use #63 round-corner cards or 3 × 5 file cards. Make matched pairs of cards, repeating the words on both ends of the cards so that they may be held either side up in the hand. A pair consists of a card containing a contraction and a card containing the contracted words.

One card—the one marked *Ain't*—has no matched word card. Call this card "Old Ain't."

Control the number of cards according to the number of players. It is difficult for a child to hold more than eight or ten in his hand.

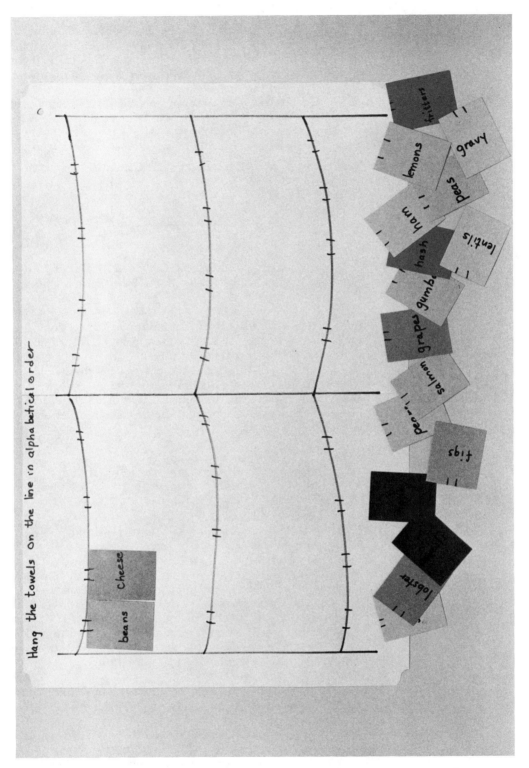

EXHIBIT 15

Deal out all of the cards. Each player examines his hand and immediately puts down any matched pairs. Players draw from each other, trying to get matched pairs and trying to avoid ending up with "Old Ain't," until all cards are on the board except "Old Ain't."

c. Wizard—Write the contractions on the top, center edge of 3 × 5 or #63 cards and write the contracted words center bottom.

```
┌─────────────────┐
│                 │
│      I've       │
│                 │
│     I have      │
│                 │
└─────────────────┘
```

Use the plastic bottle pig as described in Activity 1(d) on page 81. This is a self-checking activity for one child at a time.

14. Silent Letters—Divide a folder into four vertical sections, leaving a 3-inch space at the top. In the top space, sketch a ghost holding its forefinger to its mouth. Beside the sketch, letter the word *GHOST* with the *H* crossed out. (See Exhibit 16.)

At the top of the four columns, put the letters *b, k, w, gh*. On 20 word strips, write the following words for the student to place in the correct column to indicate the silent letters. Distractors are included.

fight	climb	knew	wrap
neighbor	limb	knee	wrinkle
straight	thumb	know	write
eight	lamb	knife	wrong
pigheaded	bomb	knock	wrote
bright	number	kingdom	whale

15. Compound Words—
a. Word Chain—Letter words that can be parts of compound words on cards or strips measuring 1 × 3 inches.

The child chooses a word, then adds a word to make a compound word. Next, using the second half of this first compound word, he tries to add another word to make a new compound word. This procedure is continued. The following list of words will make a chain:

wise, crack, up, set, back, bone, yard, stick, pin, wheel, chair, man, power, house, fly, paper, weight.

Have the child use other words and try to construct his own chain. This is a good dictionary activity.

b. Make a quad domino game for compound words. (See Exhibit 17.)

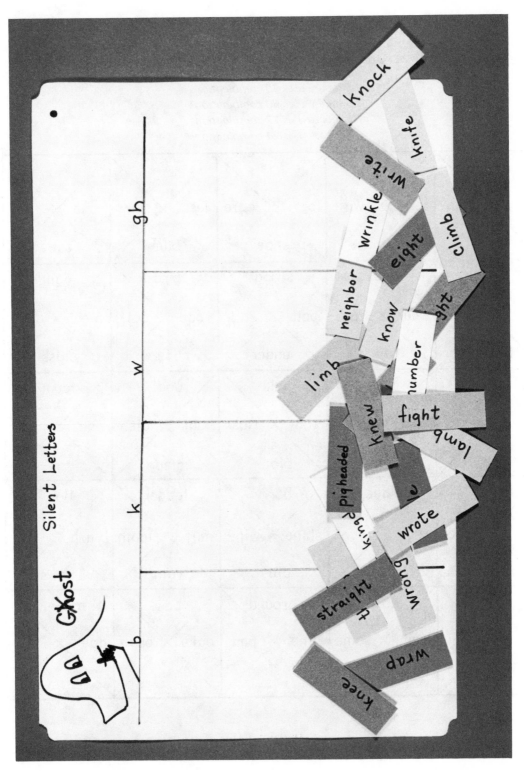

EXHIBIT 16

Quad Dominoes — Compound Words

3 square, 4, 5 or 6
5 square uses 40 combinations
6 square uses 60 combinations
3 square uses 12 combinations
4 square uses 24 combinations

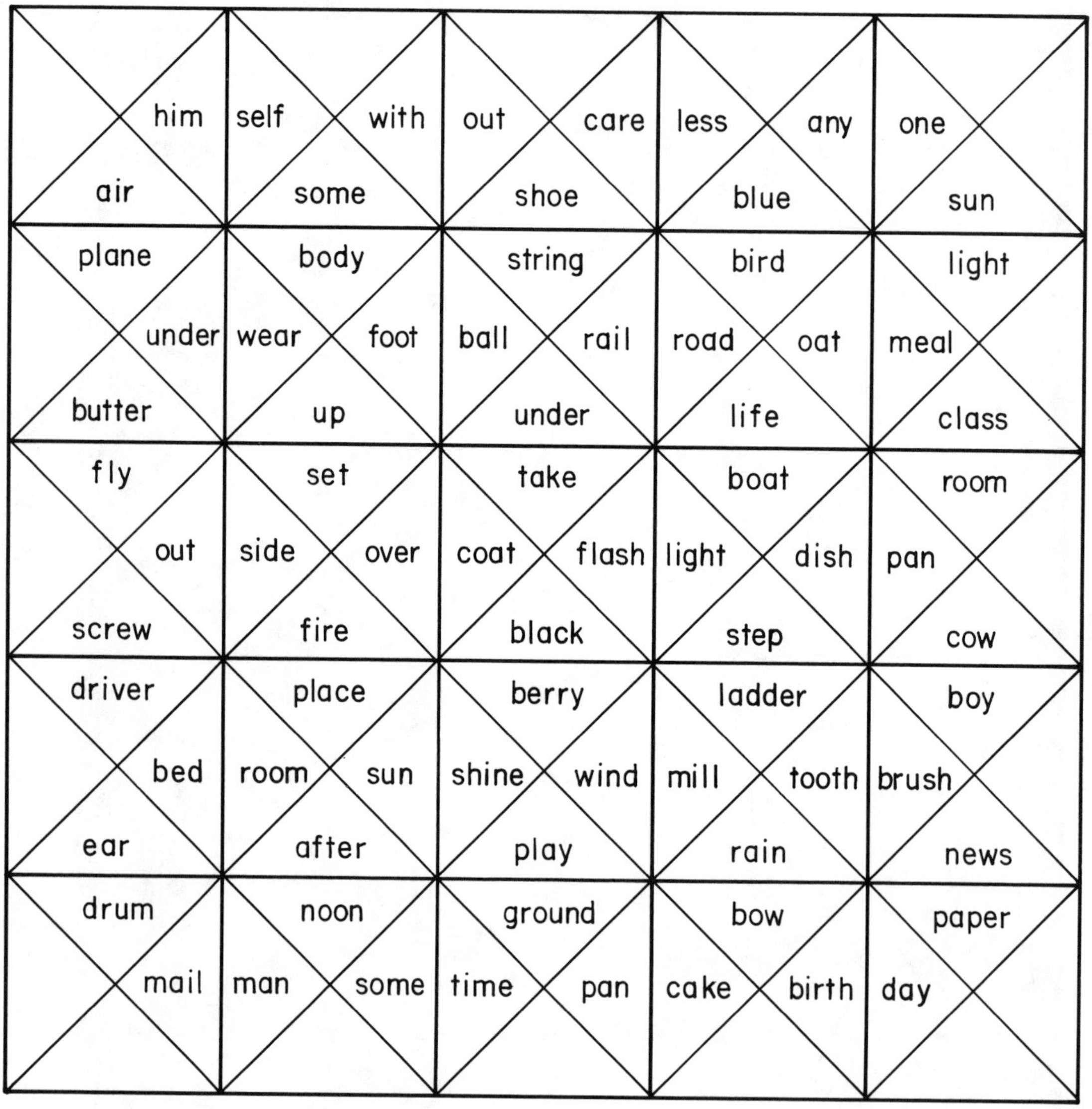

him / self / air	with / out / some	care / less / shoe	any / one / blue	one / sun
plane / under / wear / butter	body / foot / up	string / ball / rail / under	bird / road / oat / life	light / meal / class
fly / out / screw	set / side / over / fire	take / coat / flash / black	boat / light / dish / step	room / pan / cow
driver / bed / ear	place / room / sun / after	berry / shine / wind / play	ladder / mill / tooth / rain	boy / brush / news
drum / mail	noon / man / some	ground / time / pan	bow / cake / birth	paper / day

EXHIBIT 17

c. Make a domino game for compound words similar to (a), lettering one word on each end of each card.

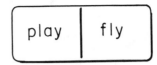

Make 25–30 cards. Be sure they are all possible parts of a compound word. Each player gets five word dominoes, and the game is played like dominoes.

16. Syllables—
    a. Dividing Words with Two Consonants—On the left side of a folder, letter a word like *swim-mer*, showing the division of syllables between the two double consonants. On the right side of the folder, letter a word like *cir-cus*, showing the division of syllables between two unlike consonants.

       Give the child a collection of picture cards to classify according to the division for syllabication. Use pictures such as the following:

hammer	basket
mitten	tractor
balloon	sandal
puppy	pencil
button	target
rabbit	window
arrow	pancake
penny	turkey

    b. Dividing Words with One Consonant—On the left side of a folder, put a word like *spi-der* (open syllable, long vowel, divided after the vowel). On the right side, put a word like *wag-on* (closed syllable, short vowel sound, divided after the consonant). On word cards for classification on the folders, put words such as the following:

pony	lilac	comic	radish
minus	label	pedal	lemon
nation	grocer	prison	model
bacon	tiger	planet	river
razor	polar	habit	cabin

    c. How Many Syllables in Your Ice Cream Cone?—On colored circles 2 inches in diameter, write flavors of ice cream:

grape	lemon	strawberry	tutti frutti
lime	orange	vanilla	pistachio
peach	maple	chocolate	vanilla nut
mint	pecan	raspberry	chocolate mint

107

On the folder, draw simulated cones with 2-inch tops. (See Exhibit 18.) On each cone, print a numeral to match the number of syllables in one of the various flavors.

Have the student match the "dips" of ice cream to the correct cones according to the number of syllables.

d. Syllable Zoo—On a folder, make five zoo cages about 4 × 6 inches. At the top of each, put a numeral 1-5.

Have the child put pictures of animals mounted on 2-inch cards in the cages according to the number of syllables in the animal name. Use pictures or words such as:

seal	lion	buffalo	rhinoceros	hippopotamus
horse	tiger	kangaroo	tarantula	boa constrictor
deer	giraffe	pelican	salamander	
bear	monkey	parakeet	caterpillar	
goat	zebra	koala		
ape	camel	octopus		

e. Syllable Bingo—Make bingo cards, each with nine spaces. In the spaces, put the numerals 1-5 twice, omitting a different number the second time on each card. Make each card with a different order of numbers. Make word cards using many words with one to five syllables. Mix the cards.

The caller selects a card and pronounces it. Players put a mark on the number showing the number of syllables in the word. Play continues until someone has a filled card.

f. Bag the Syllables—Paste five square-bottom, one-pound grocery bags to a folder. Fold in the top 2 inches of each bag for reinforcement. On the front of each bag, write one of the numerals 1-5. On a 1 × 3-inch word card, write words having one to five syllables.

Have the student put each word in the correct bag according to the number of syllables.

g. The Syllables in the 50 States—On a folder, make five 5-inch circles. In the center of each, make one of the numerals 1-5. On 50 1 × 3-inch word cards, print the names of the 50 states.

Have each student put the state's name card on the correct circle according to the number of syllables. Have the child use the dictionary or the glossary in a social studies book checking accuracy.

h. Building Words from Syllables—On 1 × 2-inch cards, letter the following syllables:

car	ton	ter
rot	key	but
ten	don	mon

The child sees how many two-syllable words he can make from these syllables. He should write each word on

How many syllables in your ice cream cone?

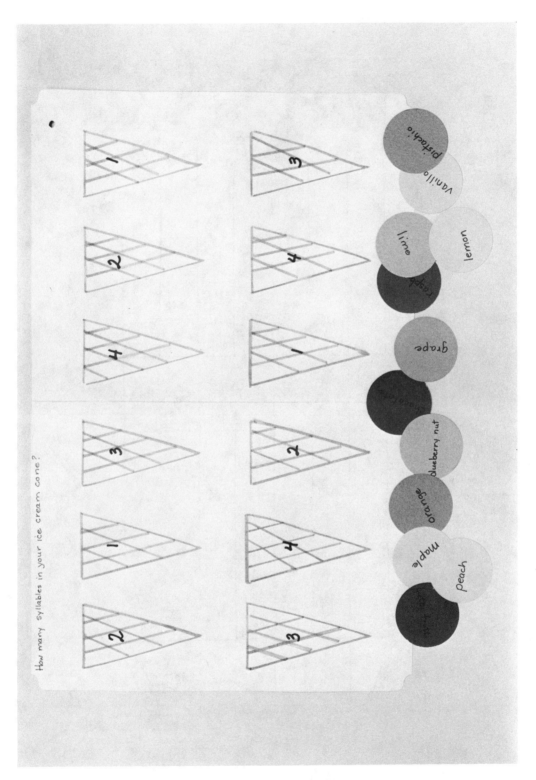

EXHIBIT 18

109

EXHIBIT 19

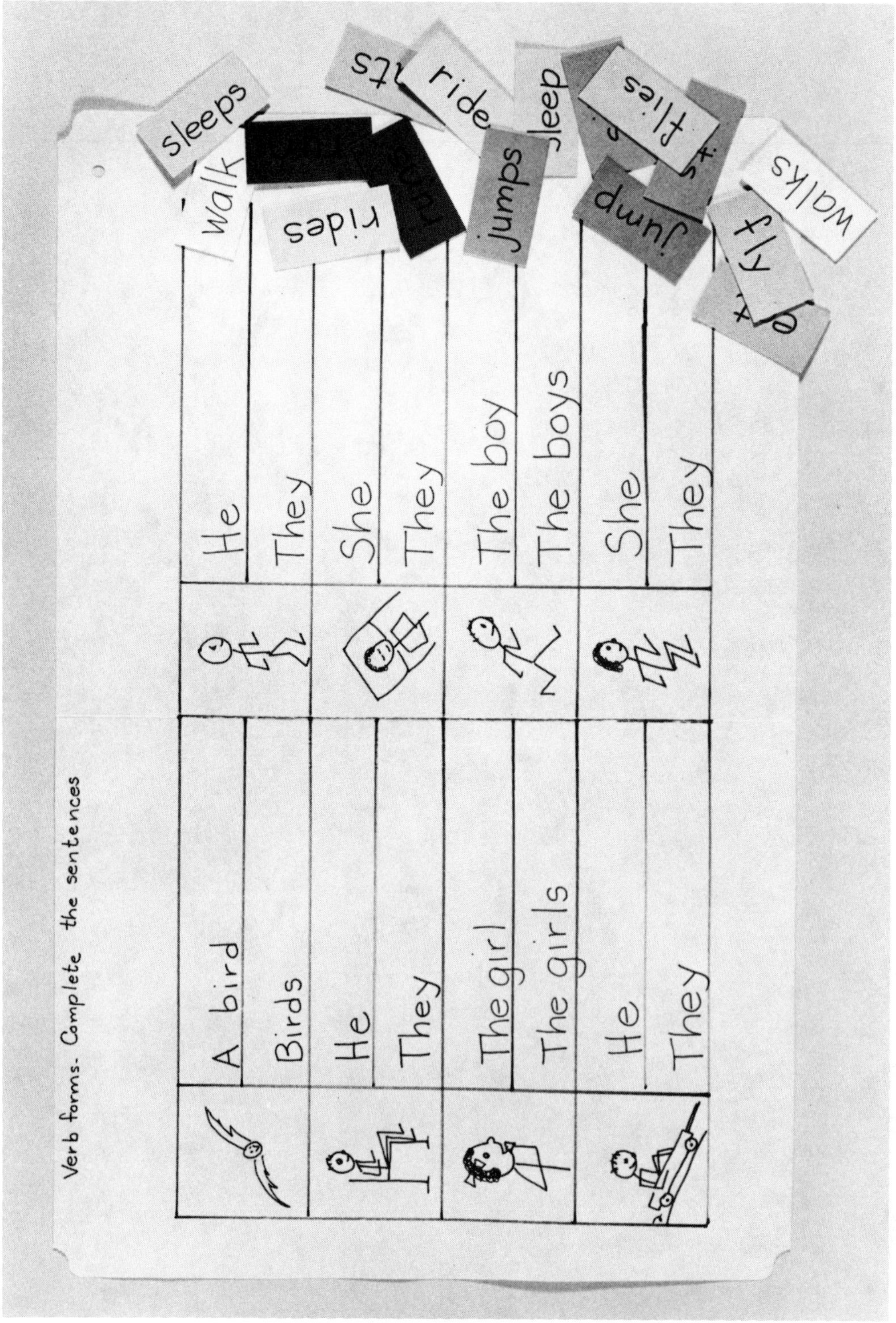
Verb forms. Complete the sentences
A bird
Birds
He
They
The girl
The girls
He
They
He
They
She
They
The boy
The boys
She
They
sleeps
walk
rides
ride
jumps
sleep
flies
jump
fly
walks

a paper as he makes it. He can use each syllable as many times as he wishes.

17. Word Endings—Distinguishing Singular and Plural Forms—Prepare a folder with four 2-inch horizontal spaces. At the extreme left of each side of the folder, in each of the four spaces make a stick figure to depict one of the following actions:

fly	run
sit	sleep
eat	walk
ride	jump

(See Exhibit 19.) Divide the space to the right of each figure into two 1-inch horizontal spaces. In these two spaces, write the start of a sentence using the singular then the plural noun form.

On 1 × 2-inch word strips, write the singular and plural verb forms to go with each stick figure.

Have the child complete each sentence by adding the word strip with the correct verb form. Although accuracy can be checked by using a Key Card, the child should read his responses out loud.

BIBLIOGRAPHY

VALETT, ROBERT E. *A Psychoeducational Inventory of Basic Learning Abilities*. Belmont, Calif.: Fearon Publishers, 1968.

WILSON, ROBERT, AND HALL, MARYANNE. *Programmed Word Attack for Teachers*. Columbus, Ohio: Charles E. Merrill Publishing Co., 1968.

7

Auditory Skills, Intermediate and Up

BACKGROUND INFORMATION

Students in the intermediate grades frequently have not mastered auditory skills and need more practice in these areas. Although the activities suggested in Chapter 6 are suitable for children in these grades, there may be a need for more mature kinds of activities in some cases. In the area of the application of auditory skills to reading, there is a need to extend beyond the skills offered in Chapter 6.

Students needing extra help in auditory skills may have fine-coordination problems as well, and therefore have a great dislike for writing answers. They have been exposed to mountains of worksheets and do not find them appealing. The use of manipulatives appeals to them as well as the game aspects of many of the suggested activities.

Most of the activities in this chapter utilize one of four techniques.

1. Folder Activities—At this level, the student will be manipulating 1 × 3-inch sentence strips containing words or phrases, and the folder will be marked into 1-inch horizontal spaces instead of the 2-inch squares used so often in the activities for younger children. (See Exhibit 1.)

    Most of the activities are of the closed-end variety and can be self-corrected by use of a Key Card made on a 5 × 7-inch file card. Be sure that the Key Cards are correctly labeled by number and code letters so that it will be easy for the student to select the correct one. Provide the student with a means of recording his successes or problems and a way of reporting his progress to you. By using the folders in this way, there will be less feeling of testing, or a need to cheat.

EXHIBIT 1

The folders should be made readily accessible to the students. Some students may wish to attempt all of the folders whereas others will try only those prescribed. As each folder is made, put the code number of the folder on the back of each sentence strip; then stray parts are easily returned to the proper folder. Plastic sandwich bags make convenient holders for the parts. These may be attached to the folder with clips or binder clamps, or both parts may be stored in 10 × 13-inch kraft envelopes. The number of horizontal lines across the folder will, of course, be determined by the activity. Eight 1-inch spaces will make for an uncrowded folder and will leave 2 inches at the top for explanation and directions.

2. Card Games—Children of intermediate grades seem especially to enjoy playing card games. Their hands are large enough to manage the cards and they usually already know the basics of several games. The card games suggested in this chapter include types of rummy, War, Go Fish, Old Maid, and Concentration.

   In rummylike games, a specific number of cards are dealt to each player, and the remainder of the deck is placed face down in the center. In turn, each player draws from the center and discards one card. The object of the game is to get runs of cards to place on the table and to get rid of all the cards in the hand. Runs consist of specified numbers of cards according to the skill being practiced.

   In War, the deck is divided equally among the players. The cards are placed face down in front of each player. All players turn up

113

a card and place it on the table. The player with the card containing the word that comes latest in the alphabet, or that has the most syllables, etc., takes all the exposed cards. Play continues until one player has all the cards.

In Go Fish, a specified number of cards is dealt to each player, and the remainder of the deck placed face down in the middle. The object is to get sets of four cards containing the same element. The first player calls on another player for a specific card he needs. If the player has the card, he must surrender it; if not, he says "Go Fish," and the first player draws the card from the center pile. Play continues until all cards are used. The player with the most sets down on the table is the winner.

In Old Maid, all cards are dealt. The object of the game is to get matched pairs. Players draw from the next player's hand and place pairs on the table. One unmatched card is included, such as "Old Ain't" in Chapter 6, Activity 13(b), p. 102.

In Concentration, all cards are placed face down in rows. Players try to pick up matched pairs. Unmatched cards are returned to their places, and players try to remember positions of cards.

3. Quad Dominoes—Quad dominoes are four-sided dominoes as explained in Chapter 6, Activity 12(b), page 100. Quad-domino games work equally well as solitaire or small-group activities. In making quad-domino games, keep in mind that 9 dominoes (3 squares) require 12 matching combinations, 16 dominoes (4 squares) require 24 combinations, and 25 dominoes (5 squares) require 60.

4. Task Cards—Tasks involving practice for needed activities for intermediate-age students can be explained effectively on attractive task cards. Means of checking can be placed on Key Cards so that the student can keep a record of his own progress. Task cards can be kept in skill or interest centers and used as needed or prescribed. Illustrations of various task cards are included, but of course the scope is unlimited.

Be sure that each task is adequately explained, that needed materials are available, and means of checking provided. If the task cards are part of a center, such as a "Dictionary Skill Center," place only those cards for a specific skill in the center at one time, then add skills as they are presented so that the center is a changing device and always applicable to the skill being learned.

Cards of colored tagboard or railroad board about 7 × 9 inches make suitable materials for task cards. If they are to be used a great deal or include pictures that are pasted on, it is a good idea to laminate the cards or cover them with clear pressure-sensitive plastic.

AUDITORY DECODING

Activities Use the activities recommended in Chapter 6.

AUDITORY MEMORY AND SEQUENCING

Activities 1. Have students take turns repeating each other's telephone numbers after hearing them once.

2. Use more difficult tongue twisters.

3. Have students make up tongue twisters using spelling, geography, or other vocabulary words and take turns trying to repeat them.

AUDITORY SKILLS APPLIED TO READING

Activities 1. Harder Beginning Sounds—Go Fish Card Game—forty cards, four cards for each beginning sound:

s	soap	scenery	city	size
p	pure	pony	pretty	pare
n	pneumonia	knife	never	gnaw
b	before	bought	born	big
g	ghost	gone	gopher	gap
t	ptomaine	target	tune	tomato
sh	sugar	sure	sharp	shelf
k	caught	kite	comrade	kitten
f	phony	felt	phantom	farce
h	whole	horse	heaven	whom

2. Final Sounds—
   a. Quad Dominoes—Sixteen 3 × 3-inch cards. (See Exhibit 2.)
   b. Final Sounds—Past Tense with Added *ed*—Prepare a folder with two sides. Label left side "Words ending with *ed* pronounced with the final sound of *d*." Label right side "Words ending with *ed* pronounced with the final sound of *t*." On sentence strips, write the following words for the students to classify:

d Sound		*t Sound*	
dated	aided	dressed	kissed
folded	blinded	peeked	snuffed
seeded	cheated	parked	kicked
boned	begged	loafed	stopped
boasted	canned	baked	hoped
hated	planned	wished	bumped
patted	skated	preached	lunched

At the bottom of the folder, write the following statements for the student to complete:

115

Left Side	*Right Side*
The *d* sound follows the letters ___ ___ ___ ___ .	The *t* sound follows the letters ___ ___ ___ ___ ___ ___ .
(*Answer: n, g, t, d*)	(*Answer: s, k, f, p, sh, ch*)

Write these letters and letter combinations on 1-inch squares for the student to place on the correct sides.

Quad Dominoes — Final Sounds

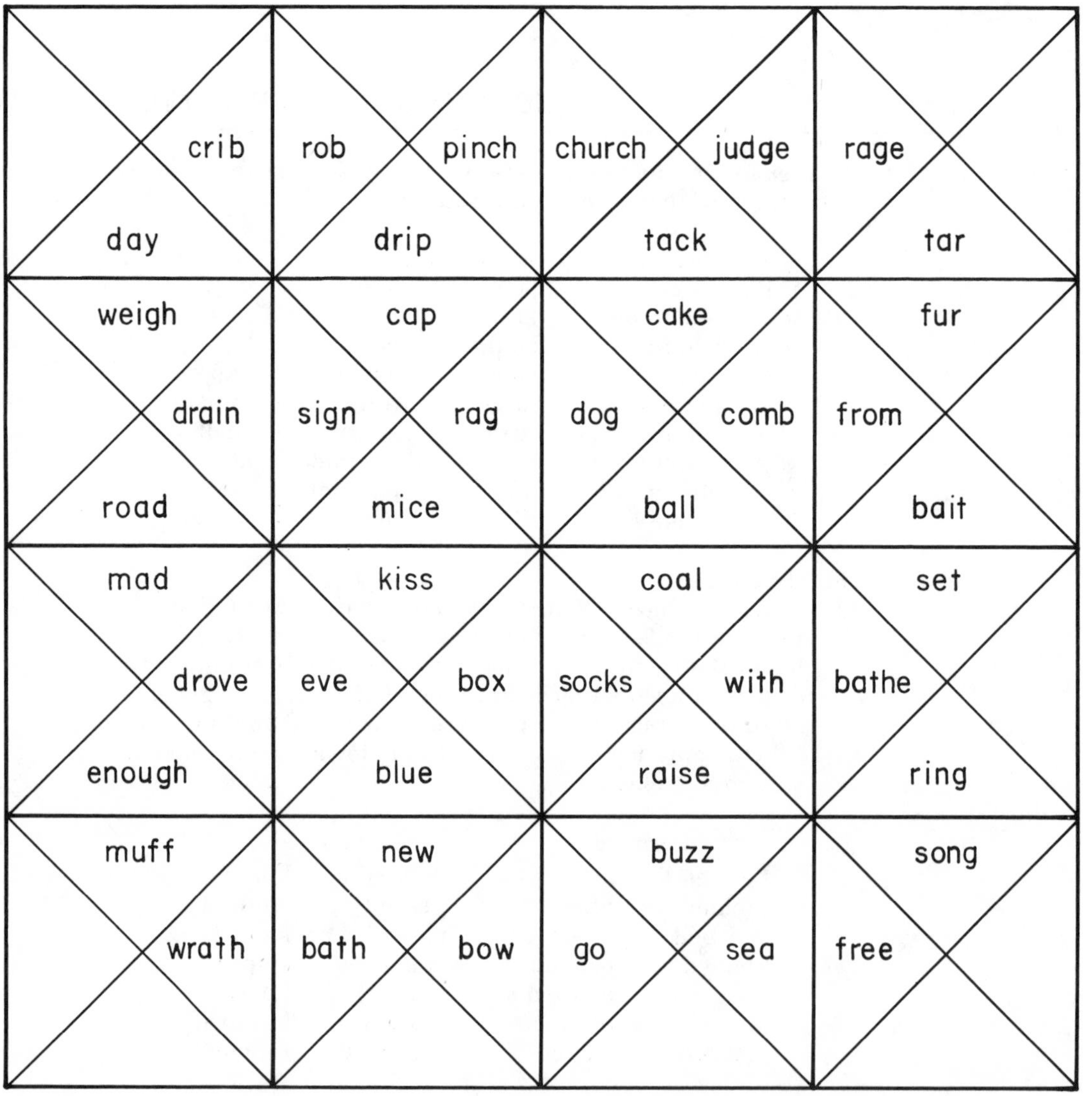

	crib	rob		pinch	church		judge	rage	
day		drip			tack			tar	
weigh		cap			cake			fur	
	drain	sign		rag	dog		comb	from	
road		mice			ball			bait	
mad		kiss			coal			set	
	drove	eve		box	socks		with	bathe	
enough		blue			raise			ring	
muff		new			buzz			song	
	wrath	bath		bow	go		sea	free	

EXHIBIT 2

3. Vowel Sounds—
   a. Ways to Spell Long Vowel Sounds—Make a folder with five vertical sections labeled *Long a, Long e, Long i, Long o,* and *Long u*. Place the following words on sentence strips to be classified on the folder according to the long vowel sound:

Long a	Long e	Long i	Long o	Long u
lake	Caesar	aisle	sew	beauty
pain	quay	aye	beau	few
gauge	be	height	yeoman	feud
break	deceive	eye	old	ewe
veil	field	ice	road	lieu
obey	key	vie	foe	you
vail	people	high	oh	queue
weigh	feet	choir	soul	suit
day	beam	buy	shoulder	mule

   b. Quad Dominoes for Vowel Sounds.

4. Alphabetical Order—
   a. Presidents of the United States—Give the student the names of the presidents to place in alphabetical order by last name.
   b. The 50 States—Give the student the names of the 50 states to place in alphabetical order.
   c. Words in Which Letters Are in Alphabetical Order—Have the student discover the words in the following groups of letters if the letters are placed in alphabetical order.

iegnb	(begin)
aotsml	(almost)
aobrh	(abhor)
iydyt	(dirty)
iymfl	(filmy)
oyrlg	(glory)
osplf	(flops)
aecntc	(accent)
ichsp	(chips)
aoscct	(accost)
eoblw	(below)
oosbt	(boost)
aiosd	(adios)
eityd	(deity)
orfyt	(forty)
otghs	(ghost)

See if the students can discover more words in which the letters are in alphabetical order.
   d. Careers A–Z—Have the students use the yellow pages of the telephone book and see if they can find careers that begin with each letter of the alphabet. If some letter is

117

missing in your particular book, try to think of careers that might start with that particular letter, e.g.,

Q   Quilting
X   X-Ray Technician

5.   Syllables—
   a.   Matching Syllables—(See Exhibit 3.) Prepare a folder with eight 1-inch horizontal spaces. Write the following beginning syllables in these spaces:

cor	par	fin	sym
mo	de	pen	
pro	dis	sim	
con	rab	can	
ro	tur	se	

On sentence strips, write the following second syllables for the students to match to the first syllables to make words:

tect	bot	bit	ple
tain	lor	key	dy
tel	file	ger	lect
ner	dain	cil	bol

(See Exhibit 1.)
In this activity, the strips are to be manipulated, and the student has an opportunity to see the words as they are matched.
   b.   Which Syllable Does Not Make a Word? In this activity, the student puts a marker on the second syllable that does not make a word. He is not able to manipulate manually the syllables, but instead must relate the sounds in his mind.
Divide a folder into 4 sections vertically and 3 sections horizontally, making 12 sections. Write the following syllables in the sections. Put the first syllable on the left and the choice of second syllables on the right. Have the student place a marker on the syllables on the right that will not make a complete word. (See Exhibit 4.)

par	ty	ex	act	ro	bot	cor	ment
	lor		pect		per		ral
	king		end		dent		ner
	fect		cite		pect		rect

mo	tain	pen	cil	cir	cle	sim	ple
	ment		dant		ret		per
	tion		tion		cus		mer
	bile		sion		rus		der

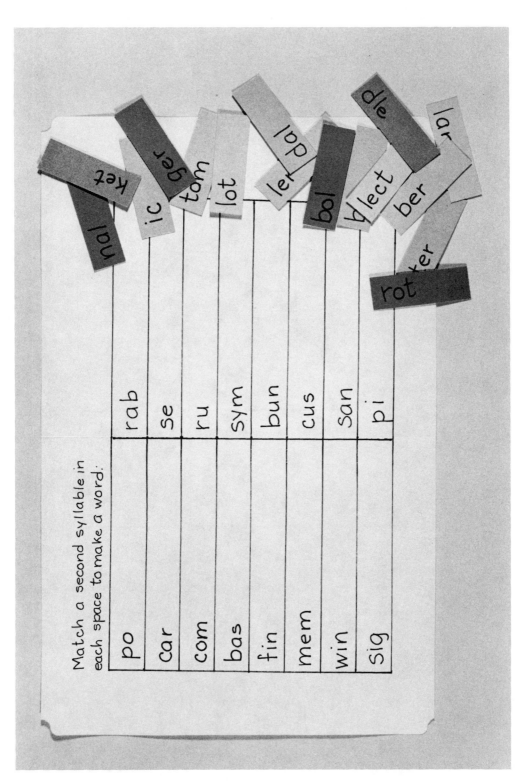

EXHIBIT 3

EXHIBIT 4

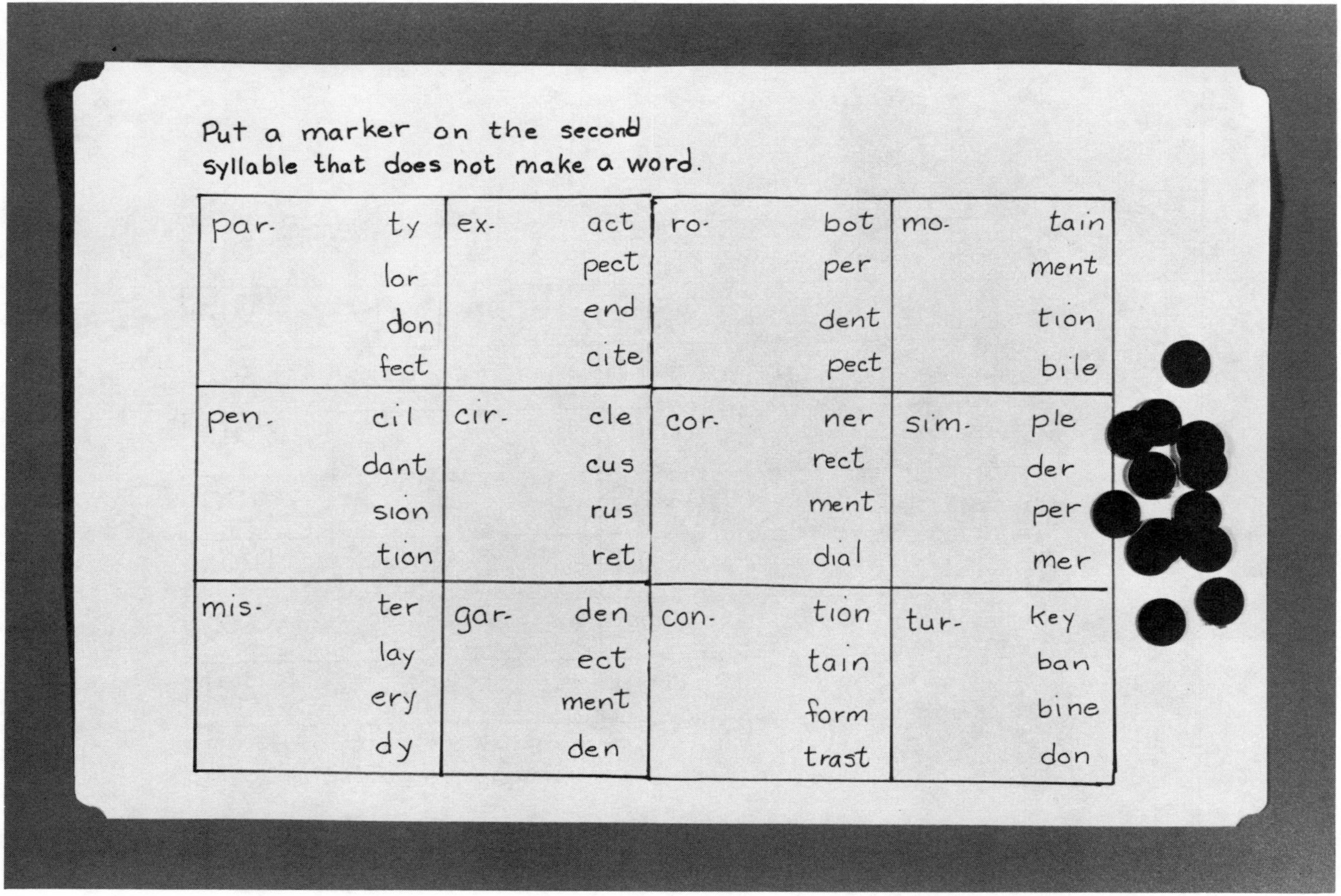

Put a marker on the second
syllable that does not make a word.

par-	ty	ex-	act	ro-	bot	mo-	tain
	lor		pect		per		ment
	don		end		dent		tion
	fect		cite		pect		bile
pen-	cil	cir-	cle	cor-	ner	sim-	ple
	dant		cus		rect		der
	sion		rus		ment		per
	tion		ret		dial		mer
mis-	ter	gar-	den	con-	tion	tur-	key
	lay		ect		tain		ban
	ery		ment		form		bine
	dy		den		trast		don

tur	key	con	tain	gar	ect	mis	ter
	ban		trast		den		dy
	don		tion		lic		ery
	bine		form		ment		lay

c. Classifying Two-Syllable Words with One Medial Consonant—Prepare a folder with two sections. At the top of the folder, letter the following directions: "Classify the words." On the left side, place words of the following category: open-syllable words, first vowel long, divide before medial consonants (*example: ba-con*). On the right, place words of the following kind: closed-syllable words, first vowel short, divide after medial consonants (*example: cab-in*).

On sentence strips, write the following words for the student to classify:

basic	profit
gravy	devil
defect	gavel
legal	novel
bison	rapid
sedan	visit
pilot	robin
motel	rivet
pupil	toxic
humid	valid

d. Syllable Rummy—Prepare a deck of 40 cards with words of one to five syllables, 8 of each. Letter the words at each end so that they can be read from either direction. Use words such as:

breath	radio
chief	television
finger	manufacture
robot	refrigerator
idea	international

The game is played by two or more players as explained at the beginning of this chapter. A run consists of five cards: a one-, two-, three-, four-, and five-syllable word. The same deck can be used by one student for classifying words by the number of syllables or as a Concentration game. In Concentration, the player would attempt to pick up two words with the same number of syllables.

e. Unstressed Syllable Ending *ən*—At the top of a folder, letter the following: "Many words end with this sound, but they have different spellings. Match the word beginning on the cards with the correct endings." Divide the rest of the folder into four vertical columns, each with eight

121

EXHIBIT 5

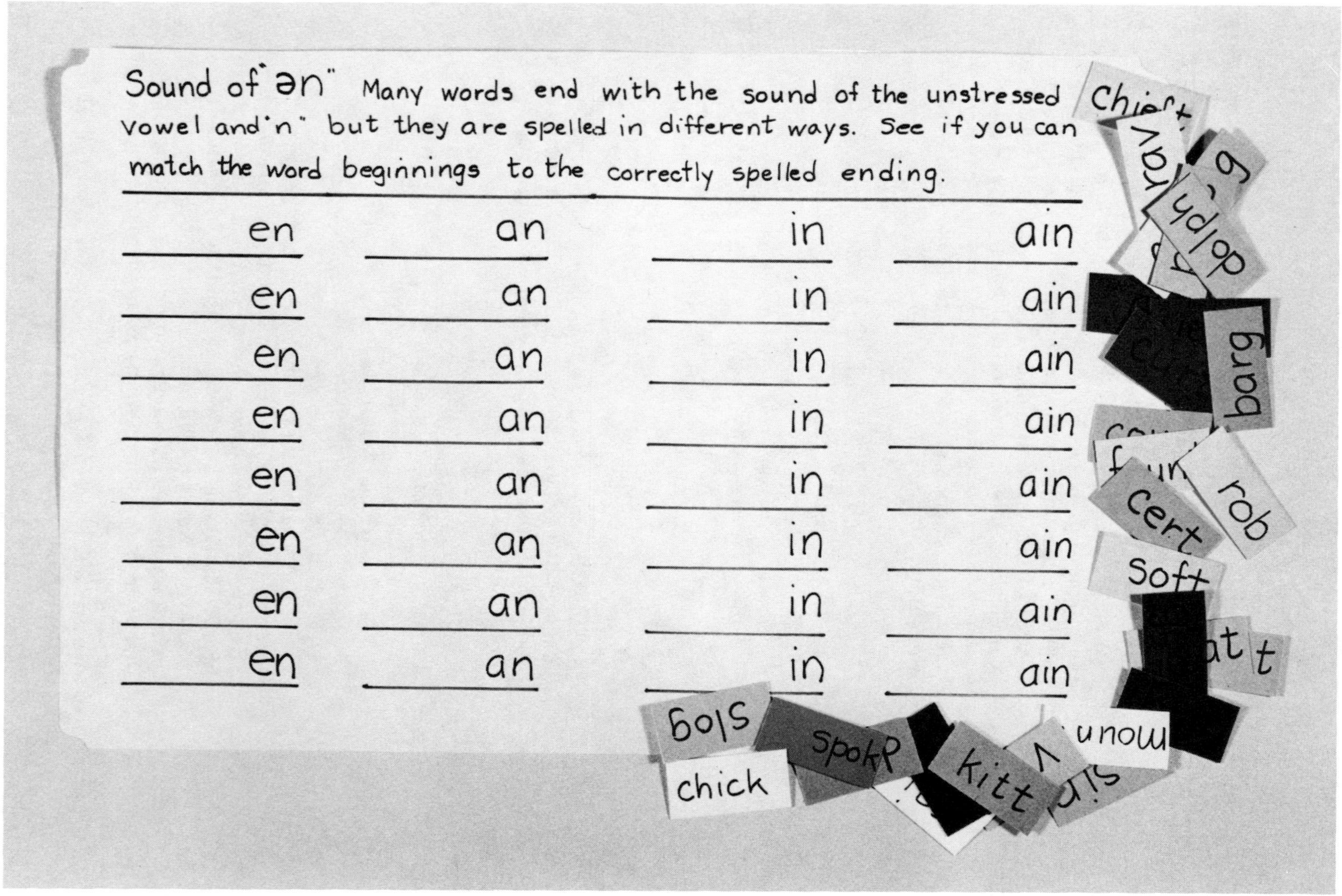

Sound of "en". Many words end with the sound of the unstressed vowel and 'n' but they are spelled in different ways. See if you can match the word beginnings to the correctly spelled ending.

en	an	in	ain
en	an	in	ain
en	an	in	ain
en	an	in	ain
en	an	in	ain
en	an	in	ain
en	an	in	ain
en		in	ain

dolph rav barg rob cert soft mount kitt spokp slog chick Chiat

1-inch spaces. At the right end of each of the 1-inch spaces in the first column, letter the ending *en*, in the second *an*, in the third *in*, and in the last column *ain*. (See Exhibit 5.)

On sentence strips, letter the following word beginnings for the student to place:

spok	veter	bas	fount
chick	slog	cab	curt
sir	Americ	dolph	chief
soft	hum	cous	capt
rav	pelic	rob	vill
list	pag	sat	barg
damp	org	rais	art

6. Accent—
   a. Recognizing Accented Syllable—Letter the following directions at the top of a folder: "Place the word strips on the correct side of the folder according to the accented syllable." Divide the rest of the folder in 2 parts. On the left side, write:

   Accent on first syllable— cir′ cus

   On the right side, write:
   Accent on second syllable—pa rade′

   Write words such as the following on the strip:

radar	static	delay	about
shiver	travel	insist	resist
motion	clinic	police	begin
artist	insect	intend	enlist
talent	gravy	direct	alarm
bacon	legal	motel	rely

   b. Meaning Changed by Accent—(See Exhibit 6.) Following the directions on the task card, the student matches heteronyms to meanings using the accent mark as the clue.

7. Prefixes—
   a. Matching Prefixes and Roots—Quad dominoes, 16 cards, 24 matches. (See Exhibit 7.)
   b. Making Words with Prefixes—Challenge Card Game—Use 24 4 × 6-inch file cards. Cut 24 4 × 4-inch cards, which leaves 24 2 × 4-inch cards. On the top left corner and bottom right corner of each 4 × 4-inch card, letter one of the prefixes on the list that follows.

123

EXHIBIT 6

Accent Changes Meaning

Besides knowing how letters sound in a word you need to know which syllable gets more stress. This is shown by a stress mark. Example: rec'ord

Many words change meaning if the accent is moved. Example: re fuse' (decline) ref'use (trash)

Number a paper to 16.
After each number write the underlined word with correct accent.

```
con' tent    con tent'
con' test    con test'
pres' ent    pre sent'
de sert'     des' ert
re' ject     re ject'
re fuse'     ref' use
sus' pect    sus pect'
min' ute     mi nute'
```

You may use a dictionary

1. I am content with my reward.
2. This cereal has high sugar content.

3. We thought the game was a fair contest.
4. The team will contest the last touchdown.

5. They will present the trophy today.
6. We gave Mother a birthday present.

7. Camels are used on the desert.
8. Please don't desert me now.

9. The teacher may reject my paper.
10. It was a factory reject.

11. How can you refuse my simple request?
12. The park was littered with refuse.

13. We would never suspect him of theft.
14. That man is our prime suspect.

15. I will be with you in a minute.
16. An atom is a minute particle.

Prefixes

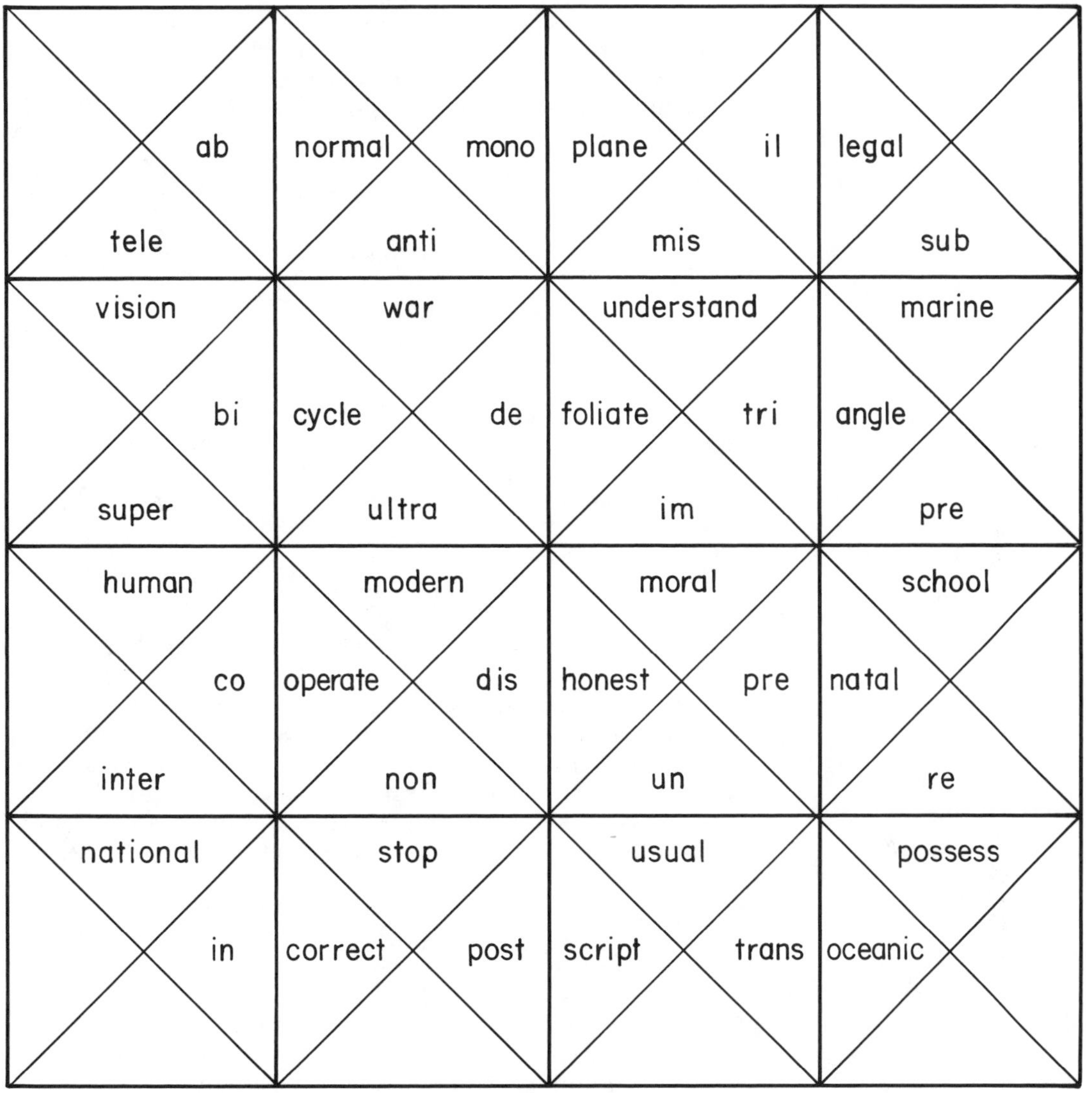

	ab	normal	mono	plane	il	legal	
tele		anti		mis		sub	
vision		war	understand		marine		
	bi	cycle	de	foliate	tri	angle	
super		ultra		im		pre	
human		modern		moral		school	
	co	operate	dis	honest	pre	natal	
inter		non		un		re	
national		stop	usual		possess		
	in	correct	post	script	trans	oceanic	

EXHIBIT 7

At the top and bottom of each of the narrow cards, letter one of the root words from the other list.

Shuffle the square cards and place them face down on the table. Deal all of the narrow cards to the players. The players take turns turning up the top card from the center pile. If it makes a word with a card in the player's hand, he places the narrow card on the square card, pronounces the word, and places the pair on the table. If the other player or players accept the word, the next player draws; if a player finds the word unacceptable, he calls

"Challenge," and the dictionary is consulted. If the challenger is correct, the player takes back his card and returns the square to the bottom of the center pile.

If the player does not try to play on the square, he says "Pass" and returns the square to the bottom of the center pile. Play continues until one player uses all of the cards in his hand.

Prefixes (four of each)

pre
non
il
un
re
dis

Root Words

own	legal	admit	school
join	literate	apply	profit
obey	logical	view	occupy
joint	legible	run	lucky
usual	stop	pay	able
real	like	sense	member

These cards may also be used for matching by one child.

c. Prefixes with the Same Meaning—The child is to match root words with the appropriate prefix meaning *not*. Mark a folder into three vertical areas. At the top of the first section, letter the prefix *dis,* the second *un,* and the third *im.* Write the following words on sentence strips for the student to place on the correct sections of the folders:

trust	common	proper
agree	happy	perfect
honest	friendly	partial
loyal	faded	moral
place	acceptable	material
claim	sure	personal
inherit	broken	patient
continues	fed	polite
own	adorned	mortal
please	beaten	porous

d. Building Words with Prefixes—This activity uses task cards. (See Exhibit 8.)

e. Getting Meaning from Prefixes—At the top of a folder, letter the following: "Understanding Prefixes: The following prefixes tell about numbers. See if you can fill in the blanks in the sentences that follow.

uni, mono—one
bi, die—two

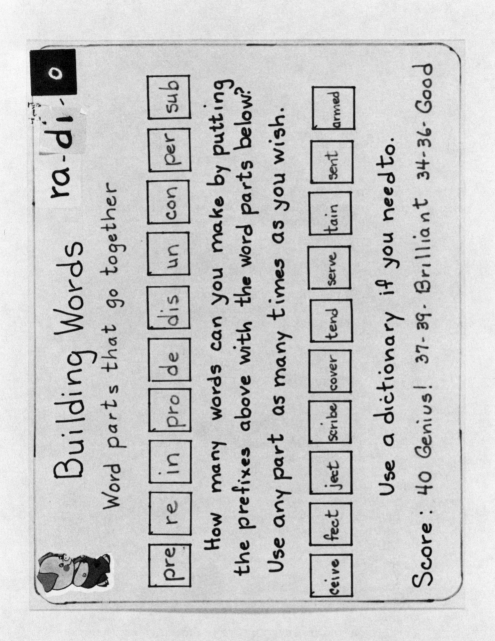

Building Words

ra-di-

Word parts that go together

pre	re	in	pro	de	dis	un	con	per	sub

How many words can you make by putting the prefixes above with the word parts below?

Use any part as many times as you wish.

ceive	fect	ject	scribe	cover	tend	serve	tain	sent	armed

Use a dictionary if you need to.

Score: 40 Genius! 37-39- Brilliant 34-36- Good

EXHIBIT 8

127

tri—three
quad—four
pent, quint—five
sex—six
sept—seven
oct—eight
non, nov—nine
dec—ten
cent—hundred

(See Exhibit 9.)

Under this information, make eight 1-inch horizontal spaces. In the spaces, letter the following sentences, leaving a space for an answer card:

1. A triangle has _____ sides.
2. An octopus has _____ feet.
3. A centennial is the anniversary after _____ years.
4. A septuagenarian is _____ years old.
5. Monoplanes have _____ wings.
6. Biplanes have _____ wings.
7. *Quadruplets* means _____ babies.
8. A decade is _____ years.
9. A duplex home has _____ apartments.
10. The Pentagon has _____ sides.
11. A sextet has _____ players.
12. A unicycle has _____ wheels.
13. *In triplicate* means _____ copies.
14. *Quintuplets* means _____ babies.
15. A novena is _____ days of devotions.
16. A century is _____ years.

On 1 × 2-inch sentence strips write the numerals to correctly complete the sentences.

The student reads the sentences and places the numerals in the spaces.

8. Suffixes—
   a. Saying Words with Suffixes—(See Exhibit 10.) This task employs flip cards. Use sixteen 3 × 5 file cards. Leave 4 cards whole. Cut 12 in half, making them 2½ × 3 inches. On the left end of each card, punch two holes so that they can be put on rings. At the right end of each of the 4 long cards, letter one of the suffixes *less, ness, ly, ment.*

   Make a pile putting 6 of the short cards on top of each of the long cards. Put ¾-inch notebook rings through the holes.

   On the six cards preceding the suffix *less*, letter the words *hope, life, worth, fear, shoe, help.*

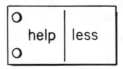

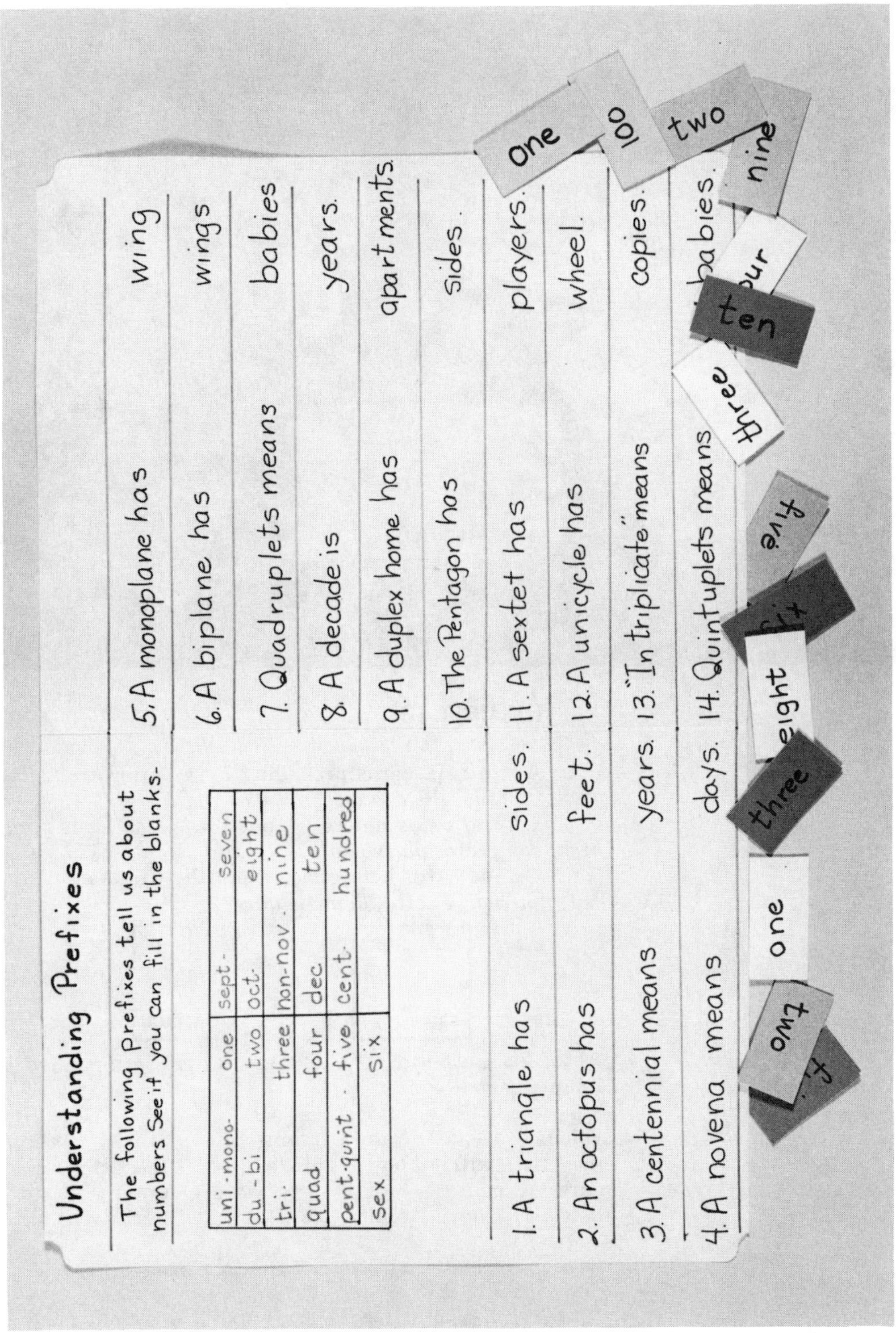

Understanding Prefixes

The following prefixes tell us about numbers. See if you can fill in the blanks.

uni-mono-	one	sept-	seven
du - bi	two	oct-	eight
tri-	three	non-nov-	nine
quad	four	dec-	ten
pent-quint -	five	cent-	hundred
sex	six		

1. A triangle has _____ sides.

2. An octopus has _____ feet.

3. A centennial means _____ years.

4. A novena means _____ days.

5. A monoplane has _____ wing.

6. A biplane has _____ wings.

7. Quadruplets means _____ babies.

8. A decade is _____ years.

9. A duplex home has _____ apartments.

10. The Pentagon has _____ sides.

11. A sextet has _____ players.

12. A unicycle has _____ wheel.

13. "In triplicate" means _____ copies.

14. Quintuplets means _____ babies.

One   100   two   nine

four   ten

three

five

six

eight

three

one

two

EXHIBIT 9

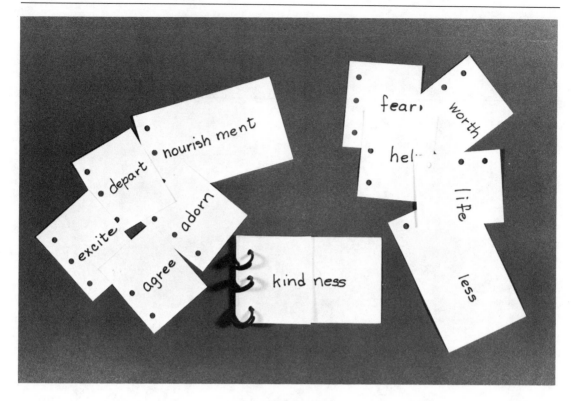

EXHIBIT 10

On the six cards preceding *ness*, letter *kind, like, great, small, white, new.*

On the cards before *ly*, put the words *love, great, nice, complete, plain, poor.*

On the cards before *ment*, put the words *pay, govern, nourish, excite, depart, agree.*

At the top and bottom of each narrow card, letter one of the following root words:

voice	great	baby	slow	grace	home
use	swift	boy	love	wonder	down
care	neat	fool	awkward	grate	up
noise	kind	child	swift	faith	sky

On square cards, put four of the following:

    less   ness   ish   ly   ful   ward

Play exactly as in 7(b), matching root words to suffixes.

9. Diacritical Marking—Mark a folder into eight 1-inch horizontal spaces. On the left of each side of the folder, letter words using the diacritical markings. Have the student place the words written on sentence strips by the correct diacritical form. Be sure to use the markings from a dictionary available to the student.

Put on Folder		*Put on Strips*	
brij	fun e	bridge	funny
skwarz	kyoob	squares	cube
brid	grat	bride	great
fiv	kof	five	cough
kam l	nif	camel	knife
kon	fo ne	cone	phony
daze		daisy	
levz		leaves	
il		aisle	
fuj		fudge	

10. Plural Forms of Words—
    a. Classifying Words by the Way Their Plurals Are Formed—Divide a folder into four vertical sections. Use these four headings:

    Add *s.*
    Change *y* to *i* and add *es.*
    Add *es.*
    Change *f* to *v* and add *es.*

    Put the following words on sentence strips for the student to place in the correct section:

boy	story	glass	leaf
cuff	baby	fish	thief
hand	army	wish	half
muff	berry	box	calf
cough	puppy	watch	loaf
flag	city	bus	scarf
fork	fairy	church	knife
table	lady	match	elf
cow	candy	brush	wife

    b. Wolf Trail Board Game—(See Exhibit 11.) Starting at the upper left corner of an open folder, make a zig-zag trail of stepping stones leading to a cave in the lower right corner. Stamp or paste a picture of a wolf at the beginning of the trail.

    On the stepping stones, letter nouns whose plurals the student should learn to spell. Provide a die or numbered cube and a marker for each student.

    A player rolls the die and proceeds the number of steps shown. He must be able to spell the plural of the noun to stay on the stone. If he fails, he must go back stone

EXHIBIT 11

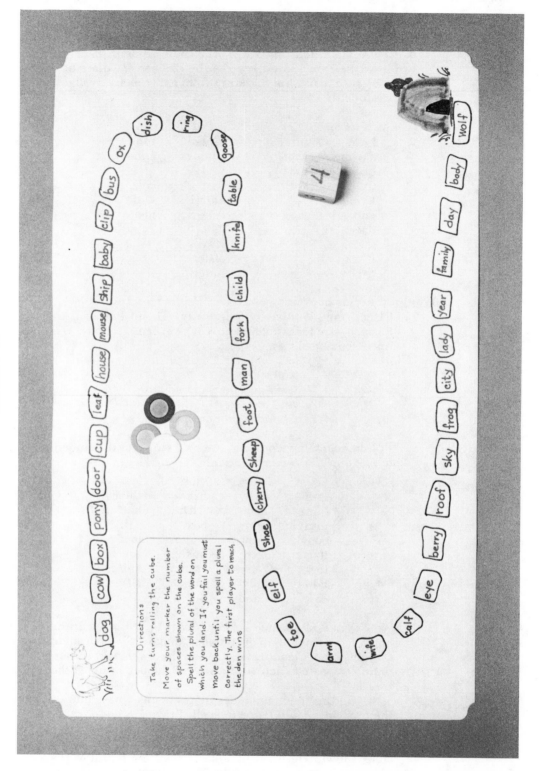

Directions

Take turns rolling the cube.
Move your marker the number
of spaces shown on the cube.
Spell the plural of the word on
which you land. If you fail you must
move back until you spell a plural
correctly. The first player to reach
the den wins

by stone until he can spell a plural correctly. The object is to follow the trail and be first to get to the wolves den.

Provide a master list of the nouns on the stepping stones with their plurals to be used for checking accuracy of responses. Include irregular plurals such as *deer, oxen, mice,* etc., if the students are ready.

11. Finding Words Everywhere—
    a. Food-Ad Pages in the Newspaper—Each student has a different food-ad page, markers, crayons, or paper and pencil as needed.
        i. Compound Words—The student draws a ring around each compound word in the food ad. For a more extensive assignment, have the student list the compound words in alphabetical order.
        ii. Syllables—Have each student find ten one-, two-, three-, and four-syllable words. What was the longest one-syllable word found? The shortest four-syllable word?
        iii. Abbreviations—Have the student make a list of all the abbreviations found on his page. After each, have him write the word that had been abbreviated.
    b. Task Cards for Finding Words—
        i. Word Go Round—(See Exhibit 12.)
        ii. Shooting Star—(See Exhibit 13.)
        iii. Double Up—(See Exhibit 14.) New words with double letters.
        iv. Looking at the States—(See Exhibit 15.) Little words in big words.
        v. Hidden Zoo—(See Exhibit 16.)

Exhibits 12-16 appear on the following pages.

EXHIBIT 12

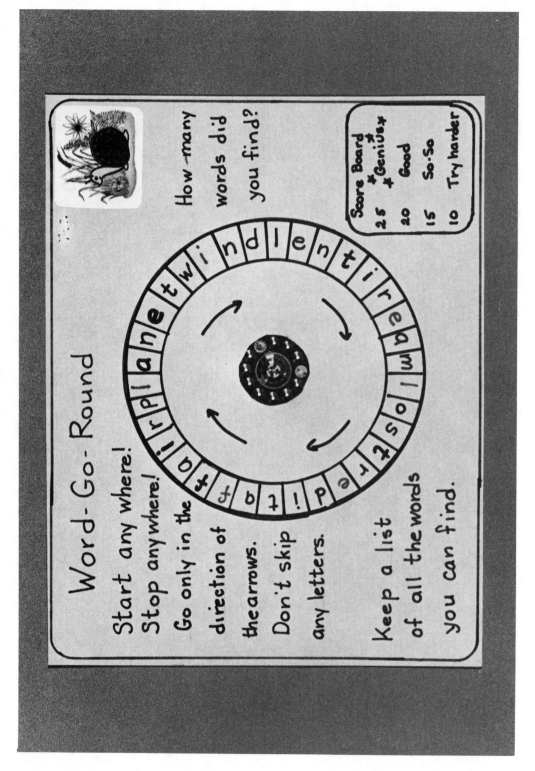

Word-Go-Round

Start any where!
Stop anywhere!
Go only in the
direction of
the arrows.
Don't skip
any letters.

Keep a list
of all the words
you can find.

How many
words did
you find?

Score Board
25 ☆Genius☆
20 Good
15 So-So
10 Try harder

Shooting Star

How many words can you find?

- Start any where.
- Stop anywhere.
- Go only on lines.
- Use each letter you come to.
- Make a list of all the words you can find.

Good Luck!

Score

40 words- Super
35   Great
30   Very Good
25   Good
20   Fair
Less than 20 Keep on looking!

EXHIBIT 13

135

EXHIBIT 14

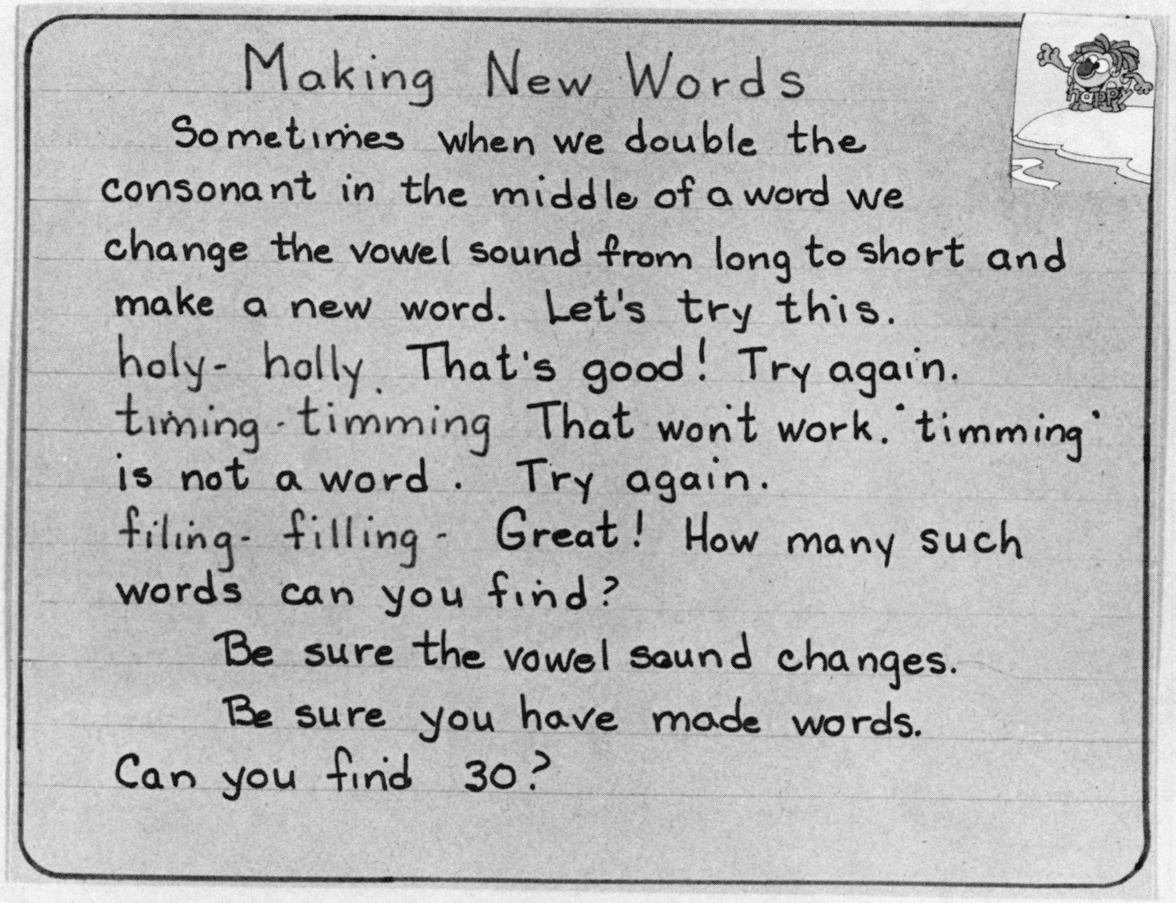

Making New Words

Sometimes when we double the consonant in the middle of a word we change the vowel sound from long to short and make a new word. Let's try this.
holy- holly. That's good! Try again. timing -timming That won't work. timming is not a word. Try again. filing- filling- Great! How many such words can you find?

Be sure the vowel sound changes.

Be sure you have made words.

Can you find 30?

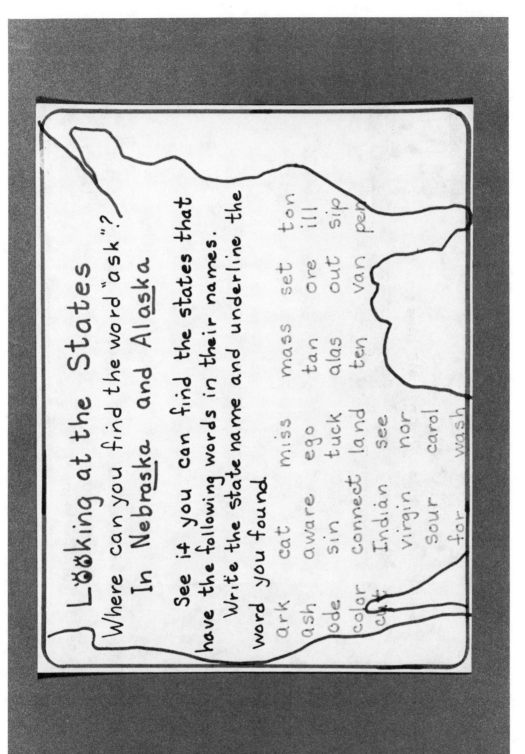

Looking at the States

Where can you find the word "ask"?
In Nebraska and Alaska

See if you can find the states that
have the following words in their names.
Write the state name and underline the
word you found.

ark	cat	miss	mass	set	ton
ash	aware	ego	tan	ore	ill
ode	sin	tuck	alas	out	sip
color	connect	land	ten	van	pen
cut	Indian	see			
	virgin	nor			
	sour	carol			
	for	wash			

EXHIBIT 15

EXHIBIT 16

The Hidden Zoo

There are enough animals hidden in the sentences below to populate a zoo. See how many you can find.

```
I'll be around, so you can go at ten if you are at the car at ten.
Waiting ahead was a risk unknown. First, I saw a small ambulance.
How do you do, Grandma. Is that a capital "I" on that sign?
You can skate on firm ice and I will not be averse to helping you.
The song was played on key but was Tom on key in the last part?
To and fro goes the swing, up and all around.
I'd like to admit my mistake but why does Tip ignore me?
Joe came later since it was a pleasant day.
Does that cow's moo seem to be getting fainter?
Will Mary and Grant elope? If so, it will be a comical farce.
That blob is from ink, I wish they made erasers that would erase that.
What size brain does a shark have? Their prestige really has grown.
I abhor seeing people murmur to each other in public.
```

Score:

27-up - Great Zookeeper	19 or less - You've lost a lot
24-26 Good Zookeeper	of animals. Keep on looking.
20-23 Fair Zookeeper	

Tactile-Kinesthetic Activities

8

The tactile-kinesthetic method as advocated by Fernald (1943) and others has much to offer nonreaders, especially those in the primary grades. In fact, Fernald demonstrated over forty years ago that adults also could learn by this method.

The tactile-kinesthetic (T-K) modality involves the sense of touch and movement. Children tracing with their fingers in sandboxes are using the T-K method. We should point out, however, that even though the sense of touch is in primary use, the child is seeing the symbol formed and probably is repeating the sound as he creates the symbol; thus, in effect, he is combining the visual, auditory, tactile, and kinesthetic modalities.

The following pages present a number of T-K activities and ways of using them.

Activities   1. Grit Tray—Put an inch or so of salt in a large cake pan and allow the child to trace letters, words, and shapes in the salt. He should say the letters or words as he makes them and name the shapes. This activity is repeated until the child masters the objective. It is especially suitable for letters of the alphabet.

You can substitute flavored gelatin for the salt, but be prepared to deal with wet fingers since the children soon learn that the taste is to their liking. Actually, a separate package can be kept for the purpose of rewarding the child when he succeeds in writing the letter or word correctly. The licking seems to relieve the boredom of tracing.

2. Sandpaper—There are many uses for the lowly sandpaper. Letters cut from the rough paper and glued to blocks of wood offer the child opportunities to trace letters and words. Children can come to understand triangles and such by tracing them with their fingers. Concepts such as *above* and *below* can be taught by placing a very rough strip of sandpaper at the top of a block and a strip of fine on the bottom. Teaching concepts of *left* and *right* follows the same procedure.

3. The Body—Children often respond well when difficult letters or words are traced lightly on their arms or in the palms of their hands. This tracing can be done with a finger or letter opener.

   Each child responds differently, and individual preferences should be considered when deciding what to trace or what part of the body to use.

   Many young children have commented that they actually feel a letter or word forming in their hand, long after they have given up the use of this touch method.

4. Clay—Clay letters can easily be made by teacher or student. Children who confuse *b* and *p*, for example, seem to respond well to this technique. With letter reversals, use different colors of clay so that not only the shape is different but the color is, too. (One child told us that she overcame her reversal problem by recalling the color of clay she used to make the letter; then, she could clearly visualize the exact shape of the letter—in living color.)

5. Concrete Blocks—These blocks, which many people use in constructing foundations for homes, can be employed to teach the alphabet. Write the letters on all sides of the block in magic marker and have the child trace the letters over and over again. The grainy texture of the blocks seems to reinforce the retention of the symbol being learned.

6. Sand Pictures—Draw outlines of several letters and particularly difficult words on black construction paper, fill the outlines with a thin coat of glue, and then sprinkle sand on the glue. (Also useful is the colored glitter you get in the dime store.) These letters and words wear rather well and allow the children an opportunity to practice on several letters on the same page. This is especially helpful on the *b-p-d* problem.

7. Pretzels—Have the children bake pretzels in the shape of various letters and use them for tracing. One of the more satisfying rewards of this approach is that the letter can be eaten once the student and teacher feel that it has been learned. A suggested recipe follows.

Pretzel Recipe

1½ cups water
1 package dry yeast   }   *dissolve*

4 cups flour
1 tablespoon sugar   }   *mix*
1 teaspoon salt

1 egg beaten slightly with 1 tablespoon of water
coarse-grained salt

Blend the yeast and flour mixture together and knead dough until smooth. Allow children to shape into letters. Place on greased pans and paint with egg-water mixture. Sprinkle with salt and bake for 25 minutes at 425°F. Should make 24 letters.

8. Foot Painting and Finger Painting—These are messy, but the daring teacher will try almost anything. Using finger paints, the child can be guided in proper formation of letters or words with the feet and hands. There is a novelty value in foot painting that should not be overlooked. And, there is something about being messy and learning at the same time that appeals to children and which should be exploited.

9. Oaktag Templates—This activity will leave you free to work with other children. Using a tape recorder, record words or letters that are giving a child trouble and make lots of letters with oaktag, covering them with a plastic laminate. Record the words at a very slow pace.

As an example, if the word is *when*, give the child the letters that spell the word and "plug" him into the tape recorder. The recording would follow like so:

You have four letters in your hand. Please lay them on the table before you. *(pause)* Pick up the W. *(pause)* Trace the outside edges of the letter with your finger. *(pause)* Please do it again. *(pause)*

The same procedure should be repeated with each letter. Then, the recording should say:

Place the letters on the table before you in the order that I tell you. W *(pause)* H *(pause)* E *(pause)* N *(pause)*. Repeat after me. W *(pause)* H *(pause)* E *(pause)* N *(pause)*. That spells *when*. Say the word. *(pause)* Say it again. *(pause)*. Now, let's trace the letters one more time. W *(pause)* . . .

Instruct the child to repeat the procedure until all letters have been traced again. Then, have him repeat the word after you several times. The lesson is at an end here, but it may be necessary to repeat the recording again and again. Persistence is the key.

10. Body Awareness—Using the body is an excellent way to teach certain words that are both abstract and concrete. For example, if the word *swallow* needs teaching, have the child feel his throat while he swallows, then have him trace the word in his grit tray as he says it. This procedure can be used for all body parts and many physical manifestations.

There are, of course, many variations of the preceding T-K activities. Although T-K is not the most efficient learning device, and although it requires a lot of effort from you and the child, the learning disabled, reading disabled, and slow learners have benefitted from this technique for years. Your responsibility is clear. The T-K method should be used if it works, no matter how painful. With success, the child will soon be able to go on to more efficient methods. You can rest assured that he will let you know when he is ready for something else.

BIBLIOGRAPHY

FERNALD, GRACE M. *Remedial Techniques in Basic School Subjects.* New York: McGraw-Hill Book Co., 1943.

Comprehension

9

BACKGROUND INFORMATION

The pot of gold at the end of the reading rainbow is comprehension. Students may be able to use phonic rules and pronounce words, but unless they can understand the meanings involved, they are not reading. Readers must associate symbols with experiences, words with experiences, then understand phrases, sentences, and paragraphs in order to appreciate the printed message. The skill of comprehension involves literal interpretation of words, phrases, and sentences and the interpretation of feelings and attitudes. It must involve implications and conclusions drawn from synthesizing an author's statements.

In order to complete the reading process, we must teach students to recognize words, understand what is being said, react from a personal viewpoint, and integrate the learnings to enhance knowledge.

The suggestions in this chapter cover a variety of techniques, many of them involving the use of manipulatives. The suggested activities are brief so they will not seem tedious, they lend themselves to self-correction for quick reinforcement, and they can be prescribed according to need or used as enrichment activities.

CLASSIFICATION

Classification involves the grouping of items according to shared characteristics. Most of the following activities can be constructed using pictures or words, depending on the level of the student.

Activities 1. Real or Make Believe—Prepare a folder with one side labeled *Real,* the other *Make Believe.* On squares, paste pictures of things such as:

An elephant doing tricks
A monkey carrying an umbrella
A seal throwing a ball
A pig building a house of bricks
A hen wearing an apron
A squirrel wearing an apron and sweeping with a broom

To make this activity for words, use sentence strips containing words such as:

fairy	dinosaur
ogre	ostrich
gnome	rocket
elf	giraffe
dragon	etc.

2. Farm or Forest—Use the same format as in (a), this time with animal pictures or names.

3. Fruit or Flowers—

4. Letters or Numerals—Use the same format with letters of the alphabet and numerals to be classified. A third category may be added using symbols (+, −, %, ?, etc.).

5. Where Do They Move—On a three-part folder with labels *In the Air, On the Ground,* and *In the Water,* have the student classify words or pictures of:

jet	submarine
blimp	raft
car	canoe
dog	etc.
snowmobile	

(See Exhibit 1.)

6. Shopping Mall—Four classes. Fasten two folders together with masking or strapping tape. On the top 2 inches of each of the four sections, make store signs with pictures that read *Furniture, Foods, Clothing, Toys.* Mark the space under each sign into 16 2-inch squares representing sections of a display window.

Put pictures or words on 2-inch squares for the student to place in the correct store window.

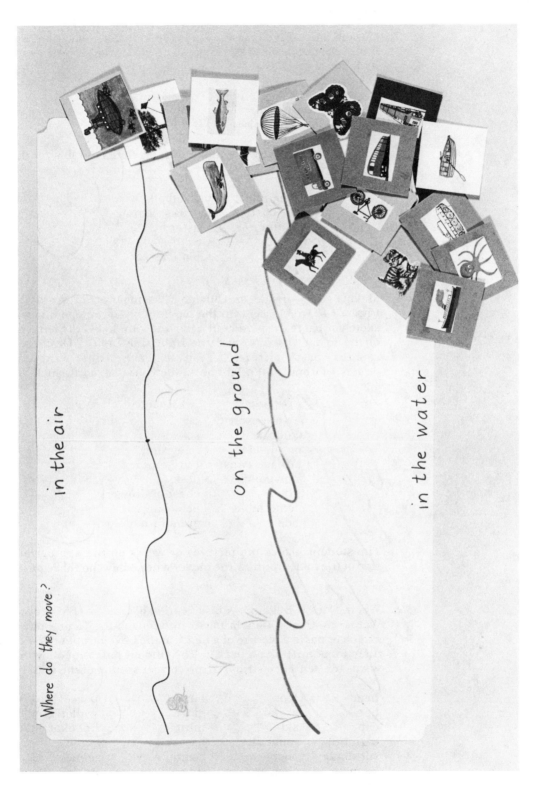

EXHIBIT 1

7. Garage Sale—Five classes. On an open folder, make five 3 × 6-inch rectangles representing tabletops. Put signs by the tops as follows:

Sports Equipment	Woodworking Tools
Clothing	Garden Tools
Kitchen Tools	

On sentence strips, write items suitable for each table for the student to classify, such as:

catcher's mitt	basketball
winter coat	hunting boots
eggbeater	toaster
drill	saw
rake	lawn mower

8. Moving Day—Inside or Outside Classification of Words or Phrases—Two classes. On the top 2 inches of an open folder, sketch or paste the picture of a moving van. Label the left side of the folder *Outside*, and the right side *Inside*. On 2-inch squares, paste pictures, or on sentence strips, write the names, of items that might be on the van. Use words such as:

Outside	*Inside*
lawn mower	bed
sandbox	sofa
long ladder	television
garbage cans	refrigerator
snowmobile	desk
grill	chest of drawers
picnic table	floor lamp
slide	grandfather clock

The student places the pictures or words on the appropriate side of the folder to show the mover where they should be put.

9. Where Does It Belong?—Classification of Objects (Pictures or Words) by Use—Divide a folder into four parts. In one put a sketch or paste a picture of a head, in the next part put a hand, then a foot, and last a pocket. The student puts the following words (on sentence strips) in the correct section of the folder:

head	foot	hand	pocket
hat	socks	glove	wallet
cap	ski	mitten	handkerchief
earmuffs	roller skate	baseball mitt	comb
sunshade	boot	boxing glove	money
helmet	shoe	ring	knife
tam	swim fin	fielder's glove	I.D. card

10. Which One Doesn't Belong Here?—Divide a folder into 12 sections—3 horizontal, and four vertical, spaces. In each of the 12 spaces, letter one of the following sets of words. The student places a marker on the word in each set that does not belong. Bingo markers or buttons are suitable. For self-checking, on the Key Card write the 12 words that should have been marked.

minute	rain	tea	(rocks)	airplane	now
hour	(heat)	coffee	trees	bus	today
(cold)	hail	milk	grass	train	tomorrow
day	sleet	(crackers)	shrubs	car	(between)
year	snow	juice	plants	(float)	later
run	lunch	skate	canoe	(cane)	sidewalk
walk	(morning)	ski	raft	torch	(hill)
(yell)	breakfast	toboggan	ocean liner	light	street
jump	dinner	(wagon)	barge	lantern	road
stroll	supper	sled	(trailer)	lamp	lane

11. Transportation—Power and Purpose—Divide a folder into seven 2½-inch vertical sections. (See Exhibit 2.) Across the top of the first two, letter *Man-Powered*. At the top of the first of these two, put *On Roads*, and at the top of the second, *On Water*. Across the top of the next three spaces, letter *Engine-Powered*, and on the three sections, letter *On Road, On Water, On Rails*. Across the next section, letter *Wind-Powered*, and on the last section, *On Runners*.

On sentence strips for the student to classify according to the correct set and subset, letter words such as:

Columns

1	2	3	4
pram	raft	jeep	tug
bicycle	canoe	lorry	speedboat
scooter	gondola	hearse	steamer
unicycle	kayak	ambulance	launch
wheelchair	umiak	jalopy	dredger
stretcher	punt	limousine	pilot boat

Columns

5	6	7
locomotive	frigate	skate
caboose	clipper	toboggan
subway	brig	sleigh
Pullman	yawl	cutter
flatcar	shell	ski
diner	caravel	sled

Encourage the use of the dictionary as needed. Have the students suggest more words for each category.

147

EXHIBIT 2

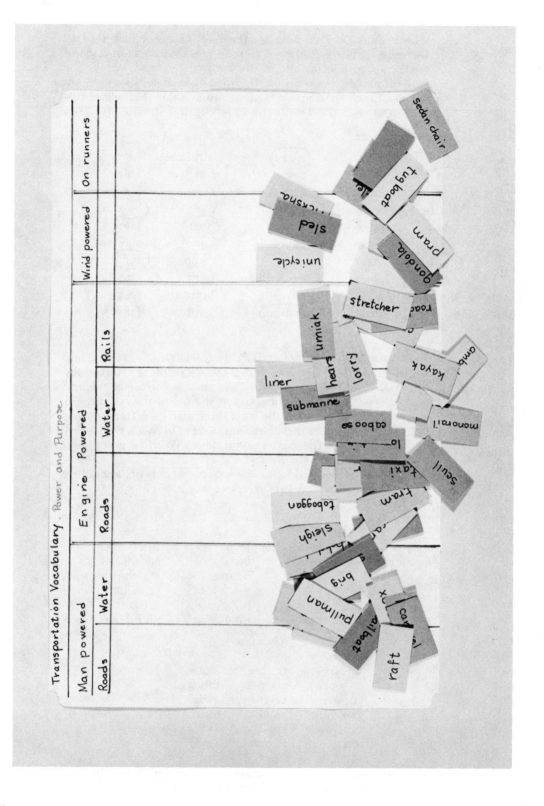

12. Classification of Phrases According to Time or Place—At the top of one side of a folder, put a picture of a clock to designate time, and on the other side, paste a small section of a road map to designate place. Put phrases to be classified on sentence strips. Suggested phrases are:

at one o'clock	at the street corner
on Sunday	on the parade stand
in the night	in the center of the pool
once upon a time	after the bridge
after his birthday	up the hill
from then on	from his window
before morning	before the ramp
three o'clock	three blocks over

The student cannot rely on the preposition, but must understand the whole phrase in order to correctly classify.

13. Which Can Grow? Label one side of a folder *These Can Grow,* the other side *These Cannot Grow.* Put words such as the following on sentence strips:

tree	seed	stone	dog house
fingernail	child	bicycle	spoon
plant	hair	hammer	wig
foot	head	hat	fence
hedge	teeth	path	shoe

14. Classification of Outcomes—Divide a folder in two and label the sides *When used, these things get smaller* and *When used, these things remain the same size.* On strips, write words such as:

pencil	soap	ruler	shears
eraser	candle	book	stapler
roll of tape	crayon	towel	marbles
lollypop	lipstick	paper clips	toothbrush
		comb	book

15. Which of My Five Senses?—Classification of Sensory Imagery—Make five vertical columns on a folder labeled *Hear, See, Feel, Smell, Taste.* Put terms such as the following on sentence strips for the student to place in the correct column:

Hear	*See*	*Feel*
transistor radio	jet trails	itch
whisper	fading rainbow	toothache
wake-up call	glistening water	hot sand
pretty melody	friendly smile	eye strain
murmur	fall leaves	sharp pain
wail	dirty windows	throb

149

Hear	See	Feel
scream	shiny	numbness
halo	dimness	slimy
echo	glare	cramp
tinkle	flash	tingle

Smell	Taste
leaking gas	bitter pickles
roasting turkey	sweet coffee
rotting potatoes	spicy pie
perfume odor	salty water
fragrance	sour milk
aroma	flavor
stink	peppery
fumes	luscious
scent	tang
reek	delicious

RELATIONSHIPS

To comprehend what is being read, the student must learn to see relationships among various words, phrases, and ideas presented in printed materials.

Activities

1. Up, Down—Opposites—No reading is required. On a folder, prepare a game board by making a wavy horizontal line across the center of the folder. On each side of the folder, make ten ¾-inch circles in random positions above the line and ten below the line. (See Exhibit 3.)

   On the six sides of a 1-inch cube, make a simple line sketch of one, two, and three fish and one, two, and three birds. Give each player 20 plastic bingo markers or buttons.

   The players take turns rolling the cube and placing markers on their side of the board as indicated by the cube. Birds represent "up," and fish represent "down." The first player to cover all of the circles on his "up" or his "down" side of the board wins. The game can be made a step more difficult by putting the words *up* and *down* on the cube instead of the symbols.

2. Opposites Words—Use the format of eight 1-inch horizontal spaces across a folder. (See Exhibit 4.) Letter words such as the following down the left edge of each side of the folder. Put the opposites of these words on sentence strips for matching.

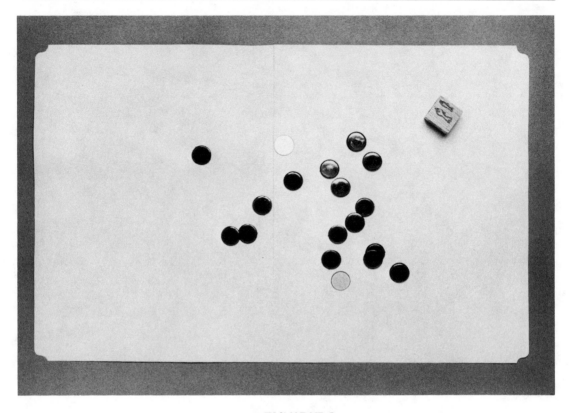

EXHIBIT 3

On Folder	*On Strips*
dark	light
night	day
right	wrong
in	out
over	under
sweet	sour
loud	quiet
fast	slow
large	small
rough	smooth
wet	dry
cold	hot
melting	freezing
sad	happy
bright	dull
full	empty

Make a Key Card on a 5 × 8-inch file card so that the activity can be self-corrected.

EXHIBIT 4

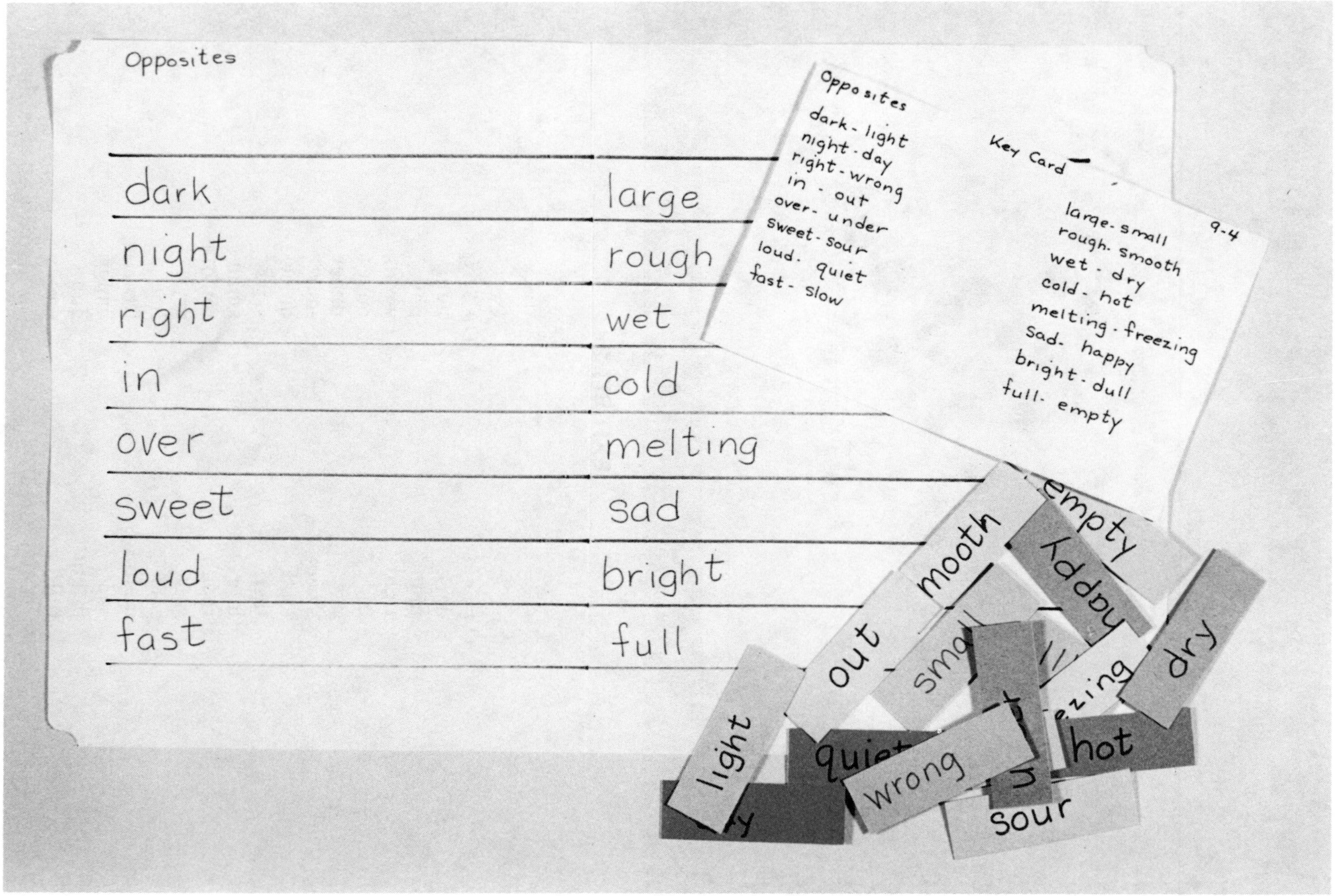

Opposites

dark

night

right

in

over

sweet

loud

fast

large

rough

wet

cold

melting

sad

bright

full

Key Card

9-4

large-small
rough-smooth
wet-dry
cold-hot
melting-freezing
sad-happy
bright-dull
full-empty

Opposites

dark-light
night-day
right-wrong
in-out
over-under
sweet-sour
loud-quiet
fast-slow

empty

happy

smooth

out

dry

hot

sour

wrong

quiet

light

3. Part-Whole Relationship—Use the same format of eight horizontal spaces as in Activity 2. Use words such as:

On Folder	On Strips
fish	fin
door	knob
horse	mane
telephone	dial
bird	feather
coat	sleeve
bicycle	handlebars
tree	leaf
hand	finger
flower	petal
foot	toe
head	eyes
elephant	trunk
cup	handle
apple	core
shoe	sole

Make similar folders to develop other relationships, such as product-source, etc. See Activity 4.

4. Determining Relationships—Mark a folder into six vertical columns labeled at the top as follows:

Product-Source
Part-Whole
Animal-Sound
Parent-Child
Container-Contents
Animal-Home

On sentence strips, write the following pairs of words. The student places these in the correct column according to the relationship between the two words.

cow-milk	can-soup	body-arm
hen-egg	box-crackers	dog-tail
pig-bacon	bottle-milk	bird-wing
wheat-flour	cupboard-dish	car-wheel
sheep-wool	purse-money	sled-runner
fish-pond	cow-calf	cow-moo
bird-nest	horse-colt	horse-neigh
cow-barn	hen-chick	pig-grunt
bear-cave	goat-kid	dog-bark
rabbit-hole	dog-puppy	hen-cackle

Make Key Cards for these activities for self-correcting. Be sure to code the back of each sentence strip with the number of the folder in order to keep parts together easily.

5. Which Two Things Can Serve the Same Purpose?—Use the format of eight 1-inch horizontal spaces on the folder and the sentence strips for matching.

On Folder	On Strips
stairs	escalator
hat	helmet
boat	raft
bed	cot
lamp	lantern
furnace	fireplace
shoe	slipper
mitten	glove
box	suitcase
wagon	van
zipper	gripper
tent	cabin
watch	sundial
slingshot	bow and arrow
hatchet	axe
pencil	pen

6. Which Two Things Could You Use To _____ ?—Same format as Activity 5. Put each member of the pairs of words to go on strips on a separate strip. The student places two strips after each word on the folder.

On Folder	On Strips	
paint	brush	roller
write	pen	pencil
eat	fork	spoon
read	newspaper	book
tell time	clock	watch
climb	ladder	stairs
drink	glass	cup
cut paper	shears	paper cutter
cut wood	saw	hatchet
color	crayon	paints
dig	shovel	spade
ride	pony	bicycle
hear news	radio	television
sew	sewing machine	needle and thread
pound	hammer	maul
provide power	gas	oil

7. Relationships—Use the format in Activity 5. Add a third related item on the strips. Examples follow. Adjust the difficulty of the words used to the skills of the child. For young children, use colors, numbers, coins, pets, etc.

On Folder	On Strips
girl	boy, children, tots
gas	coal, wood, oil
sandal	shoe, slipper, boot
mosquito	fly, ant, bee
syrup	honey, sugar, candy
orange	apple, banana, pear
steak	hot dog, bacon, sausage
biscuit	muffin, roll, cracker
dagger	knife, sword, cutlass
yacht	steamer, cruiser, liner
shotgun	pistol, revolver, rifle
great	big, large, huge
cousin	sister, father, uncle
silver	iron, gold, tin
pine	maple, oak, elm

8. Do I Hear or See?—At the top of the left side of a folder, letter the words *I see*. On the right side, letter *I hear*. On sentence strips, write phrases such as the following for the student to place on the correct side of the folder:

Hear	See
thunder	signal flags
car horn	blinding light
train whistle	dim figures
tea-kettle whistle	spiral of smoke
motor roar	steam from kettle
howling wind	flying kite
radio signal	jet trail
baby's cry	waving scarf
creaking steps	sand castle
jingle of bells	snow falling
crashing	broken glass
clock striking	sparkling diamond
alarm	daybreak
distant drums	shooting star

9. Analogies—This activity can be made using pictures or words. In each type, the first three items are put on the folder and the student adds the fourth.
   Suggested pictures:

   small red circle, large red circle, small blue square, large blue square
   front of coin, back of coin, girl's face, girl's back
   whole bottle, broken bottle, whole carton, smashed carton
   bird in cage, bird in tree, fish in bowl, fish in pond
   etc.

155

Suggested words:

cork, bottle, lid, jar	
stool, sit, bed, sleep	
gas, car, food, body	*Purpose*
eye, see, ear, hear	
wee, small, great, large	
weary, tired, level, even	
dingy, dull, bright, gleaming	*Synonyms*
conceal, hide, expose, reveal	
black, white, night, day	
pretty, ugly, bold, shy	
complicated, simple, scarce, ample	*Antonyms*
clear, muddy, clever, stupid	
rain, wet, snow, cold	
heat, warm, poverty, hunger	
hurt, pain, wound, bleed	*Cause-effect*
slow, late, fast, early	
hat, head, ring, finger	
mountains, land, waves, ocean	
tennis, court, bowling, lanes	*Place*
swim, water, fly, air	
wing, bird, arm, man	
nut, shell, bean, pod	
antler, elk, tusk, elephant	*Part-whole*
prow, boat, snout, pig	
pain, agony, thirst, crave	
cub, bear, sapling, tree	
mouse, lion, goldfish, shark	*Degree*
joy, ecstasy, sad, grief	
do, did, go, gone	
prettier, prettiest, better, best	
slow, slowly, swift, swiftly	*Grammatical*
its, their, table's, people's	

SEQUENCE

All readers need to develop the ability to organize events or ideas in a logical sequence. The student needs to understand time relationships and organize happenings in the order of their occurrence.

Activities   1.   Pictures—On 4 × 6-inch or larger file cards, make sketches to show sets of four sequential happenings. Have the student put the cards in the correct order.
Suggested pictures:

Apple—one bite gone, half gone, core
Large snowball, second ball on top, third ball, finished snowman

Candle being burnt
Jack-o'-lantern
Sun rising or setting
Piece of pie being eaten—last picture crumbs only

2. Comic Strips—Paste comic strips with clearly sequential happenings on tagboard, then cut the panels part. Have the student reassemble them.

3. Words and Pictures—(See Exhibit 5.) Mark a folder into eight parts by dividing each side in half vertically and horizontally. At the top of each section, draw or paste a picture of the following:

cake	campfire
milk	telephone
fish	ear of corn
letter	watermelon

Divide the space under the picture into three vertical sections. At the top of each section, put the words as listed in the following.

Give the student 1-inch squares numbered 1, 2, and 3. A set is needed for each picture. The student places the numerals under the words in the order that the actions would take place.

cake	*milk*	*fish*	*letter*
eat	buy	catch	stamp
cut	drink	eat	write
bake	pour	clean	mail

campfire	*telephone*	*ear of corn*	*watermelon*
put out	dial	eat	cut
let burn	talk	cook	pick
build	listen	pick	eat

4. Phrases—Prepare a folder with eight 1-inch horizontal spaces. Write the following sentences in each strip. Put the first part of the sentence on the left side of the folder, and the second part on the right side. Leave enough space at the end of each sentence part for the student to place a 1-inch square with the numeral 1 or 2. The student reads the sentence, then places the numeral squares to indicate the order of events.

Suggested sentences:

Bob went to school / after he fed his pets.
Before she left for school / Mary got her lunch money.
Father washed the car / then looked for dents.
Joe got up and dressed / as soon as the alarm rang.
Mary wished for luck / then presented her idea.
He put his hand in his pocket / and discovered it was empty.
The teacher closed the door / when the children were gone.
The dogs heard the sound / and began to bark.

EXHIBIT 5

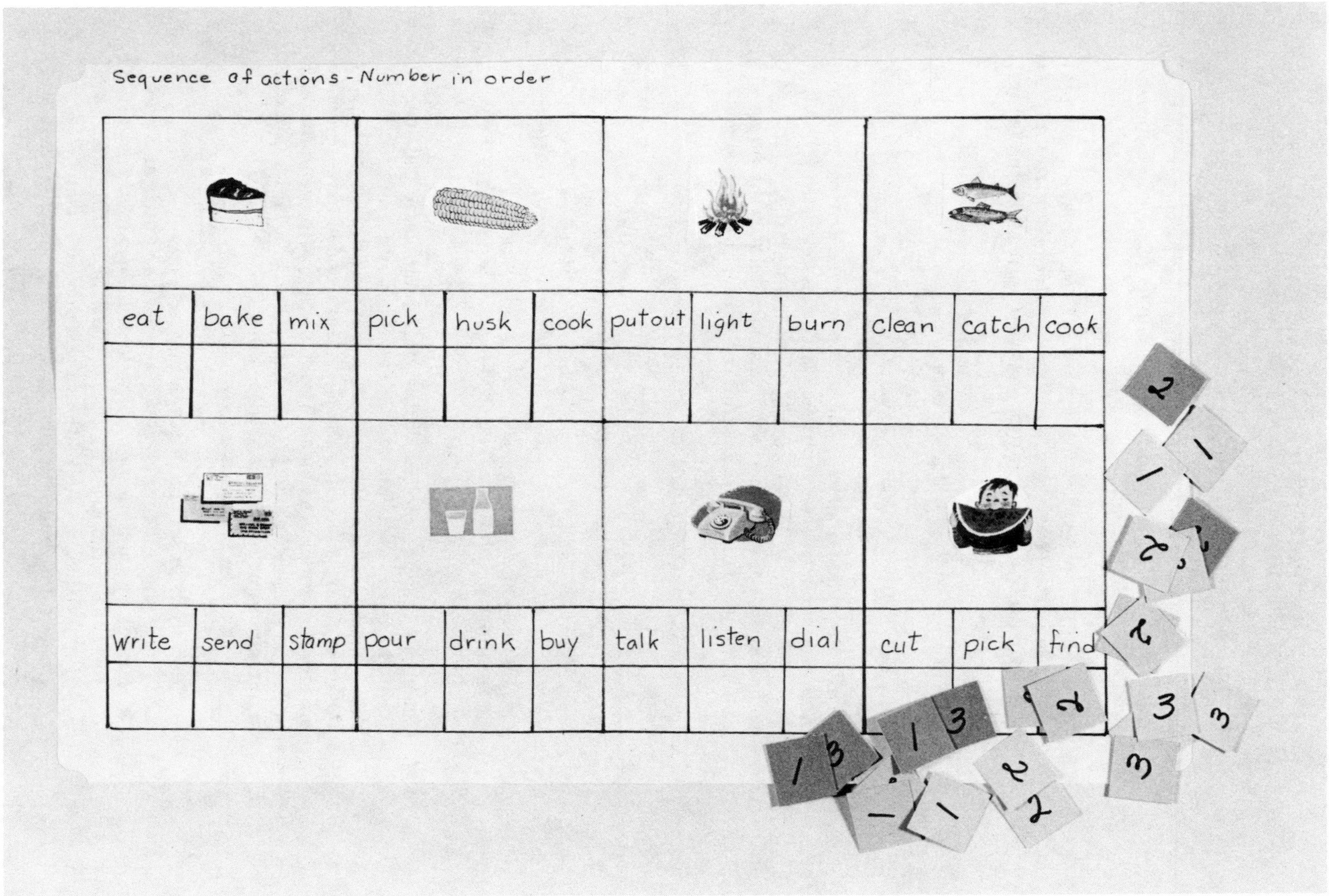

Sequence of actions – Number in order

	eat	bake	mix		pick	husk	cook		putout	light	burn		clean	catch	cook
	Write	send	stamp	pour		drink	buy	talk		listen	dial	cut		pick	find

5. Sentences—Prepare a folder with four 2-inch horizontal spaces. Write two sentences in each space, leaving space at the end for the student to place 1-inch squares with the numerals 1 and 2 to indicate the order the sentences would have occurred.

Suggested sentences:

The candles were blown out.
Nothing was left but crumbs.

He was dripping wet.
The boy fell in a puddle.

The lights went out.
It became dark.

The garden was bare.
The children picked all of the flowers.

The window broke.
The ball sailed toward the house.

She bit the candy bar.
She opened her mouth.

He opened the door.
He unlocked the door.

He pulled on his socks.
He tied his shoes.

6. Sequence of Events—Mark a folder into eight parts by dividing each side in half horizontally and vertically. At the top of each section, write one of the following sentences followed by the events that occurred in the sentence. The student places a 1 × 1-inch numeral square in front of each event to show the order of happening.

After he asked his mother, Mark put a rope on his dog and took him for a walk.
_____ took a walk
_____ asked his mother
_____ put a rope on the dog

Mary showed her father the new coat, then put it back in the box.
_____ bought a coat
_____ put it back
_____ showed it to father

The camper made a shelter out of the wood he found after the storm.
_____ made a shelter
_____ found some wood
_____ there was a storm

159

The fire fighters washed the truck after they drove home from putting out the fire.

_____ washed truck

_____ drove home

_____ put out fire

When night came, the girl tied her horse and made a fire.

_____ night came

_____ tied horse

_____ made fire

The flood caused by the rainstorm did great damage to the town.

_____ flood came

_____ rainstorm

_____ damage to town

Before morning, the rain stopped, and then we got some sleep.

_____ morning came

_____ rain stopped

_____ we got some sleep

After mother left, the children got frightened and ran and hid under the bed.

_____ mother left

_____ children became frightened

_____ children ran and hid

7. Seed Packets—At the top center of each side of a folder, paste an empty vegetable or flower seed envelope. On sentence strips, write the directions given on each packet, one step on each strip. There are usually five to seven steps in the directions, such as:

> soften ground
> make trench
> place seeds one inch apart
> cover seeds lightly
> press down soil
> water well
> thin young plants

Have the student put the strips in the correct order under each seed packet.

8. Recipes—Clip a recipe from a magazine and paste it on a folder. Write the directions one step at a time on sentence strips. Have the student put the strips in the correct order as given in the recipe.

9. Sequence in a Story—Clothespin activity. Put the following sentences about ½ inch apart on a strip of tagboard or cardboard. Have the student slip ten numbered spring

clothespins down the right edge of the cardboard to show the order of events.

> Mother put the dishes back in the cupboard.
> The dinner party was over.
> She washed each dish carefully.
> Mother asked Mary to do the dishes.
> The girls dried the dishes.
> Mary said, "I'll be glad to. Can Josie help?"
> They took all of the dishes to the kitchen.
> Mary filled the sink with hot water.
> After being washed, the dishes were rinsed.
> She put some soap in the hot water.

LITERAL COMPREHENSION

Literal comprehension is the ability to get the direct, stated meaning from a reading unit. The student must be able to master this skill before he proceeds to analytical and critical comprehension.

Activities
1. Picture to Sentences—Cut eight small pictures involving simple actions from old workbooks and paste them on 2 × 2-inch squares. Mark a folder into 2-inch horizontal spaces. At the left of each space on each side of the folder, write a simple sentence describing the action in one of the pictures. Have the child read the sentence and then place the correct picture in the space after the sentence.

2. True or False—Label the two sides of a folder *True, False* or *Yes, No.* Have the student read sentences from sentence strips and place them under the correct heading. Use sentences such as:

A fish can run.	A baby can grow.
We sleep in a garden bed.	Pencils can break.
Colors have smell.	Grass can be green.
Every chicken lays eggs.	All rain is wet.
Dogs are always brown.	Some birds sing.
All children can read.	All animals eat.
Grass can be white.	Snow is always cold.
Table legs wear socks.	A ball can ring.
Wheels are square.	You can hear a story.
You hear a picture.	Some dogs swim.

3. Who Did What?—Mark a folder with ten 1-inch horizontal spaces. On the left side of the folder, write a simple sentence in each space. Divide the right side with a vertical line down the

center. At the top of one of these sections, write *Who,* and at the top of the other, write *Did What.* On 20 sentence strips, put the simple subjects and simple predicates from each of the ten sentences.

The student reads a sentence, then selects from his array of 20 cards the two that tell "who" and "what was done" in that sentence and places the cards in the correct spaces after the sentence. Use sentences such as:

	Who	*Did What*
Some children climbed into the animal's cage.	children	climbed
Over the hill ran the rabbit.	rabbit	ran

4. Signs of Spring—Sentence Completion—Mark ten 1-inch horizontal spaces across the folder. On the left side of the folder, write sentence beginnings, and on sentence strips, write the endings for each to be matched with the sentence in the space on the right side of the folder.

Examples are:

On Folder	*On Strips*
The snow	melts away.
The birds	build nests.
The nights	get shorter.
The weather	gets warmer.
The seeds	are planted.
The trees	turn green.
The days	get longer.
The thermometers	go up.
The children	fly kites.
The bees	make honey.

Depending on the ability of the children, you may add distractors to matching activities. Sample distractors for this folder would be:

turn brown
fly south

5. Football Signals—Reading Pictures—(See Exhibit 6.) Get a college football program. Cut out the 5 football signals with their meanings and paste them on 2 × 2-inch squares. Mark a folder into five 2-inch spaces horizontally and three 5-inch spaces vertically.

In the left 3 inches of each section, write one of the following literal descriptions of the signals. Have the student match the squares to the descriptions.

Right arm extended from side of body, forefinger pointing out.
Right arm extended over head, open hand facing forward.

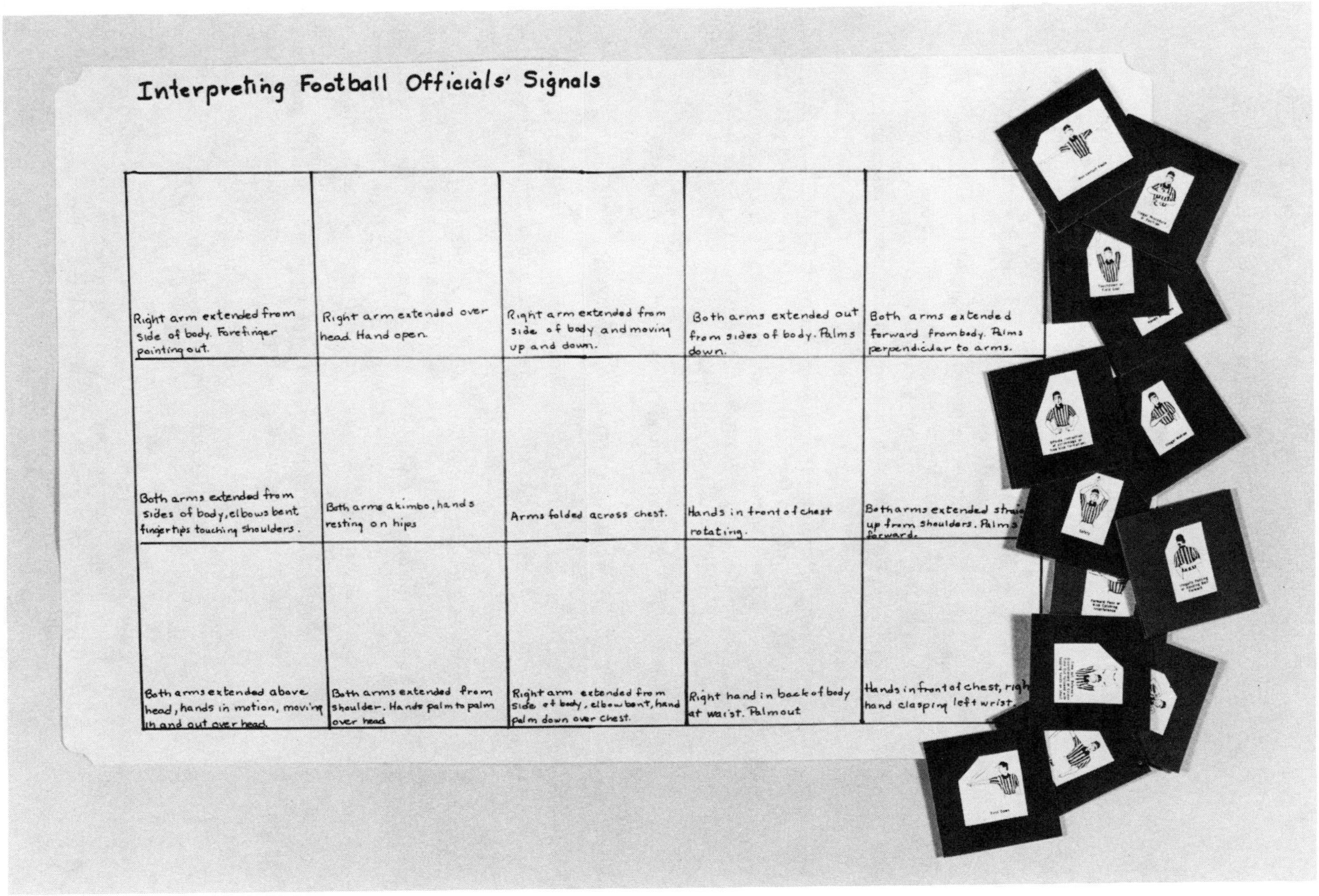

Interpreting Football Officials' Signals

		Right arm extended over head. Hand open.	Right arm extended from side of body and moving up and down.	Both arms extended out from sides of body. Palms down.	Both arms extended forward from body. Palms perpendicular to arms.
		Both arms akimbo. Hands resting on hips	Arms folded across chest.	Hands in front of chest rotating.	Both arms extended straight up from shoulders. Palms forwards.
Right arm extended from side of body. Forefinger pointing out.	Both arms extended from sides of body, elbows bent, fingertips touching shoulders.	Both arms extended above head, hands in motion, moving in and out over head.	Both arms extended from shoulder. Hands palm to palm over head	Right arm extended from side of body, elbow bent, hand palm down over chest.	Hands in front of chest, right hand clapping left wrist.
Right hand in back of body at waist. Palm out.

EXHIBIT 6

Right arm extended from side of body, palm down, arm moving up and down.

Both arms extended from sides of body, palms down.

Both arms extended forward, palms facing forward.

Both arms extended from sides of body, elbows bent, fingertips touching shoulders.

Both arms akimbo, hands resting on hips.

Arms folded across chest.

Hands in front of chest, rotating.

Both arms extended straight up from shoulders, palms forward.

Both arms extended above head, hands in motion, moving in and out over head.

Right arm extended from side of body, elbow bent, palm of hand down on chest.

Right hand in back of body at waist, palm out.

Hands in front of body, right hand clasping left wrist.

6. Using the Classified Ads—Reading for Details—Cut many ads from the classified section of the newspaper and paste them on 1 × 2-inch sentence strips. Mark two ½-inch vertical columns on the folder, heading each one with one of the headings from the classified pages, such as:

Lost and Found	Furnished Apartments
Help Wanted	Unfurnished Apartments
Situations Wanted	House for Sale
Room and Board	etc.

Have the students place the ads in the correct column.

7. Reading a Catalog—Reading for Details—Cut a page or section from a catalog showing several items identified by number with descriptions given below. Paste this section on the left side of a folder. Mark the right side of the folder into 1-inch horizontal spaces. In each space, describe one of the items from the catalog.

The student places a 1-inch square beside the description identifying the object by number. Use descriptions such as:

17-jewel man's watch, radium dial _____

Boy's watch, shockproof, waterproof _____

8. Reading about Sports—Cut several short stories from the sports page of the newspaper. Give the student a fine-point, colored, felt-tip marker and have him mark each word in the story that identifies the sport written about. Words to be marked might be *inning, base hit, outs;* or *forward pass, punt, touchdown;* etc. Words used with many or all sports should not be marked (*score, player, uniform,* etc.).

FOLLOWING DIRECTIONS

Activities 1. Primary—Prepare a folder with five 2-inch horizontal spaces. In the left half of each side of the folder, letter some simple directions such as the following:

> Put a star over the chimney of a house.
> Place an animal between two children.
> Put a ball between two trees.
> Put an x between two animals.
> Put a tree on both sides of a house.
> Put a little tree to the left of a house.
> Make three stars in the sky above a house.
> Put a dog to the left of a tree and a ball to the right.
> Make a fence between two trees.
> Put two animals beside a boy.

On 2 × 3-inch cards, make diagrams following the preceding directions. Use simple sketches, gummed seals, or workbook pictures. Make two extra cards with different arrangements to be used as distractors.

Give the child the folder and the cards and have him match the cards to the spaces beside the lettered directions on the folder.

2. Post Office—

a. Primary—Take 3 × 5 file cards to the U.S. Post Office and have them stamped with the messages the workers use to mark undeliverable mail, such as:

> Incomplete Address
> Insufficient Postage
> Addressee Unknown
> Postage Due ____¢
> etc.

Give each child a card and have him deliberately prepare an envelope to match the message on his card. Use green stamps or used stamps as postage. Put the envelopes and cards together and have the children take turns matching cards with envelopes.

b. Intermediate—Get forms from the Post Office to be used for change of address and holding mail, or a kit to be used when moving. If you can get only one copy of each, make facsimiles. Have the children fill out the various forms and check one another's work.

3. Careers—

a. Primary—Make and duplicate application forms for the various helper jobs that you assign in your classroom. Simulate regular job application forms. Have the children apply for the jobs they would like to do and have them state inter-

165

est, experience, background, etc. If your group is large enough, have a personnel committee review the applications and award the jobs.

b. Intermediate—Procure job application forms from local businesses, grocery stores, or employment agencies. Have students fill them out, then, as a committee, review the applications for accuracy in following directions.

4. Credit—Intermediate—Procure forms for application for credit from mail-order houses, department stores, and banks. Have the students fill them out, then review them individually or as a committee for accuracy in following directions.

5. Word Games—More-complicated games for following directions are suitable for older students. After you have presented one or two similar to the following, have the students make up their own puzzles and challenge each other.

Sample game:

REGGIE JACKSON

A B C D E F G H I J K L M N O P Q R S T U V W X Y Z

Directions:
a. Print this man's name, last name first.
b. Print the name again as you did in Step 1, but this time reverse the order of the letters in his first name.
c. Take out the double letter and substitute the twentieth letter of the alphabet doubled.
d. Substitute the fourteenth letter of the alphabet for the third letter of the alphabet.
e. If the fifth letter of the alphabet occurs twice, use two of that letter instead of the word that means "male child."
f. Cross out the first letter in your puzzle and put the twenty-fifth letter of the alphabet in its place.
g. Substitute the eighth letter of the alphabet for the fifth letter the first time it occurs in the second word and you should have a description of Reggie Jackson.

COMPARING AND CONTRASTING

The activities that follow have the students compare statements about two different items and place them on a folder to show if they do compare or contrast.

Activities 1. Dogs and Cats—Make a horizontal line across a folder 4 inches from the bottom. Make a center line in the area above, making two sections. Label the top left section *Dogs Can,* the top right section *Cats Can,* and the bottom section *Dogs and Cats Can.* On sentence strips, write phrases such as the following for the students to place in the correct area:

Cats Only	*Dogs Only*
Sharpens claws	Used by hunters
Purrs	Is a canine
Is a feline	Barks
Climbs trees	Sometimes guides people
Sees well at night	Used to guard homes
Meows	Likes to gnaw bones
Can retract nails	Likes to bury bones
Sharpens claws	Whines

Both
Is a mammal
Is playful when young
Has many colors
Has four legs
Breathes and eats
Has fur
Is often a pet
May catch mice

2. Tennis and Golf—Prepare a folder as in Activity 1. Put statements about these two sports on strips for the student to classify.

3. Basketball and Football—Same as Activity 2.

4. Birds and Mammals—For older students, prepare a folder as in Activity 1, and on the strips write statements with more scientific information relating to those two classes of animals.

5. Products—On the left side of a folder, paste the information panel from two pain-relievers, toothpastes, or cereals. On the right side, in ten 1-inch horizontal spaces, write questions to be answered by reading the information panels. (See Exhibit 7.) Sample questions are:

Which has the most calories?
Cost per ounce?
Percentage of daily requirement of calcium?
Percentage of daily requirement of iron?

Leave the last two spaces for comparison:

In how many ways is Product A superior? _____
In how many ways is Product B superior? _____

167

EXHIBIT 7

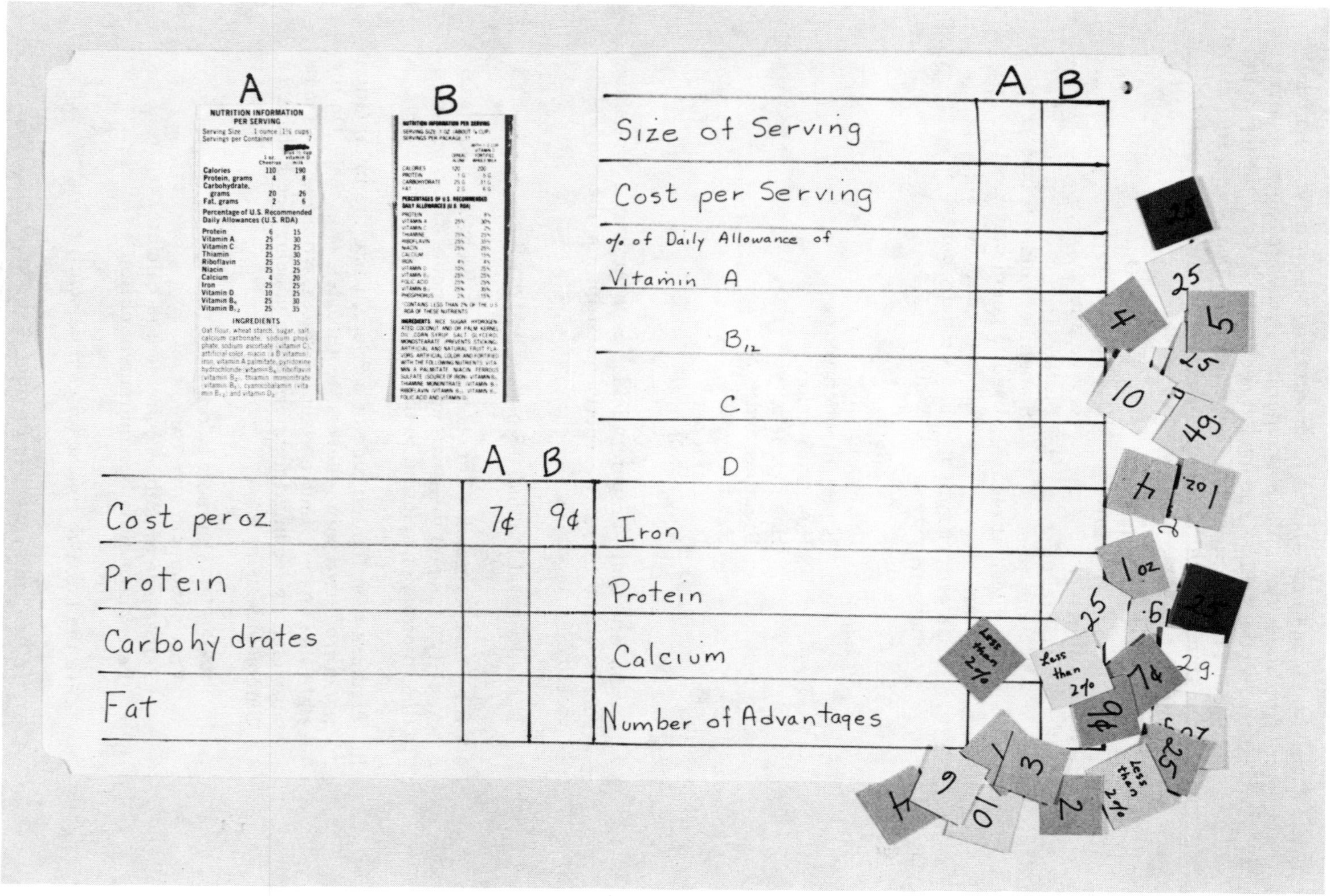
A
B
A
B
Size of Serving
Cost per Serving
% of Daily Allowance of
Vitamin A
B12
C
D
Iron
Protein
Calcium
Number of Advantages
A
B
Cost per oz
7¢
9¢
Protein
Carbohydrates
Fat

MAIN IDEAS

The ability to distinguish between the central core of a passage and the informational details is very difficult for some children. The concept *main idea* is quite abstract. To clarify the concept *work sets of objects*, put in front of the child some common objects such as a marble, a ball, a toy car, and a doll. Ask the question, "What is one word we could use to describe all of these items as a group?" The child can see that they are all toys. They cannot be grouped by color, shape, or size, but all do serve the same function. Through the use of pictures, the main idea of homes could be developed with pictures of a nest, cave, house, and log cabin.

Pictures of a person using a rope and pick to climb a mountain, people riding an escalator, a man on a ladder, and someone climbing stairs can result in a statement that these are all ways to get to a higher level or elevation. Make a sentence about each picture. Then the child can understand that the title *Ways to Climb* could represent the main idea of the sentences.

Activities 1. Words—Make 12 3 × 4-inch squares on a folder by making 3 horizontal 3-inch spaces and 4 vertical 4-inch spaces. (See Exhibit 8.) In each of the squares, letter four words, one of which tells the main idea of the other three. The child places a marker (bingo marker, button, etc.) on the main-idea word. At an easy level, use word groups such as:

big	purple	nine	round	walk
small	pink	numbers	squares	run
tiny	violets	one	triangle	move
size	colors	two	shape	jump

At a more difficult level, use:

rain	baton twirler	books	knight	whale
sleet	drum major	novels	sailor	stingray
hail	tuba player	paperbacks	pioneer	jellyfish
precipitation	school band	encyclopedias	people	sea animals

2. Words—Adding Supporting Details—Mark a folder with 12 spaces as in Activity 1. At the top of each space, write one of the following:

desk	car trunk
cleaning closet	toy chest
jewel box	cupboard
cutlery drawer	refrigerator
workbench	lunch box
medicine chest	wallet

EXHIBIT 8

Main Idea

Put a marker on the word in each space that tells the main idea.

red color	number two	dime nickel	bird robin	bang buzz
blue green	one seven	penny money	wren jay	boom noise
little small	home city	pear fruit	juice milk	coat shirt
big size	places town	apple banana	beverage tea	pants clothing
foot wear shoe	dog sheep	corn beans	hamster pets	light sun
boot slipper	goat animals	vegetables peas	canary kitten	candle lamp

On 1-inch sentence strips, write the names of items that will support the main idea. The following words can be used:

ink	broom	ring
pencil	dustpan	necklace
ruler	mop	bracelet
spare tire	rag doll	cup
jack	football	plate
jumper cable	blocks	bowl
knife	vise	bandages
fork	hammer	disinfectant
spoon	saw	pills
milk	thermos	money
eggs	sandwich	driver's license
meat	cupcake	credit card

3. Sentences—Mark a folder into 12 spaces as in Activity 1. In each space, write four sentences, one of which states the main idea of the group. Have the student place a marker on the sentence which states the main idea.

   Suggested paragraphs are:

   There is a place called Turtle Creek. In the west, there is a Snake River. One place is named Deer Lake. Many places have animal names.

   There are many ways of sleeping. Birds can sleep sitting in a tree. Horses sometimes sleep standing up. Fish sleep with their eyes open.

   Birds like a sand bath. Elephants spray themselves with water. Even animals like to keep clean. Monkeys groom each other with their paws.

   We get milk from some kinds of animals. Many animals help us in different ways. Dogs can lead blind people. Horses and elephants pull heavy loads.

4. Go Fish—Main Idea with Supporting Details—Card game for one to four players. Use two colors of cards, 12 of one color and 36 of the second. On the 12 cards of the first color, write (at both ends) the following main ideas:

kinds of birds	means of communication
kinds of beverages	kinds of coins
parts of a car	parts of the face
kinds of clouds	parts of a tree
kinds of storms	kinds of homes
means of transportation	parts of a book

   On the cards of the second color (both ends), write the following supporting details:

engine	fly	mouth	index
wheels	ride	eyes	pages
body	sail	nose	cover

171

roots	cottage	cumulus	lark
leaf	den	stratus	wren
branch	house	cirrus	robin
nickel	rain	conversation	water
dime	wind	telephone	juice
penny	hail	letter	milk

Shuffle the cards and deal 8 to each player. If a player has in his hand the three supporting details for one main idea, he tries to get the main-idea card. If he has main-idea cards, he tries to get the supporting details. The dealer calls on any player and requests, by color, the main idea for his supporting details or a detail card. The player called on must give the cards if he has them, or if he does not, he says, "Go Fish." The dealer then draws a card from the center pile. The play goes on to the next person. Whenever a player gets a book (one main idea, three details), he lays it on the table. The first person to get two books down wins the game.

5. Paragraphs from Textbooks—A similar, but slightly more difficult, activity can be made by cutting paragraphs from old science textbooks. Start with second- and third-grade texts, even for older children, then advance to more difficult levels and textbooks for other subjects, such as social studies. Be sure to select well-organized paragraphs.

6. Newspaper Articles—Matching Titles to Stories—Collect many brief human-interest articles from the newspaper. Clip off the titles and paste the articles on cards. Paste the titles on separate sentence strips. Have the students read the articles, then select the correct titles.

7. Newspaper Articles—Writing Titles—Collect human-interest stories as you did in Activity 6, but keep the titles separate. Have the students read the articles and write suitable titles. Compare the titles different children write for the same article. Select the most appropriate title. Then, show the newspaper's own titles and compare to the ones the students have written.

CONTEXT CLUES

Most readers get the meaning of an unfamiliar word by reading the whole passage and perceiving what the word must mean. This skill is especially important in understanding our language since so many words have multiple meanings.

Activities 1. Words with More Than One Meaning—Mark a folder with four 2-inch horizontal spaces. (See Exhibit 9.) In the left side of the space on each side of the folder, write a sentence containing a word with more than one meaning. In the right part of the space, write two of the meanings. Have the student read the sentence, then place a marker on the meaning used in that sentence.

Examples:

Jim tried to pet the animal.
    1. pet with love
    2. an animal kept in a home

He came to a fork in the road.
    1. utensil for eating
    2. place where a road branches

Cinderella danced at the ball.
    1. a round toy
    2. a formal dance

He thought the decision fair.
    1. just and honest
    2. an exhibition of products

She was so tired she wanted to drop.
    1. fall down
    2. a small amount

2. Which Word Will Fit Both Sentences?—Mark ten 1-inch horizontal spaces on a folder. Write two sentences containing two different meanings of the same word on the two sides of the folder. Instead of the word, leave a blank in both sentences. Leave a space in the center of the folder between the two sentences for the student to place a word strip containing the word that would correctly fill both blanks. Here are sentences that could be used:

Left sentence	Word	Right sentence
The car went over the _____ .	bank	He put his money in the _____ .
The toddler took a few _____ .	steps	The _____ led to the door.
He tried to _____ the ball.	duck	A _____ swam in the pond.
The gun wouldn't _____ .	fire	We built a hot _____ .
I tried to _____ my dog.	train	Father rode the _____ .
She cooks on a gas _____ .	range	Horses were loose on the _____ .
She tried to _____ a horse.	draw	The horse could _____ the wagon.

173

EXHIBIT 9

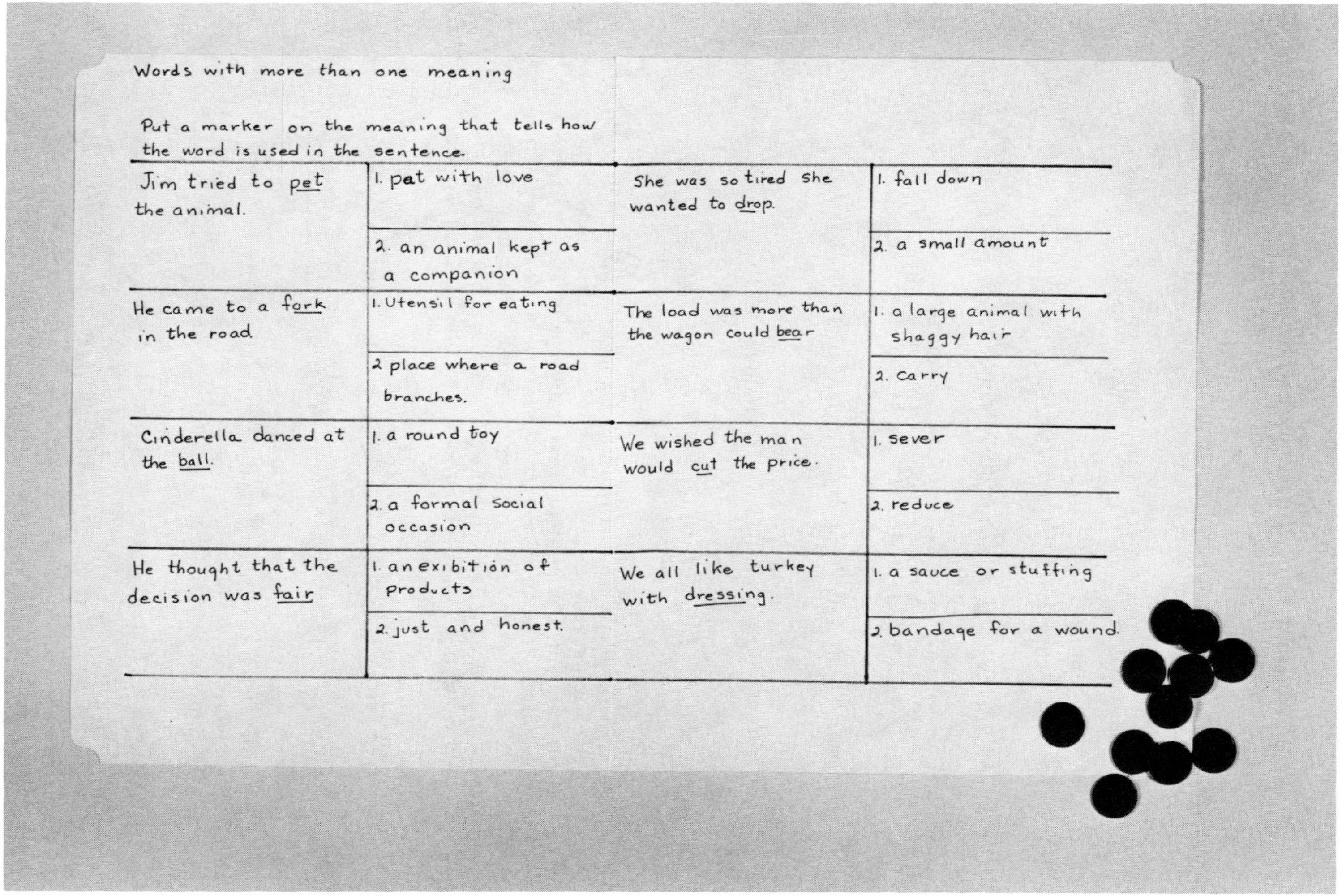

Words with more than one meaning

Put a marker on the meaning that tells how the word is used in the sentence.

Sentence	Meaning 1	Meaning 2
Jim tried to pet the animal.	1. pat with love	2. an animal kept as a companion
He came to a fork in the road.	1. Utensil for eating	2. place where a road branches.
Cinderella danced at the ball.	1. a round toy	2. a formal social occasion
He thought that the decision was fair.	1. an exibition of products	2. just and honest.
She was so tired she wanted to drop.	1. fall down	2. a small amount
The load was more than the wagon could bear.	1. a large animal with shaggy hair	2. carry
We wished the man would cut the price.	1. sever	2. reduce
We all like turkey with dressing.	1. a sauce or stuffing	2. bandage for a wound.

Mother wrote a _____ .	note	He sang a very high _____ .
Many _____ were at the game.	fans	It took many _____ to cool the room.
The orange was perfectly _____ .	round	The men played a _____ of golf.

3. Matching Sentences That Use the Same Meaning of a Word—
   Put the first ten sentences that follow on 1-inch spaces on the left
   side of a folder. Write the next ten on sentence strips to be
   matched to the first ten by placing the strips on the right side of
   the folder in the space opposite each sentence.

   On the Folder
   Two men were going to box.
   Jo sat on the wooden box.
   They hope to strike oil.
   The workers went out on strike.
   He tried to strike my hand.
   That horse is very fast.
   Make sure the horse is tied fast.
   Some people fast on Fridays.
   The deer's hide was sent to be tanned.
   We tried to hide the gold.

   On the Strips
   They use heavy gloves when they box.
   He kept his tools in a large box.
   Sutter made a great gold strike.
   Never strike a snarling dog.
   The shortage was caused by the truckers' strike.
   A fast truck will get there in time.
   Make sure the gate is fast.
   They decided to fast for twelve hours.
   My shoes are of cowhide.
   It is hard to hide an elephant.

4. Put Up the Signs—Matching signs to explanations—Mark 3
   3-inch spaces across a folder horizontally. Make vertical lines 4
   inches apart, making 12 spaces. In each of the spaces, write one
   of the messages that follow, leaving a 1-inch strip at the top
   where the student can erect the sign. A few pictures in some of
   the spaces will make the folder more attractive.
      Make the signs on 1 × 4-inch strips. Have the children
   match the signs with the messages.

   Messages:

   Mr. Brown just finished painting the front steps.
   New grass is coming up in the yard.
   This is the place where you come in to see the show.
   The farmer has some kittens to give away.

175

The baby is having his afternoon nap.
The man has some young dogs to sell.
This is the place to get the bus.
These people have garden produce to sell.
Here is where people cross the street.
Some wild animals are loose in the field.
The front door cannot be opened.
This is the area around a school.

Signs:

WET PAINT	FRESH VEGETABLES
BUS STOP	STAY OUT
SCHOOL ZONE	QUIET PLEASE
PUPPIES FOR SALE	STAY OFF
FREE PETS	USE OTHER DOOR
ENTER HERE	PEDESTRIAN CROSSING

5. Where Are They Going?—Matching Actions to Purpose—Mark five 2-inch spaces across a folder. Write the sentence containing the purpose in the left end of each side of the folder, leaving a 2-inch space at the end where the student can place the card on which the destination is written.

Sentences:

She put a stamp on the letters and walked to the corner.
They packed lunch in a basket and got in the car.
Mother wrote a list, picked up her purse, and left.
The children got into their suits and took some floating toys.
The boy picked up his homework and lunch and told his mother goodbye.
Bobby's tooth hurt so much that his mother was taking him for some help.
First they saw smoke, and then the red truck whizzed by.
Roy's hair was so long, he was going to get it cut.
The table looked so bare that Mother took her scissors and went outside.
The aerial was bent over, so he got the ladder.

Destinations:

mailbox	barber shop
school	flower garden
picnic	roof
beach	fire
dentist	shopping

6. You Can Tell What This Word Means—Meanings of Unfamiliar Words—Mark five 2-inch spaces across a folder. On the left of both sides, write sentences containing words that are unfamiliar to the child but that can be understood by the context of the sentence. Underline the unfamiliar words. Leave a space after each sentence for the student to place a card containing the meaning of the word as used.

Sentences that could be used are:

> She heard the *peal* of the bells.
> The sale was so *lucrative* our pockets were filled.
> The man was a *charlatan* selling cheap imitations.
> He was so *obese* he rolled out of his clothes.
> The dog took care of the kitten and became a *surrogate* mother.
> Although the fabric Mother made was coarse, Mary was proud of her *linsey-woolsey* dress.
> The words were so scrawled and blurry they were *illegible*.
> The men came in starving, so she hurried and put the *victuals* on the table.
> We saw whales and other *denizens* of the deep, blue sea.
> Nothing was decided because the committee would not get serious, but engaged in *persiflage*.

Meanings:

sound	fraud
profitable	substitute
overweight	impossible to read
food	homespun fabric
inhabitants	frivolous chatter

INFERENCE

A reader must often make inferences from unstated facts. This involves a process of problem solving. The reader assembles the stated facts in his mind, makes inferences, tests them, and makes changes as necessary.

1. Inferences from Pictures—From workbooks or magazines, collect pictures such as the following. Pictures can also be sketched.

   > Person with suitcases
   > Man setting alarm clock
   > Person putting up umbrella
   > Child crying, holding part of body
   > Drooping plants
   > Animal tracks in snow
   > Door of house, newspapers in a pile
   > Woman running, carrying briefcase
   > Person lying on street surrounded by packages
   > Child putting chair in front of high window

   On sentence strips, print the following inferences that can be made from the pictures:

An animal was here.
He is going away.
He wants to get up at a certain time.
She is too small to see out of the window.
She is late.
It is raining.
The child is hurt.
They need water.
The street is slippery.

2. What Is Happening?—Matching Inferences to Sentences—Mark a folder into five 2-inch horizontal spaces. At the left of each side of the folder, write one of the following sentences, leaving space for the student to place a card to show the inference.

Sentences:

The three horses came around the bend, with the black horse in the lead.
The two men smiled and shook hands.
The boy picked up his flattened bike from the driveway.
They ran as fast as they could from the monster.
The children stopped at the corner and waited.
The children dressed in their best clothes and bought presents.
A police officer tried to stop them from hitting each other.
Her hand hurt, so she quickly let go of the pan.
They ran down the field after the ball.
She put her arm around the crying boy.

Inferences:

It is a race.
They are friends.
A car ran over it.
They were afraid.
A car was coming.
It was a party.
They were fighting.
It was hot.
It was a game.
She felt sorry.

3. Where Are They?—Action/Location—Inferences from Sentences—Prepare a folder with five horizontal two-inch spaces. At the left of each side of the folder, write one of the sentences that follow, leaving a 2-inch space at the end for the student to place a card bearing the location.

Sentences:

They fed the chickens and gathered the eggs.
The children ran down the street and stopped at the light.
They looked at clowns and saw elephants doing tricks.
The jungle animals were all in barred cages.

It was so dark, the usher helped them find a seat.
They swam awhile, then played with a float.
Father ordered from the menu first.
They took the books to the desk to get them signed out.
Bobby paid the driver and found a seat by the window.
They picked some bread and sweet rolls, then paid the man.

Location inferences:

bakery	bus
theater	restaurant
farm	pool
city	zoo
circus	party

4. What Did They Use?—Action/Tool—Inferences from Sentences—Use the same folder format as in Activity 2.

Sentences:

He put the button back on his sweater.
They washed the dirt from the driveway.
He speared some meat from the platter.
The children carried water to the garden.
They peered through the dark at the distant stars.
The boy cleaned up the broken glass.
The girls gathered leaves from under the trees.
Mother peeled the potatoes.
Jo threw the cap in the trash and drank the soda.
Peter ate the soup for lunch.

Tool inferences:

needle and thread	broom
telescope	rake
hose	bottle opener
pail	fork
knife	spoon

5. What Happens Next?—Cause/Effect—Inferences from Sentences—Use same folder format as in Activity 2.

Sentences:

A car ran over broken glass.
The gas tank was empty.
He blew into the balloon.
She lost her money.
The egg rolled off the table.
The man stepped on a roller skate.
He didn't hear the alarm.
He pricked the balloon with a pin.
There was a sudden rain shower.
Joey lost his mittens.

179

Effect inferences:

people got wet	flat tire
cold hands	car stops
late for work	can't buy ticket
it gets larger	he falls
it bursts	breaks on floor

6. Syllogisms—Inference Involving Logic—Prepare a folder with five 2-inch horizontal spaces with 1-inch spaces at the right of each space. (See Exhibit 10.) In each of the 2-inch spaces, write two statements, the first requiring two answers, the second requiring one. The answer to the second statement is a logical conclusion drawn from the answers to the first.

On 1 × 1-inch pieces of cardboard, write the answers, allowing at least two extra repeats for distractors.

Statements:

Space 1—It is a numeral, so it can be _____ _____
It is more than three, so it is _____

Space 2—It is a color, so it can be _____ _____
It is not the color of grass, so it is _____

Space 3—You can drink it, so it can be _____ _____
It comes from a cow, so it is _____

Space 4—You eat it, so it can be _____ _____
It came from the garden, so it is _____

Space 5—You can ride it, so it can be _____ _____
It is alive, so it is _____

Space 6—It can fly, so it can be _____ _____
It lays eggs, so it is _____

Space 7—It is a toy, so it can be _____ _____
It is round, so it is _____

Space 8—You wear it, so it can be _____ _____
It goes on your foot, so it is _____

Space 9—It is a part of your head, so it can be _____ _____
You use it to see, so it is _____

Space 10—You use it to tell time, so it can be _____ _____
It goes on your arm, so it is _____

Answers: (two of each):

two	five	green
blue	milk	water
corn	meat	bike
pony	bird	airplane
doll	ball	hat
shoe	eyes	ears
clock	watch	

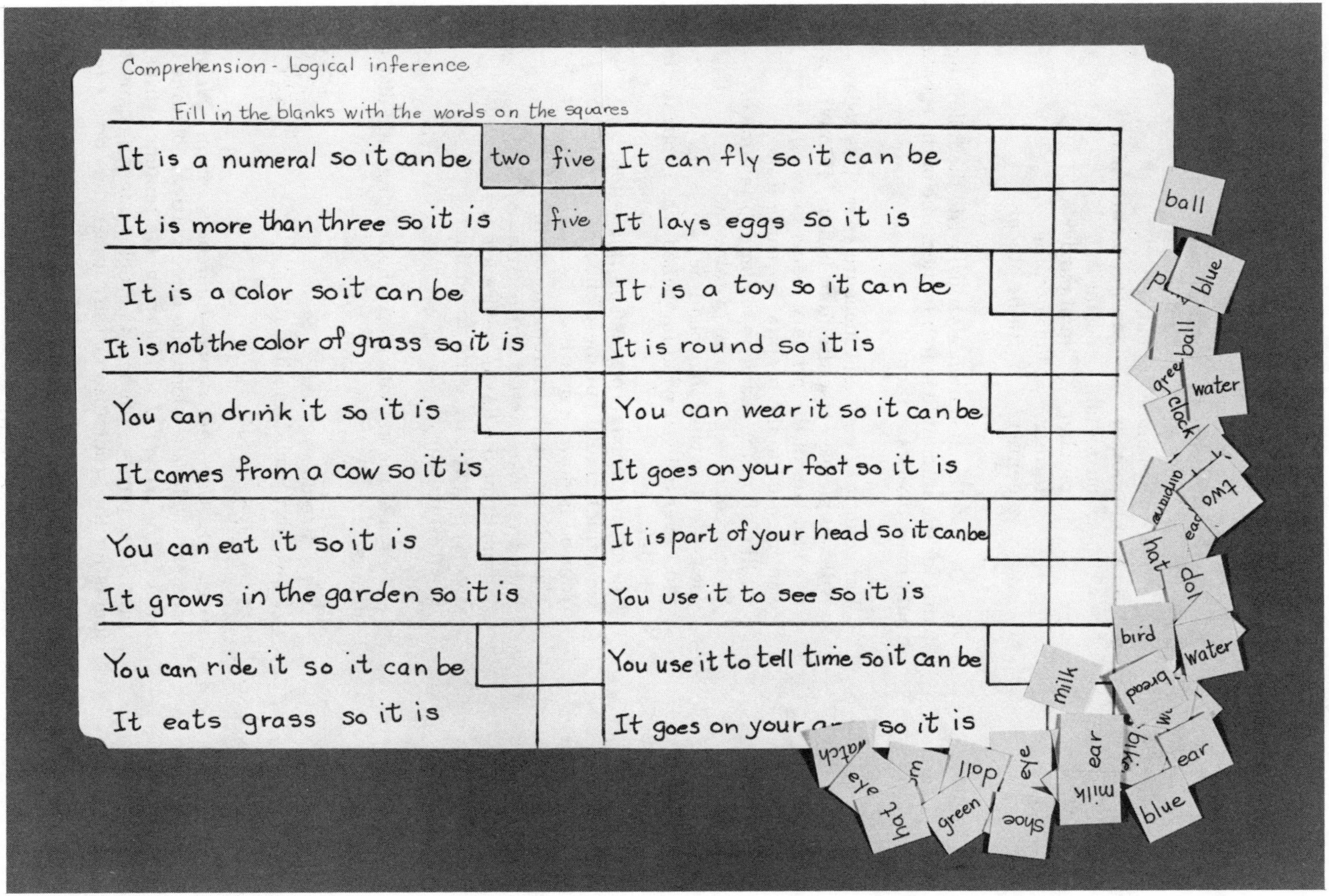

Comprehension - Logical inference

Fill in the blanks with the words on the squares

two	five	It can fly so it can be
	five	It lays eggs so it is
		It is a toy so it can be
		It is round so it is
		You can wear it so it can be
		It goes on your foot so it is
		It is part of your head so it can be
		You use it to see so it is
		You use it to tell time so it can be
		It goes on your arm so it is

	It is a numeral so it can be
	It is more than three so it is
	It is a color so it can be
	It is not the color of grass so it is
	You can drink it so it is
	It comes from a cow so it is
	You can eat it so it is
	It grows in the garden so it is
	You can ride it so it can be
	It eats grass so it is

ball · blue · water · green ball · clock · two · airplane · hat · doll · water · bird · bread · bike · ear · milk · blue · milk · eye · shoe · green · doll · hat · eye · watch

EXHIBIT 10

181

7. Who Said It?—Message to Speaker—Mark a folder with eight 1-inch horizontal spaces. On the left edge of both sides of the folder, list the following speakers:

grocer	school nurse
teacher	banker
principal	baker
mother	gas station attendant
custodian	doctor
butcher	mail carrier
farmer	grandfather
dentist	traffic officer

On 1 × 4-inch sentence strips, write the following statements for the student to match to the name of the speaker who would most likely say them:

I'm going to weigh and measure your class today.
Will you please erase the front boards, Jimmy?
I've still got all the primary rooms to sweep.
You must go to the hospital for some tests.
I'd like all of the teachers to come to my office.
Your account seems to be overdrawn.
Joey, it's way past your bedtime.
Did I ever tell you what happened when your mother was little?
There's not enough postage on this letter.
How thick shall I cut these chops?
Your oil is down a quart.
These buns are fresh from my oven.
Would you like canned or frozen peas?
We must get the hay in before it rains.
You were going over the speed limit.
Open wider now.

To make the activity more challenging, add distractors, such as:

What size do you take?
How short would you like it?

8. Causes of Car Accidents—Inferences from Newspaper Statements—Mark a folder into three vertical columns labeled *The Car, The Driver, The Highway.* On sentence strips, write sentences or phrases from news articles inferring causes of accidents for the student to classify under the correct heading. Samples are:

The car brakes were faulty.
The driver fell asleep.
The horn failed.
The tires seemed to be smooth.

Unmarked hazard
Faulty accelerator pedal
Patches of ice
Burnt-out headlights
Failed to negotiate curve
Under influence of alcohol
Slow-moving vehicles on a hill
Glaring headlights
Missing warning signs
Potholes
Defective steering apparatus
Passing on hill
Oil slick on road
No center line
Excessive speed
Unlicensed driver
Car on wrong side of road
Drunken driver

VOCABULARY EXPANSION

Besides learning basic vocabulary and sight words, the good reader must expand his vocabulary so that he can read in and understand a wide range of materials.

Activities   1. Homonyms—(See Exhibit 11.) On a folder, draw randomly on both sides at least 20 2 × 2-inch squares. In the top half of each square, write one of the following words, leaving space for the student to place a 1 × 2-inch word strip to show the homonym.

eight	wrap
grown	steel
reign	through
seen	vein
flour	wade
plain	waist
haul	wave
night	would
peace	bow
maid	write

On the cards for the student to match, write the homonyms:

ate	rap
groan	steal
rein	threw

183

EXHIBIT 11

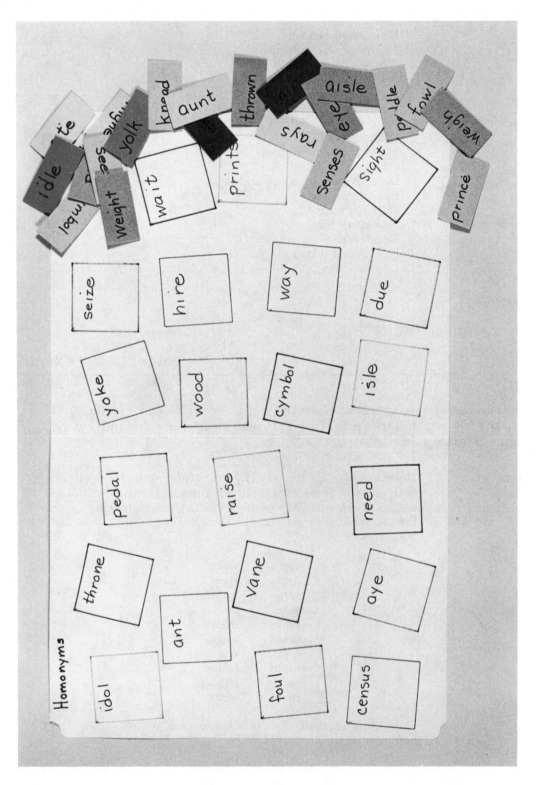

184

scene	vane
flower	weighed
plane	waste
haul	waive
knight	wood
piece	bough
made	right

2. Synonyms—Prepare a folder with 20 randomly placed 2 ×
    2-inch squares as in Activity 1. On the top half of each square,
    write one of the following words, leaving space at the bottom
    for the student to place the synonym on a 1 × 2-inch word
    strip.

On Folder		On Strips	
actual	conceal	real	hide
aim	decay	goal	rot
abundance	evil	plenty	wicked
allow	far	permit	distant
arrest	gather	stop	collect
beg	height	plead	altitude
frightened	idle	afraid	inactive
ancient	mature	old	ripe
bald	noise	hairless	clamor
certain	peculiar	sure	odd

3. Antonyms—Folder activity. Prepare a folder as in Activity 1
    using words such as:

On Folder		On Strips	
adapt	cheap	reject	expensive
advance	genuine	retreat	imitation
broad	bright	narrow	dull
bland	pale	harsh	vivid
cause	question	effect	answer
sloppy	timid	neat	bold
save	weak	spend	strong
accept	wild	reject	tame
remain	wrap	leave	uncover
stop	young	start	old

4. Which One?—Homonyms, Synonyms, Antonyms—Mark a
    folder with three vertical columns. Head them *Homonyms,
    Synonyms, Antonyms.* On 2-inch squares or 4-inch sentence
    strips, write pairs of words for the student to classify and to
    place under the correct heading. Use word pairs such as:

Homonyms	Synonyms	Antonyms
weight, wait	thrifty, saving	tidy, sloppy
guessed, guest	whole, total	wild, tame
tax, tacks	wrong, incorrect	worn, new
dense, dents	yield, surrender	vague, clear
leased, least	vacant, empty	expand, contract

Homonyms	Synonyms	Antonyms
I'll, aisle	permit, allow	temporary, permanent
chews, choose	rude, insolent	reduce, increase
crews, cruise	shelter, protect	question, answer
threw, through	moist, damp	punish, reward
rows, rose	mend, repair	opaque, transparent

5. Homonym Hokum—Making Sense with Homonyms—Mark a folder with eight 1-inch horizontal spaces. Letter the following story in rather large print in these spaces. Write the homonyms for the words used on 1 × 2-inch sentence strips for the student to lay over the words in the story so that the story makes sense.

The story:

The blew none and the buoy with read hare tolled hymn that they new that they had scene and herd bear feat in the haul weigh awl threw the knight. Of coarse sum tax throne on the floor mite help them no if the strange guesseds came again or nought.

6. Matching Synonyms—Card game with 40 cards. Use ten sets of four words each, all four words in a set with the same meaning. For each set, write all four words on 4 cards, placing a different word on the top of each card. For instance, the words for one set of cards would be arranged at the top of the 4 cards like this:

Card 1	Card 2	Card 3	Card 4
merry	*jolly*	*gleeful*	*jovial*
jolly	gleeful	jovial	merry
gleeful	jovial	merry	jolly
jovial	merry	jolly	gleeful

Shuffle the cards, deal 8 to each player, and place the remainder in the center face down. A player tries to get all four cards in a set by calling for a specific card from another player. The word at the top of the card is the call word. If a player holds Cards 1, 2, and 3 as described, he calls on any other player and requests *jovial*. If that player has the card, he must surrender it; if not, he says "Draw," and the caller takes a card from the center. The object of the game is to get the most sets. By having to name the wanted cards, the player gets practice in reading the words.

Suggested word sets:

giant	quiet	rage	odor	get
huge	still	anger	aroma	obtain
large	silent	fury	scent	receive
big	noiseless	wrath	smell	win

danger	talk	tear	small
hazard	say	rip	wee
peril	utter	rend	tiny
jeopardy	speak	rive	little

Have the students find other sets of words to be used.

7. "Shall I Eat It or Wear It?"—Classifying Words by Meaning—Put the following words on 1-inch strips to be classified on the correct side of a folder. Put a picture of a food at the top of one side, and a garment on the other. Have the students use the dictionary when necessary.

Eat		*Wear*	
mousse	borsch	peplum	bolero
canape	ragout	ruffle	boa
bouillon	gherkin	epaulet	fez
omelette	truffle	sari	ruff
croquette	fricasse	stole	jerkin
torte	ricotta	cloche	sarong
timbale	macaroon	tutu	kilt

8. Adjective—Complimentary or Derogatory?—At the top of one side of a folder, write *Thank You;* on the other, write *How Dare You?* Put the following words on sentence cards for the student to place on the side of the folder to show his response if that word were used to describe him.

perspicacious	unctuous
vapid	august
devious	repugnant
eccentric	gregarious
eminent	benevolent
urbane	callous
forward	affluent
mordant	maundering
sagacious	amicable
intrepid	malicious
indolent	alluring
astute	callow

9. Where Do These Words Belong?—Social Studies Words—Mark a folder into four vertical columns headed *Natural Landforms, Artificial Formations, Water Formations, Map and Globe Terms.* Put the following words on strips for the student to place in the correct columns:

island	bridge	ocean	degree
cape	dock	lake	diameter
desert	dike	sea	circumference
cave	levee	river	latitude
volcano	dam	pond	longitude

canyon	canal	bay	meridian
isthmus	road	stream	topography
crater	highway	brook	precipitation
peninsula	ramp	pool	contour
mesa	moat	whirlpool	route

10. A Challenge—Matching Specialists to Their Area of Study—Mark a folder into ten 1-inch horizontal spaces. On the left edge of each side of the folder, letter the following words, leaving space for the student to match the sentence strip with the area of study:

Specialist	*Area of Study*
herpetologist	snakes
numismatist	coins
philatelist	stamps
orthodontist	teeth
archeologist	ancient peoples
botanist	plant life
podiatrist	feet
criminologist	crime
ornithologist	birds
paleontologist	fossils
psychologist	mind and behavior
astronomer	stars and heavenly bodies
astrologist	influence of heavenly bodies on human affairs
oculist	eyes
otologist	ears
genealogist	family ancestry
bibliophile	books
audiologist	hearing
apiarist	bees
zoologist	animals

11. Winners and Losers—Using the Newspaper—Have the student examine the sports pages from several newspapers and cut out the captions denoting winners and losers. Paste all of the captions that denote winning on one side of a folder and the captions that denote losing on the other. Captions for losers are usually scarce, so you will need many papers to get a collection of these. The captions can be pasted on sentence strips and used in a classification activity.

12. Matching Phobias with Their Meanings—Task cards. (See Exhibit 12.)

13. Idioms, Those Strange Expressions We Use That Cannot Be Taken Literally—Prepare a folder with ten 1-inch horizontal spaces. Write the following sentences in the spaces, leaving at

188

Do You Have a Phobia?

phobia- "an irrational fear of some
particular thing or situation."

Match the listed
phobias with
their meanings.

claustrophobia

nychtophobia

ophidiophobia

pyrophobia

cynophobia

ailurophobia

microphobia

dentophobia

agoraphobia

triskaidekaphobia

Make a phobia collection.

snakes

fire

dogs

cats

germs

darkness

closed places

number thirteen

open spaces

dentists

EXHIBIT 12

189

least 2 inches at the right end of each for the student to place the explanation. Underline the idiom in each sentence.

Who will *see to* my pets while I'm gone?
Last night the attendance *fell off.*
We all *fell in* with the idea of a trip.
The boy *takes after* his father.
The boss will be *tied up* all morning.
Father *blew up* when he saw the fender.
The problem had *blown over* by morning.
Mother was not *taken in* by my excuse.
Money is hard to *come by.*
I *ran across* an old friend.
When you arrive, *drop me a line.*
This will help you to *throw off* your cold.
The thaw caused the skating plans *to fall through.*
The baby had just *dropped off.*
The teacher *put his foot down.*
How did the play *come out?*
She always *throws cold water* on my plans.
The police officer *threw her weight around.*
Father said he would *look into* my problem.
Please *take down* my suggestions.

Explanations to be placed on strips:

resembles	fallen asleep	became angry
write down	used her authority	end
write to me	take care of	fooled
met	busy	get

was firm	get rid of
been forgotten	fail
agreed	discourages
became less	examine

14. When It Comes Right Down to It, Perspiration Is Sweat!—Euphemisms—Explain to the children that, to make reality seem less harsh, writers often use a pleasanter wording, called a euphemism. Sometimes euphemisms are used to make a job sound more important. Have the students match the direct meanings to the euphemisms on the folder. Use 1-inch horizontal spaces on the folder.

On Folder

Left Side	*Right Side*
(to cover blunt reality)	(to make a job sound more impressive)
memorial garden	canine warden
passed away	landscape architect
dentures	lubrication expert
ermine	custodian
between jobs	mortician

Left Side	*Right Side*
inebriated	cosmetologist
dismissed	educator
rest room	
perspiration	
refuse	

On Strips

graveyard	dog catcher
died	gardener
false teeth	grease monkey
weasel fur	janitor
out of work	undertaker
drunk	beautician
fired	teacher
toilet	
sweat	
trash	

15. Qualifiers—Some words are used to make a statement less positive and leave room for doubt. Other words make positive statements and state a definite message. Mark the two sides of a folder *Sure, Unsure* and have the student classify the following qualifiers:

Sure	*Unsure*
accomplished fact	alleged
absolutely	believed to be
guaranteed	probably
undoubtedly	presumed
positive	supposed
irrefutably	implied
certainly	attempted
undeniably	likely
conclusive	assumed
precisely	suspicioned
specifically	theoretically
definitely	inferred

16. Hinky Pinky—Make 20 2 × 2-inch outlines at random on a folder. In the top half of each, letter one of the following descriptions. On 1 × 2-inch word strips, write the rhyming definitions. Have the student place a strip in the square with the correct description.

On Folder	*On Strips*
obese feline	fat cat
costless shopping	free spree
home for small rodents	mouse house
ill-mannered city man	rude dude
scarce rabbit	rare hare
night bird's scream	owl's howl
sad antelope	blue gnu

191

On Folder	On Strips
unusual female horses	rare mares
sharp hassock	cool stool
large amount of money	read bread
finer epistle	better letter
dull shellfish	drab crab
insane flower	crazy daisy
wet canine	soggy doggy
reducing panic	diet riot
happy river boat	merry ferry
boxing glove	hittin' mitten
speechless hobo	dumb bum
smashed souvenir	broken token
ground work	soil toil

CRITICAL READING

Activities

1. Fact and Opinion—On squares or sentence strips, write descriptive phrases for the children to classify on the two sides of a folder. The statements can be simple for young children:

Red is prettier than blue.	Red is darker than pink.
This is a good pie.	This is an apple pie.
You are a fine boy.	You are in my way.
Apples are better than pears.	Apples can be green.

    or more difficult for older students:

He is our greatest politician.	He has been in Congress.
This was the biggest story of the year.	This was about politics.
The price of coffee is too high.	The price of coffee has gone up.
Everyone should start jogging.	Jogging is a form of exercise.
That is dangerous to society.	This is good for everyone.

2. Facts Can Change—Readers must examine when information was written and who the writer was before being sure of facts. The following statements are to be classified as to whether they will remain facts or if they may change with time.

    This is the cheapest car on the market.
    Neil Armstrong took the first step on the moon.
    The Chrysler Building is the tallest in the world.

The Cardinals won the World Series.
The weather is warmer in Florida than in Maine.
The Atlantic Ocean is east of the United States.
The Democrats control the Senate.
Marconi invented the radio.
George Washington was our first president.
That man is the tallest man that ever lived.
Hawaii was the last state to be admitted to the Union.
Crabs were good this year.
The dollar has gone down in value.
The rate of population growth changes.

3. Facts and Opinions—Using the Newspaper—Give the student brief news articles to read. Have him mark factual statements with one color marker and opinions with a second color.

4. Facts and Opinions—Advertisements—Make a collection of all kinds of advertisements from magazines and newspapers. Cut statements from the ads that are facts and opinions. Paste the statements on cards to be classified. The statements that are opinions can be further classified as to type of appeal, such as:

   Is it a testimonial from a well-known person?
   "_____ says, 'My family loves it.' "

   Is it a glittering generality?
   "We offer you more."

   Does it infer everyone is doing it?
   "50,000,000 people can't be wrong."

   Does it use snob appeal?
   "Makes you feel rich."

   Is a well-known person shown in the advertisement?
   Not speaking, but shown using the product.

   Does it use unpleasant words?
   "Don't be skinny!"

5. Fact and Superstition—Mark one side of a folder *These statements are facts,* and the other side *Some people believe these superstitions.* On strips, write statements like the following for the student to classify:

Tea leaves can tell your future.	A nail may cause a flat tire.
Toads cause warts.	Too much candy can make you sick.
Killing a ladybug brings bad luck.	Running water flows downhill.
Cats have nine lives.	Thunder means there has been lightning.
Thunder makes milk turn sour.	Camels can go for days without water.

193

Eating bread crusts will give you curly hair.

Peas should be planted in early spring.

Dropping a fork will bring company.

Magnets attract nails.

It is unlucky to walk under a ladder.

Plants grow from seeds.

Thirteen is an unlucky number.

Many hotels do not have a thirteenth floor.

Groundhogs can predict spring.

Ground Hog Day is February 2.

Stepping on a crack will break your mother's back.

Ice is frozen water.

Eating fish will make you smart.

Every area seems to have its own superstitions. Have the students collect these.

Alternative Approaches for Older Children and Adults

10

It is important to keep in mind that the same rule that applies to elementary-age children also applies to older children and adults, i.e., if they failed in a typical school reading (basal) program, the remediation must take another tack. The most important thing to expect in attempting remediation for older students is the "mock" resistance that you are going to encounter—and you can be sure that you will come up against it. Adolescents are likely to say how much they hate reading and how boring it all is. Sufficient to say, this is a defense mechanism and nothing else. Ignore it. Personally, we have never met a person who did not want to know how to read.

Since this resistant attitude prevails, it is extremely important that the students' first ventures into reading be successful. Forget about phonics and anything else that deals with words in a synthetic way. They want to read. They have no interest, per se, in a consonant digraph, diphthong, or an esoteric thing called word attack. Spache and Spache (1977, p. 391) state that, ". . . there is little doubt there are some children who do not profit from much of our phonics instruction for a variety of reasons." These older children have failed in phonic-oriented programs.

To insure that these older children (and adults) can read after their first encounter, you must set a stage that will guarantee success. To do so, run an interest inventory similar to the one in Exhibit 1. The results should give you an idea for selecting a book or magazine that will have impact on the student. Better yet, allow the student to select from a

---

EXHIBIT 1

Check the kinds of things you like to read about (as many as you wish).

love stories _____   how to make things _____

baseball _____   football _____

criminals _____   teenagers' problems _____

war stories _____   nature stories _____

murder mysteries _____   scientific experiments _____

famous people _____   basketball _____

mathematics _____   dictionaries _____

historical tales _____   horses _____

mythology _____   space travel _____

true-life adventure _____   cowboy stories _____

poetry _____   travel articles _____

movie stars _____   encyclopedias _____

essays _____   politics _____

---

variety of paperbacks on topics that the inventory indicates. Encourage the remedial reader to select any book that catches his attention. It does not matter how difficult it is.

The following approach is guaranteed to have the student reading meaningful material during the first session.

ECHO IMPRESS

Echo impress is a method advocated by Heckelman (1974), among others. It is a simple procedure and one that has always worked for us and our graduate students in our own modified version for young children as well as adults.

After selecting the book, read a sentence or short paragraph aloud to the student with verve and gusto at your normal reading pace. Then, ask a few questions about the content, such as, "What was Bill doing?" or, "What color was the car?" In essence, these questions require simple, literal recall. If no answers are forthcoming, there is no need to become excited. Simply read the same sentence or paragraph again, but at a slightly faster pace. Without asking any questions, reread at an even faster pace. Repeat this procedure three or four times, each time reading faster but distinctly pronouncing each word.

After reading the selection several times (the student has not yet seen the print), ask if he can recall any words that were read. For each one he recalls, display pleasure and point it out to him in the book. If the student cannot recall any words, then repeat the initial procedures. You will finally wear him down.

As soon as the student can recall a few words, you can begin a variation of echo impress. While holding the book for the student, begin reading aloud the same short selection. Read it several times. After you are convinced that he can almost repeat it from memory, ask him to read along with you. At first, your voice will dominate, but as you read the selection again and again, you must allow his voice to begin to be heard above yours. When you are utterly convinced that the student knows at sight every word in the selection, then ask him to read it alone. If he makes an error and becomes frustrated, then allow a new start. If he makes a mistake but does not show any frustration, then allow him to continue through the selection. Let the selection be read several times until it is mastered.

This will be your method of operation for several days (or weeks if necessary). However, do not spend more than 10 or 15 minutes each day. The important aspect to remember is that the student must leave the reading scene only after having been totally successful with that day's offering. Nothing else is permitted.

As the days (or weeks) go by, you will notice that many words become easy for the student to pronounce. They are recognized immediately. At this point, you are ready for the process called neurological impress.

NEUROLOGICAL IMPRESS

One of the more intriguing techniques used by many teachers has been the approach with the lofty title of neurological impress. The simplicity of the task belies the impressive name. It is, beyond a doubt, one of the easiest, yet most productive remedial techniques ever encountered. It is to be used with students who have some words in their sight vocabulary (100 or more) and should not exceed ten minutes a day according to the

---

EXHIBIT 2

Neurological Impress

The purpose of this exercise is to reinforce the match between audition and vision in the reading process. The method would be to use a book new to the child. The procedure is as follows:

1. The child sits slightly in front of the parent (or teacher). Both have the same book.

2. Then, the parent and child read aloud in unison. Initially, it is expected that the parents' voice may lead the child's voice. Eventually, the child should be encouraged to take the vocal lead.

3. The parent should use one finger as a pointer, and it's important that the finger he pointed at the end of a word as it is sounded.

4. No stumbling. No pauses are allowed as the two read together. Any word the child does not know is immediately read by the parent, thus leaving the child no time to struggle with pronunciation.

5. The pace of normal reading flows on unimpeded. The only time a pause occurs is when the child's voice tires.

6. The child is encouraged to discuss the reading when completed, but he is not asked specific questions about the text of the material.

7. Eventually, as improvement is noted, the child uses his finger to point. Later, he may take the vocal lead and do the pointing while the parent reads softly in unison and fills in any words that the child may not know. The rhythm of the prose is to be maintained.

The following aspects are to be emphasized:

1. The child should follow material well with his eyes.

2. The child's voice should match the parent's as they read.

3. Smoothness and rhythm are encouraged.

4. Good lighting and good posture are to be maintained at all times.

5. The parent should alternate reading into the child's right ear and left ear.

6. It is absolutely essential that the finger movements, voice, and words all be synchronized.

latest research (Cook, Nolan, and Zanotti, 1980). Heckelman (1974) and others have had great success with this procedure with the very young as well as with older students. A description of the technique is presented in Exhibit 2.

One of the difficulties in gaining acceptance for this procedure has been its simplicity. It appears to most people that if something is easy enough for most anyone to do, then it could be of no value. What a tragedy. We have used child-to-child tutoring using this method and have had impressive results. We have trained parents to do the procedure with equally impressive results. However, we must enter a word of caution regarding parents. Make certain that the parent is one of even temperament. If they are quick to lose their temper, then the results will be of no value. Similarly, you must realize that frustration or disapproval on your part during neurological impress is forbidden. If you do not have the patience to carry out this procedure in a pleasant, easy manner, then forget it. Why punish the child further?

A STRUCTURED PAPERBACK-BOOK APPROACH

A most successful research project carried out in our clinic involved the use of paperback books from various publishers. The research was carried out with a clinician working with one, two, or three children at a session. Each student selected the book he wanted to read, and the clinician built the daily lesson plans around that particular book.

Using results obtained from a series of tests, the teacher created a lesson plan that resembles the one in Exhibit 3. As you can see from the exhibit, no matter what the student needed in the way of remediation, it all came from the paperback book. It is a highly structured program, but one that effectively demonstrated that children who had gained only six to eight months the previous semester under individual clinician-selected remedial approaches gained from one to three years on post-tests in six weeks' time under the present method (Cook, Zanotti, & Cook, 1980).

Along with the lesson plan presented in Exhibit 3, the clinician kept a sheet to record daily errors. (See Exhibit 4.) This sheet enabled the clinician to jot down anything that cropped up during the teaching that had not been unearthed in prior testing, insured that the clinician would not forget the weaknesses, and enabled their supervisors to make certain that the problems were attacked in future lesson plans.

The Daily Record sheet is also ideal in large-group instruction. It can be kept handy and used in the fashion indicated in Exhibit 5. This format enables the teacher to keep the weaknesses of a particular group together on one sheet and simplifies the skill work for the next day's lesson. Additionally, it is a very powerful device to show parents and convince them that you are aware of their child's problem and are attempting to do something about it. Parents appreciate concerned teachers.

199

EXHIBIT 3

Daily Lesson Plan

DATE _March /2_

NAME _John L._   TIME __4:30__   CLINICIAN __Christine P.__

Goal	Objectives	Behaviors	Methods and Materials	Evaluation
Comprehension.	To develop literal, inferential, and critical comprehension through a cloze exercise.	John will be able to supply 15 of 20 deleted words in an instructional cloze exercise following instruction in synonym and antonym signals.	Materials: Teacher-made cloze exercise containing synonym and antonym pairs. The exercise will be related to the social studies content area on the first Thanksgiving. Motivational device: "Your goal is to pluck 15 out of 20 feathers correctly to beat the turkey to the finish line." Use DRA Format. 1. Set background with Thanksgiving coming. "How did it get started in the United States?" "Can you give me some facts?" Have John write answers down. They will be used in the study-skill activity. 2. Vocabulary Development. With the turkey, flash Tachistoscope and sentence with the vocabulary words: *festivals, holiday, Plymouth, proclaim, colonists, slaughtered, decreed, harvest.* Present words. At this point, teach John to use the synonym and antonym signals to get meaning of the words to understand context. For synonyms, present the *j* (arbitrary signalling device to indicate synonyms). For antonyms, have him find the antonym for underlined words. Teach him to use the signals. *Example:* Sue did	John attained an 80% on both synonym and antonym identification. He understands the use of analogies and signals such as the word *or* to clue the unknown or upcoming word. John was a little disappointed that he missed 2 questions in each exercise. He said he could have done better. His errors came because he was confused over the word's meaning. He overlooked the obvious. After discussion of what the pair (synonym and antonym) were, he could describe the relationship. This was obvious since his understanding of the concepts of synonym and antonym was tested in the cloze exercise. He completed the cloze exercise with 75% accuracy. The substitutions were grammatically correct. John supplied 2 nouns instead of 2 adjectives and verb for a noun. The substitutions were not semantically acceptable. The meaning change was minimal. After orally reading the sentence and with clinician direction, he corrected the error in 4 out of 6 cases.

		not leave through the exit *but* through the entrance. "Circle the antonyms." Give him practice in identifying word meanings by having him find synonym and antonym pairs in 10 sentences. Have him restate the signals he should watch out for when he reads. 3. Set Purpose. Tell John that when he completes a cloze, he will have a story about the first Thanksgiving. Tell him to look out for synonym and antonym analogies, and to watch out for signals so that he supplies the correct words. Some facts discussed in background will be asked for. 4. Have John silently read the cloze. 5. Check his comprehension, have him complete the cloze. 6. Have John orally read the cloze cases with the deleted words supplied. The clinician will correct and evaluate.	
Comprehension (Study-Skill Development.)	To develop the study skill of outlining by selection of main ideas and details.	John will be able to fill in, with at least 80% accuracy, a skeletal outline form with the main ideas and facts on the Thanksgiving story found in the cloze exercise previously done.	Materials: Skeletal outline form; cloze exercise; red pencil; green pencil. 1. Review with John the makeup of an outline. 2. Have John supply the title on the title line. 3. Have him circle with the red pencil the main idea of each paragraph of the cloze. Then, have him underline the facts of each paragraph that go with the main idea.	John was able to select the main idea of each paragraph found in the cloze exercise. This will be continued on 12/6 for the outline work. Main idea is grasped, so we can dispense with any further *directed* activity. Teach indirectly as reinforcement.

EXHIBIT 3 (cont.)

Daily Lesson Plan

DATE _March 12_

NAME _John S._   TIME _4:30_   CLINICIAN _Christine P._

Goal	Objectives	Behaviors	Methods and Materials	Evaluation
			4. Give John main-idea and detail strips the clinician has found. Have John check the clinician's choices. 5. Discuss any differences. 6. Have John fill in the skeletal outline with his main ideas and details. He is to use phrases. Check his outline.	
#3 Reading Fluency.	To develop reading fluency through NI.	John will be able to read along with the clinician in a fluent and even manner, concentrating on phrasing and sentencing.	Materials: Book: _The Martians Are Coming_, pp. 1–2–3. Method: NI; John will be encouraged to keep up with the clinician.	

EXHIBIT 4

Daily Record

DATE *March 12*

NAME *John S.*

Problem	How Diagnosed	Remediation
Comprehension: During the cloze exercise, John's substitutions were neither grammatically nor semantically correct in 5 deletions. A 75% accuracy rate was attained in the cloze exercise. Looking at the 5 errors grammatically, John substituted 2 nouns for 2 adjectives, 2 nouns for 2 nouns, 1 verb for 1 noun. Semantically the errors changed only minimally his under understanding of the story. The meaning change was slight. In one instance — "All the Pilgrims, ____, ____ and ____, worked together to prepare the feast." — John completed the deletions with *prepared, food,* and *fires.* There was a change in meaning. John failed to read the remainder of the paragraph to clue for the answers — *men, women,* and *children.*	Observed during evaluation of the cloze exercise.	Have John continue to develop comprehension by completing cloze exercises. Concentrate on filling in deletion with adjectives. Can use maze exercise to begin this skill development. Encourage him to write his answers out to sharpen his writing ability.

EXHIBIT 5

Daily Record

NAME _Group Three – Scott, Foresman Level 9   3-3_

Problem	How Diagnosed	Remediation
Tom — unable to handle multisyllabic words.	While doing oral reading, missed every word of three syllables or more.	Will do some work on structural analysis prefixes, suffixes, root words.
Sally — eyes seem to water when reading.	Observed rubbing eyes during silent reading.	Have school nurse check eyes.
George — does not know how to handle consonant digraphs *ch.*	During oral reading was unable to pronounce beginning sound of *Charles, chance, choose, chimney* (only four words in story with *ch* sound).	Try *Phonics We Use* workbook, Level H, p. 6.
Ralph — child is suddenly reading word by word.	Oral reading.	Level 9 is just beginning. Maybe too hard for him. Will wait a few days to see if fluency improves. If not, will try a lower level in another series.
Jim — ignores punctuation.	While reading aloud, he completely ignored periods.	Will have Jim do a language experience story. I'll make the periods, etc. giant size until he begins to realize value.

THINGS NOT TO BE OVERLOOKED

Activities   There are many useful materials available from governmental and other agencies that can be used to assist the disabled reader in developing the motivation necessary to overcome obstacles in reading. Some will be discussed in the following pages along with suggested techniques of application.

1. The Federal Bureau of Investigation (F.B.I.) publishes informational bulletins on their role in society. Among these publications are: *The Story of the Federal Bureau of Investigation, The F.B.I. Laboratory, Know Your F.B.I.,* and *Fingerprint Identification.* The preceding books are well illustrated and provide considerable information on the F.B.I. They can be obtained by writing to the Federal Bureau of Investigation, United States Department of Justice, Washington, D.C. 20535. For suggested activities on how to use the manuals, see Exhibits 6 and 7, which are simple task cards suggesting areas of investigation by interested students. You would develop additional cards detailing questions and answers for self-checking.

2. Each state harbors a game commission in its state capital, and each commission has a number of brochures on hunter safety. These are available free of charge and interest older children and adults. You would make a task card on each topic (see Exhibit 8 for types of topics), and the student could set his own pace.

3. Sewing patterns are often of interest and should not be overlooked. By placing a few patterns in a folder and setting up tasks, you are again providing reading activities under a different guise.

EXHIBIT 6

Federal Bureau of Investigation

The Story of the Federal Bureau of Investigation

1. Write questions involving significant dates and places in the history of the F.B.I.
2. Read about the F.B.I. and espionage.

The F.B.I. Laboratory

1. Describe units and some case studies.
2. Write questions concerning the tasks of each unit.
3. Read case studies and match to unit involved.

Units

Firearms	Explosives	Neutron Activation
Serology	Chemistry	Instrumental Analysis
Mineralogy	Toxicology	Microscopic Analysis
Metallurgy	Shoe and Tire	Document
Cryptanalysis	Fraudulent Checks	

EXHIBIT 7

Federal Bureau of Investigation

Know Your F.B.I.

Use questions that compare the activities performed in the different divisions.

Divisions:

Training	General Investigative	Intelligence
Identification	Specific Investigative	Administrative
Laboratory	Files and Communications	Inspection
Computer Systems	Legal Counsel	

Fingerprint Identification

Topics:

Purpose	Method	Files	Classification

Have students make fingerprint cards, and classify and compare prints.

EXHIBIT 8

Activities on Hunting, Gun Safety

Pa. Hunter Education Program Training Guide (free)

Topics:

Game Management	Gun Handling
Pa. Game Laws	Bow Handling
Guns and Ammunition	Trapping

Make task cards or activity sheets on each topic. Answers to be found in the brochure.

N.R.A. Gun Safety Series, Posters (free) (Set of 20 posters depicting safe and unsafe practices)

Identify and write or tell the reason for the practice.
Both sets of materials available free of charge.

4. Football and basketball programs offer another way of motivating students to read. Almost all colleges and high schools prepare programs for every game, and these are natural for catching the interest of students.

5. A very important aspect of living is knowing how to deal with local banking institutions. The banks affect our lives in many ways, so we should "get to know them." Any bank will be happy to supply you with brochures, deposit tickets, blank checks, and its other paraphernalia. You could also deal with credit-card and loan applications. Much more information can be obtained from various agencies on banking. The addresses of some follow:

> Publications Services
> Division of Administrative Services
> Board of Governors of the Federal Reserve System
> Washington, D.C. 20551

> Research Department
> Federal Reserve Bank of Atlanta
> Atlanta, Ga. 30303

> Administrative Services Department
> Federal Reserve Bank of San Francisco
> San Francisco, Calif. 94120

6. Bicycling is an important and healthful sport that has millions of participants in this country. It also becomes an easy lead into reading if several brochures on bicycles are placed in your reading corner. All major manufacturers of bicycles have consumer relations departments that will be happy to send out information free of charge. Two of the larger producers can be contacted at the following addresses:

> Consumer Relations Department
> Panasonic Company
> One Panasonic Way
> Secaucus, N.J. 07094

> Consumer Relations Department
> Schwinn Bicycle Company
> 1856 North Kostner Avenue
> Chicago, Ill. 60639

Additionally, most state departments of education produce booklets on bicycle safety that are yours for the asking. Simply contact the department of education in your state capital.

7. Money interests all of us, readers and nonreaders alike. There are many fascinating readings to be found by investigating U. S. currency. You should make task cards and have:

    1. Questions that can be answered by examining money. (What president is on the quarter, etc.?)

2. Questions that can be answered by reading booklets from the Department of the Treasury.

Further, you can have reports on money by:

1. Having students interview someone at a local bank about counterfeit money.
2. Getting a local coin collector to talk to the class.

Excellent booklets on the topic of money are:

1. *Facts about United States Money,* available for 25¢ from Superintendent of Documents, U.S. Government Printing Office, Washington, D.C. 20402
2. *Fundamental Facts about United States Money,* available free of charge from Research Department, Federal Reserve Bank of Atlanta, Atlanta, Ga 30303
3. *Our American Coins,* available for 25¢ from the Superintendent of Documents, U.S. Government Printing Office, Washington, D.C. 20402

8. Product labels offer fascinating reading for disabled readers. They provide opportunities for teaching critical reading, allow readers to compare and contrast products, and can go a long way in developing vocabularies. How many of you know what "insoluble sodium metaphosphate" is?

9. Many of us receive numbers of specialty catalogs each year and generally throw them away. Teachers have found it very profitable to place them in our learning centers without any instruction on what to do with them. Students invariably pick them up and thumb through. It is painless to them in that there are no assignments to deal with. In fact, some children put much more energy into something like this than into assigned material. Five particularly delightful catalogs that you can write for are:

Greyhound Gift House
7178 NW 12th Street
Miami, Fla. 33126

American Archives
1112 Seventh Avenue
Monroe, Wis. 53566

Brownstone's Studio, Inc.
342 Madison Avenue
New York, N.Y. 10017

Holiday Gifts
67 Holiday Building
4975 Miller Street
Wheat Ridge, Colo. 80036

Stratford House
P.O. Box 289
277 Ferry Boulevard
Stratford, Conn. 06497

10. Travel brochures and booklets intrigue adults as well as children. They offer opportunities to:

    1. Gain knowledge of other parts of the world.
    2. Compare prices on group and single tours.
    3. Discover why certain hotels are considered better than others.
    4. Experience cultural differences (Spanish flamenco dancers on one page and great Greek tragedies on the next!).
    5. Appreciate beautiful photography.
    6. Learn geography from maps showing airline connections between major cities of Europe and Asia.

    These brochures are available (most free of charge) from local travel agencies, airline and shipping-line offices, and the American Automobile Association offices. They offer a bit of Europe, a taste of Asia, and a smattering of Polynesia. They create a wanderlust in us and spark the imagination.

11. Postal cards from various parts of the country (and the world) is another subtle way of teaching reading painlessly. Almost all cities and towns in this country have postal cards extolling their virtues. We are reminded of the young student who became so enamored with postal cards from the Pennsylvania "Dutch Country" that he was moved to check out simple books on the Amish, and was not even unhappy when he discovered they were not Dutch. The student became so enthralled that the parents took the child on a vacation to that area the next summer.

    The point here is that we never know what will inspire the child to read, but as teachers, we should be prepared to use the kitchen sink if necessary.

12. One of the more interesting things that we have found in our travels around the country has been restaurants. It is not, we hasten to say, due to the fact that we are either gourmets or gourmands, but rather that the colorful and educational placemats used by many restaurants are a natural lead into reading. We have many from all over the country, and our students revel in them. Most restaurants we have asked have been willing to share, but if you want an instant package of 75 different designs, send your check for $10.00 to:

    Springhurst Paper Products Company
    504 West Euclid Avenue
    Springfield, Ohio 45501

    We laminate the placemats to increase their life, and almost every student shows uncommon interest in them.

    Menus offer unusual opportunities to teach reading. Many are attractive, colorful, and chock-full of things that interest all of us—foods. You can ask for one, and most restaurants will provide them free of charge or at a small cost. The Big Boy chains and Howard Johnson restaurants have particularly appealing ones.

In using a menu, the students could be directed to the following specifics:

a. Place an order and figure the cost.
b. What can you order if you have $2.00?
c. Categorize types of meals.
d. Classify types of food, meat, fish, poultry, etc.
e. Adjectives—List descriptive words used.
f. Classify beverages—Dairy, fruit, etc.
g. How many ways of cooking?—Boil, broil, etc.
h. Which meal has the most calories?
i. Which meal has the fewest calories?
j. Which foods listed need refrigeration?
k. Which foods are served cooked?
l. Which foods are served raw?
m. Which foods are served hot?
n. Which foods are served cold?
o. Write a radio/television commercial for this place.

BIBLIOGRAPHY

COOK, JIMMIE E.; NOLAN, GREGORY; AND ZANOTTI, ROBERT. "Treating Auditory Perception Problems: The NIM Helps." *Academic Therapy,* March, 1980.

COOK, JIMMIE E.; ZANOTTI, ROBERT; AND COOK, PAMELA J. "Structure, Trade Books, Reading Specialist, and Reading Disabled Students." *Carolina Journal of Educational Research,* Fall, 1980.

HECKELMAN, R. G. "Using the Neurological Impress Method Remedial Reading Technique." *Academic Therapy Quarterly,* 1 (1966): 235–39.

SPACHE, GEORGE D.; AND SPACHE, EVELYN B. *Reading in the Elementary School.* Boston, Mass.: Allyn and Bacon, 1977.

More Alternative Techniques for Older Children and Adults

11

If a child reaches the middle grades and has not learned to read successfully in traditional approaches, it is probably time to abandon those approaches and try something else. We do not mean a "shotgun effect" wherein you blast away and hope to hit something. We do mean that it is necessary to give thought to the situation based upon your informal analysis as explained in Chapter 2 and to proceed from there.

It has been our experience that the activities listed in this and the preceding chapter work, but be selective, and do not overwhelm the students with all of them at one time. Give as much as they enjoy, and no more. Get to work.

WHAT LANGUAGE DO YOU SPEAK?

Activities   One of the more fascinating things we found is that middle school-age children respond well to the idea of the English of England versus the English of the United States. The children think they speak English, so they are intrigued by the large number of items for which the two countries have different descriptive words. For instance, if you were to ask a group of American children what a vest is, they would respond that it is a part of a three-piece suit, whereas English children think of it as a T-shirt. In the United States, a bonnet is a hat worn by a woman, but to the English, it is the hood of a car.

We have found that children generally respond with alacrity to this "different" way of studying words or, heaven forbid, of reading. It is simply a matter of introducing them to the concept and allowing them to take it from there.

A suggested list of words and phrases to whet the appetite follows. The Appendix is a bibliography that will help you find many more.

United States	England
absorbent cotton	cotton wool
admit to the bar	call to the bar
aisle (in theater)	gangway
alcohol lamp	spirit lamp
ale	beer; bitter
alumnus	graduate
apartment	flat
apartment, hotel	service flats
apartment house	block of flats
ashcan	dust bin
ashman	dust man
automobile	motor-car
baby carriage	perambulator; pram
baggage car	luggage van
bakery	baker's shop
bathrobe	dressing gown
beach	seaside
blowtorch	brazing lamp
boulevard	arterial road
bowling alley	skittle alley
boxcar	covered waggon
briefcase	portfolio
business suit	lounge suit
candy	sweets
candy store	sweetshop
cane	stick
carnival	fun-fair
catnip	catmint
check (in restaurant)	bill
checkers (the game)	draughts
cheesecloth	butter-muslin
cigarette butt	cigarette end
closet	cupboard
clothespin	clothespeg
commencement	speech day
cone (for ice cream)	cornet
corporation	limited-liability company
custom made	made to measure
denatured alcohol	methylated spirit
detour	road diversion
dishpan	washing-up bowl
dock	wharf
druggist	chemist
dumbwaiter	service lift

United States	England
dump	refuse tip
editorial	leading article
elevator	lift
engineer	engine driver
expelled (from college)	sent down
faucet	tap
filling station	petrol pump
fire department	fire brigade
fish dealer	fishmonger
flophouse	doss house
frame house	wooden house
fraternal order	friendly society
freight car	goods waggon
gasoline	petrol
ginger ale	stone ginger
hallway	passage
hardware store	ironmonger
hash	shepherd's pie
highball	whiskey and soda
hockey	ice-hockey
horn (auto)	hooter
hospital	nursing home
information bureau	inquiry office
insane	certifiable
insurance (life)	assurance
intermission	interval
legal holiday	bank holiday
lifeguard	life-saver
life preserver	life-belt
long distance (telephone)	trunk
low gear (of an automobile)	first speed
mail	post; letters
molasses	treacle
monkey wrench	spanner
movie	cinema
newsstand	bookstall
overcoat	greatcoat
paraffin	white wax
parking lot	car-park
period (punctuation)	full stop
phonograph	gramophone
police officer	constable
poolroom	billiards-saloon
poorhouse	almshouse
postpaid	post-free
prison guard	warden
public school	council school
racetrack	race course
radio	wireless
railroad	railway
raincoat	waterproof
rare (of meat)	underdone

213

United States	*England*
recess (in school)	break
roast (of meat)	joint
round trip	return trip
scrambled eggs	buttered eggs
scratch pad	scribbling block
shoes	boots
silent partner	sleeping partner
silverware	plate
slacks	bags
soda fountain	soda-bar
spool (of thread)	reel
stenographer	shorthand writer
store	shop
straw hat	boater
streetcar	tram
street cleaner	road sweeper
sugar bowl	sugar basin
suspenders	braces
taffy	toffee
taxes (local)	rates
telephone booth	callbox
truck	lorry
truck farmer	market gardener
tube (radio)	wireless valve
vaudeville	variety
vaudeville theater	music hall
warden (of a prison)	governor
weather bureau	meteorological office
white collar (worker)	black coat
windshield	windscreen
witness stand	witness box
wrecking crew	breakdown gang

THE CHANGING NATURE OF WORDS

Activities   Another interesting device that we have used successfully with children in the middle grades has been the fact that words change in their meaning over time. What was meant by *nice* in 1078 is not meant by *nice* now. Children are excited to find that *nice* in an earlier time in English history meant *stupid*. This type of approach to reading has been enjoyed by reluctant readers in grades 4–12. Perhaps that they can shout to students from other classes, "You were a nice guy in 1078," accounts for their enthusiasm—we do not know. We simply accept the fact that it is a tremendous motivating factor in getting children to read.

Students in our classes have written books on the changing nature of words and have shared them with the class. We even have seen them meander (there is a river in Caria in Asia Minor named

214

Meander, and its slow, lazy pace gave its name to all streams and people who take circuitous routes) through books in search of information that previously would have brought tears of anger because of its length and complexity. The method is effective.

You will have to teach a few definitions before proceeding with the children. Certain words must be defined and clearly understood before embarking. First, introduce the concept of the changing nature of words and discuss with the class that word meanings do not necessarily remain stagnant. Then, define the following:

- *Pejorative Words* (pej.)—words that have changed from having a pleasant or neutral meaning to having a negative impact
- *Ameliorated Words* (am.)—words that have changed from a negative to a positive meaning
- *Specialized Words* (sp.)—words that have changed from a general meaning to a specific meaning
- *Generalized Words* (gen.)—words that have changed from a specific meaning to a general meaning

Examples of the above are as follows:

Word	Current Meaning	Past Meaning	Classification
abominable	detestable	away from man	pej.
adieu	goodbye	God be with you	gen.
amazon	tall, strong, aggressive woman	person without a breast	sp.
artifice	clever device	something made through skilled workmanship or craft	pej.
austere	stern in manner or appearance	dry; quality of making the tongue dry and rough	pej.
awkward	not graceful	difficult	pej.
bead	small ball or bit of glass, metal, plastic or other material	to pray	sp.
bewilder	to confuse completely	to lose in pathless places	gen.
bomb	container filled with an explosive	buzzing or humming noise	sp.
bonanza	rich mass of ore in a mine	fair weather; prosperity	sp.
bonfire	large fire built outdoors	fire of bones	gen.
canny	shrewd and cautious in dealing with others	quality of being able	pej.

215

Word	Current Meaning	Past Meaning	Classification
clean	free from dirt or filth; not soiled	little; puny	am.
conspire	to plan secretly with others	to breathe together	pej.
crazy	having a diseased or injured mind; insane; mad	to break or crush objects	pej.
cunning	clever in deceiving	knowing	pej.
deer	a particular animal	any small animal	sp.
disheveled	not neat; rumpled; mussed	having hair out of bounds	sp.
dismal	gloomy	of evil days	gen. and am.
elegant	showing good taste; refined; beautifully luxurious	term of reproach used of a dainty foppish male	am.
enormous	very, very large	deviating from ordinary rule or type	sp.
eschew	to avoid; to keep away from	to fear; to terrify	sp.
etch	to engrave	to eat	sp.
fiasco	complete or ridiculous failure	flask or bottle	pej.
fond	loving; affectionate; tender	lost its flavor; sickly flavored	am.
grocer	person who sells food and household supplies	wholesaler, who bought and sold in the gross, in large amounts	sp.
hello	exclamation to express greeting	to fetch	sp.
lewd	indecent	unlearned	pej.
lido	fashionable resort	shore or beach	sp.
minister	a pastor	anyone who served others	sp.
minstrel	singer	buffoon	am.
nice	pleasant	ignorant	am.
odd	left over	the third man who gives the deciding vote	sp.
pantry	small room in which food, dishes, silverware, or table linen are kept	a storeroom for bread	gen.

Word	Current Meaning	Past Meaning	Classification
paradise	abode of God, the angels, and the righteous; heaven	enclosure or park	sp.
pavilion	light building, usually one somewhat open, used for shelter, for pleasure	tent or canopy, gaily set up in all its rich blaze of color to shelter knights and ladies at the jousting	gen.
pedagogue	teacher of children; schoolmaster	servant who led a well-to-do Greek boy to school	gen.
pedigree	list of ancestors of a person, animal, or plant; family tree	crane's foot	sp.
penicillin	very powerful drug for destroying bacteria (Penicillin is shaped like pencils)	paint brush, pencil	sp.
person	man, woman, or child; human being	mask used by a person	gen.
picayune	small; petty, mean; paltry	U.S. silver five-cent piece	pej.
pirate	thief	one who ventured forth	pej.
prestige	reputation, influence, or distinction based on one's abilities, achievements, opportunities, or associations	illusion; deceit; imposture; juggling tricks	am.
pretty	pleasing	deceitful	am.
prevaricate	to lie	to straddle	pej.
propagandize	mislead	inform	pej.
restaurant	place to buy and eat a meal	to restore or repair	sp.
rummage	to search thoroughly by moving things about	to arrange cargo in the hold of a ship	sp.
scruple	feeling of doubt about what one ought to do	little pebble	gen.

217

Word	Current Meaning	Past Meaning	Classification
ship	move by land, air, or sea	move by sea	gen.
slave	person who is the property of another	one of the Slavic race captured and made a bondsman	gen.
sycophant	servile or self-seeking flatterer	informer or slanderer	sp.
tabloid	newspaper in compressed form	concentrated drugs	sp.
tall	higher than average	swift; prompt; ready; active	sp.
tide	rise and fall of the ocean every 12 hours caused by the attraction of the moon and the sun	fixed time of flood and ebb; not dictated by sun and moon	gen.
uncouth	not refined	unknown	pej.
very	much; greatly; extremely	true	gen.
wanton	reckless; heartless; malicious	undisciplined	pej.
wretch	very unfortunate or unhappy person	person banished from his native country; an exile	gen.
zest	pleasant or exciting quality to give flavor	piece of lemon peel to give taste	gen.

There are many more examples that you and your students will find interesting reading. They provide another opportunity to awaken an interest in words. Sources are given in the appendix.

WHAT'S IN A NAME?

Activities   To paraphrase a well-known poet of the last century, there is no sweeter flesh than our own. In understanding human nature, it is important to know that everyone sees some worth in their own person. For example, have you ever tilted your head a certain way while looking in a mirror and said to yourself, "If I hold my head this way, I look so much more attractive/handsome?" We have.

Understanding this led us to another way of teaching reading. We simply selected a list of male and female names with their meanings. Every student would like to know what his name means as well as the names of his friends, parents, siblings and other relatives. Following is a partial listing of names and their meanings. We believe the children will participate.

Name/Female	Meaning
Abigail	a source of joy
Ada	joyous; prosperous
Adabelle	joyous and fair
Adrienne	woman of the sea
Agnes	pure; chaste; gentle
Aileen	light
Aimee	beloved
Alda	rich
Alice	truth
Almira	princess; the exalted
Althea	wholesome; healing
Amanda	lovable
Amber	jewel
Ann	grace
Ava	bird
Barbara	mysterious stranger
Beatrice	she brings joy
Belinda	wise and immortal
Bernice	she brings victory
Bertha	shining; bright
Beth	place of God
Beverly	ambitious
Bonnie	sweet and good
Brenda	fiery
Bridget	mighty; strong
Camilla	noble; righteous
Candace	pure
Carla	one who is strong
Carol	joyous song
Celeste	heavenly
Charlotte	strong
Christine	fair Christian
Claudia	the lame
Colleen	girl
Cynthia	moon goddess
Daisy	the day's eye
Darlene	dearly beloved
Deborah	the bee
Deana	pure goddess of the moon
Dolores	our Lady of Sorrows
Donna	lady
Dora	a gift
Doreen	golden girl
Doris	sea goddess
Dorothy	God's gift
Edith	rich gift
Edna	rejuvenation
Elaine	light

219

Name/Female	*Meaning*
Elizabeth	consecrated to God
Emily	industrious
Emma	one who heals
Erica	of royalty
Esther	a star
Eunice	gloriously victorious
Eve	life
Faith	trusting
Fanny	free
Felicia	happy
Flavia	yellow-haired
Florence	to flower and bloom
Frances	free
Freda	peace
Frederica	peaceful
Fritzie	peaceful ruler
Gabrielle	woman of God
Genevieve	pure
Georgiana	earth lover
Geraldine	ruler with a spear
Gertrude	spear maiden
Gladys	frail; delicate
Gloria	the glorious
Grace	the graceful
Guinevere	fair lady
Gwendolyn	white browed
Hannah	full of grace, mercy, and prayer
Harriet	mistress of the home
Heather	a flower
Helen	light
Helga	holy
Hesper	night star
Hilda	battle maiden
Holly	good luck
Hope	optimistic and cheerful
Hortense	garden worker
Ida	happy
Imogene	an image
Ingrid	daughter
Irene	peace
Iris	rainbow
Irma	strong
Isabel	consecrated to God
Isadora	a gift
Isolde	the fair
Ivy	a plant or a vine
Jacqueline	the supplanter
Jane	God's gracious gift
Janet, Janette, Janice	God's gracious gift
Jasmine	fragrant flower
Jennie, Jennifer, Jenny	fair lady

Name/Female	Meaning
Jessica	rich or grace of God
Joan	God's gracious gift
Jocelyn	the fair
Josephine	she shall add
Julia	youthful
Katherine	pure
Kay	rejoice
Kim	noble or glorious leader
Koren	young girl
Lara	well-known
Laura	the laurel
Laverne	springlike
Leah	the weary
Leona	the lion
Linda	beautiful
Lois	battle maiden
Lucy	light
Lydia	cultured
Madeline	a tower of strength
Madra	mother
Maida	maiden
Margaret	a pearl
Mary	bitter
Melanie	darkness; clad in black
Melody	song
Myra	the wonderful
Mirabel	of great beauty
Monica	adviser
Nadine	hope
Naomi	sweet; pleasant
Narda	joyous; gay
Natalie	child of Christmas
Nerissa	of the sea
Nicole	victory of the people
Noel	a Christmas child
Nola	famous; well-known
Nona	the ninthborn
Norma	the model or pattern
Octavia	the eighthborn
Odelia	prosperous
Odele	a melody
Odette	home lover
Ola	daughter or descendant
Olga	holy
Olivia	peace
Ophelia	wise or immortal
Oriole	fair
Ottilie	battle heroine
Pamela	loving; kind
Patience	patient
Patricia	of the nobility; well-born
Paula	little

Name/Female	Meaning
Pearl	precious gem
Penelope	weaver
Phoebe	the wise, shining one
Phyllis	a green bough
Priscilla	the ancient; of long lineage
Prudence	the prudent; cautious
Queena	a queen or a woman
Quenby	wife; womanly
Quinta	the fifth
Rachel	naive and innocent
Rebecca	the captivator
Renee	reborn
Rita	a pearl
Roberta	of shining fame
Rosalind	fair rose
Rose	a rose
Roxanne	dawn
Ruby	precious red stone
Ruth	a beautiful friend
Sabrina	a princess
Samara	watchful; cautious
Sarah	princess
Sheila	musical
Shirley	from the white meadow
Sophia	wisdom
Stephanie	a crown of garland
Susan	a lily
Sybil	the prophetess
Sydney	the enticer
Tabitha	the gazelle
Tamara	the palm tree
Teresa	the harvester
Thelma	nursing
Theodora	God's divine gift
Theola	heaven-sent
Timothea	honoring God
Tobey	God is good
Thalia	blooming
Tallulah	vivacious
Tara	tower
Ula	sea jewel
Ulrica	ruler of all
Una	all truth is one
Undine	of water
Ursula	she-bear
Valda	battle heroine
Vanessa	the butterfly
Vania	God's gracious gift
Veda	wise
Verna	spring-born
Veronica	true image

Name/Female	Meaning
Victoria	the victorious
Violet	modest; shy
Virginia	maidenly; pure
Vita	life
Vivian	lively; full of life
Wanda	the wanderer
Wilda	the untamed
Wilfreda	firm peacemaker
Wilhelmina	protectress
Willa	desirable
Winifred	friend of peace
Wynne	the fair; the white
Xanthe	blonde
Xena	hospitable
Xylia	of the wood
Zabrina	of the nobility
Zandra	friend or helper of humankind
Zebada	gift of the Lord
Zerlina	serene and beautiful
Zora	dawn
Zuluka	fair

Name/Male	Meaning
Aaron	light; high mountain
Abraham	father of many; exalted father
Adam	red earth; man of earth
Alan	harmony
Alexander	protector of men
Alfred	wise as an elf
Andrew	manly
Arnold	strong as an eagle
Arthur	strong as a rock
Avery	ruler of the elves
Barnaby	son of consolation
Barry	spear
Basil	kingly
Baxter	the baker
Benedict	blessed
Benjamin	son of my right hand
Bernard	grim bear
Bradley	from the broad meadow
Brian	powerful
Bruce	from the brushwood thicket
Calvin	bald
Cameron	bent nose
Charles	man
Chester	of the fortified camp
Christopher	Christ-bearer
Clark	scholarly
Clifford	from the ford near the cliff

Name/Male	Meaning
Clyde	heard from a distance
Conrad	brave counsel
Craig	of the crag or stony hill
Daniel	the Lord is judge
Darrell	beloved
David	beloved
Dennis	lover of fine wines
Desmond	worldly; sophisticated
Dominic	the Lord's
Donald	ruler of the world
Duane	singing
Earl	nobleman; chief
Edgar	lucky spear; fortunate warrior
Edmund	fortunate or rich protector
Edward	prosperous guardian
Edwin	wealthy friend
Eli	the highest
Ellsworth	lover of the earth; farmer
Eric	kingly
Esmond	gracious protector
Eugene	noble; well-born
Fabian	prosperous farmer
Farrell	the valorous one
Ferdinand	bold venture
Fergus	best choice; strong man
Firman	traveler to distant places
Fletcher	arrow maker
Forrest	from the woods
Francis	free
Franklin	a free man
Frederick	peaceful chieftain
Gabriel	God is mighty
Galvin	the sparrow
Geoffrey	God's peace; peace of the land
George	farmer; tiller of the soil
Gerald	mighty spearman
Glen	from the valley
Gordon	from the cornered hill
Grant	great
Gregory	vigilant
Guy	guide
Hamilton	from the mountain hamlet
Hanley	of high meadow
Harold	army commander
Harvey	bitter
Henry	home ruler
Herman	noble warrior
Howard	chief guardian
Hubert	shining of mind
Humbert	bright home
Humphrey	a protector of the peace

Name/Male	*Meaning*
Ichabod	the Lord has departed
Ignatius	the fiery and the ardent
Igor	hero
Ingram	the raven
Inness	from the island
Ira	watcher
Irvin	sea friend
Isaac	laughing
Israel	the Lord's warrior or soldier
Ivar	military archer
James	the supplanter
Jared	the descending; descendant
Jason	healer
Jeremy	exalted by the Lord
Jerome	holy
Jesse	God's gift or grace
Joel	Jehovah is God
John	God's gracious gift
Jonathan	gift of the Lord
Joseph	he shall add
Kane	bright; radiant
Keith	a place
Kelsey	from the water
Kendall	chief of the valley
Kendrick	royal ruler
Kenneth	handsome
Kenyon	fair-haired
Kevin	kind; gentle
Kirby	from the church village
Kirk	of the Church; living close to the Church
Lance	spear
Lawrence	laurel; crowned with laurel
Lee	meadow; sheltered
Leo	lion; brave as a lion
Leslie	from the gray fort
Lewis	renowned in battle
Lincoln	from the place by the pool; riverbank
Lloyd	gray; dark
Lowell	beloved
Luther	renowned warrior
Mac	the son of
Malcolm	dove
Mallory	luckless
Mark	belonging to Mars; a warrior
Matthew	God's gift
Meredith	sea protector
Michael	Godlike
Montgomery	mountain hunter
Morgan	from the sea; sea white
Murray	sailor
Nathaniel	gift of God
Neal	champion

Name/Male	*Meaning*
Nero	black; dark
Neville	from the new town
Newton	from the estate
Nicholas	victory of the people
Nigel	dark; black
Noah	rest; comfort; peace
Norman	man from the north
Norton	from the north place
Ogden	from the oak valley
Olaf	peace; reminder
Oliver	olive; peace
Orson	bear
Osborn	divinely strong
Oscar	divine spear
Oswald	divine power
Otis	keen-eared
Otto	wealthy; prosperous
Owen	young warrior
Palmer	the palm bearer; the pilgrim
Parry	guardian; warder; protector
Patrick	noble; patrician
Paul	little
Pembroke	from the headland
Perry	pear tree
Peter	rock; stone
Philip	lover of horses
Porter	doorkeeper or gatekeeper
Preston	of the priest's place
Quentin	fifth
Quelon	sword
Quincy	from the fifth son's place
Radcliffe	from the red cliff
Ramsey	from Ram's island
Randolph	protected; advised by wolves
Raphael	healed by God
Raymond	wise protection
Reginald	mighty ruler
Reuben	behold, a son
Richard	wealthy and powerful
Robert	of bright, shining fame
Roger	renowned spearman; famous warrior
Samuel	name of God
Saul	longed for desire
Scott	a Scotsman
Sebastian	respected; reverenced
Sheldon	from the hill, ledge, or shell valley
Silas	of the forest
Stephen	crown; garland
Stewart	keeper of the estate
Tate	cheerful
Terence	tender
Theodore	gift of God

Name/Male	Meaning
Thomas	the twin
Thornton	from the thorny place
Thurston	Thor's jewel or stone
Timothy	honoring God
Todd	the fox
Titus	safe; saved
Tyler	maker of tiles or brick
Tyrone	of uncertain meaning
Ulysses	angry one
Upton	from the hill town
Urban	from the city; urbane; sophisticated
Uriah	the Lord is my light
Valentine	healthy
Vaughan	the small
Vernon	growing green; flourishing
Victor	the conqueror
Vincent	the conqueror
Virgil	strong; flourishing
Vito	vital
Wallace	a foreigner
Walter	powerful; mighty warrior
Warren	gamewarden
Watson	warrior's son
Wayne	wagonmaker
Webster	weaver
William	determined protector
Winston	from the friendly town
Wyatt	a guide
Wylie	beguiling; charming
Xavier	bright
Xenos	stronger
Xerxes	king
Yale	payer; yielder
Yancy	Englishman
Yates	the gate dweller or protector
Yves	an archer
Zachariah	the Lord's remembrance
Zebulon	dwelling place
Zelig	blessed
Zeke	God's strength

I DUB THE SURNAME

Activities As much interest as there is in our first names, much more has been generated in last names since Alex Haley's *Roots* was published. We found children eager to know the origin of their names and those of their friends. Likewise, adults were motivated to get into the act. It is our judgment that there exists within each one of us a fierce pride in our own family (in spite of a few skeletons in the closet) and we want to know about it. Thus, a motivating, stimulating influence is brought to bear in an effortless manner. Following is a list of surnames (by no means exhaustive) with their meanings.

Surname	Meaning
Abbate	one who was a member of an abbot's entourage
Abdullah	the servant of Allah
Abel	one who was a servant to Abel (breath; vanity)
Abernathy	one who came from Abernathy (at the narrow opening), in Perthshire
Abrams	English descendant of Abram (high father)
Ackerman	one who plowed the Lord's land and tended his plow teams
Ackroyd	dweller at the oak clearing
Adams, Adamson, Addams, Adam	the son of Adam (man of earth; red earth)
Agnew	dweller at the sign of the lamb; one who was angelic or lamblike
Aiello	one who experiences bad luck
Albright	one who came from Albright (Eodbeorht's homestead), in Shropshire
Alexander	descendant of Alexander (helper of humankind)
Allen	name of rivers in Cornwall, Dorset, Northumberland, and Stirlingshire
Allen, Allan, Alan	descendant of Alan (harmony); dweller near the Allen (green plains)
Andrews	descendant of Andrew (manly)
Armstrong	the strong-armed man
Atkins, Atkin, Atkinson	the son of little Ad, a pet form of Adam (man of earth; red earth)
Atwood, Attwood	dweller at or near a wood
Axe	one who lived on or near the Axe, the name of two rivers in England
Babbitt	descendant of Little Babb or Babba (descendant of baby); pet form of Barbara (mysterious stranger)
Babich, Babick, Babicz, Babic, Babij	one with the characteristics of a woman; one who loved women; a casanova; descendant of Baba (grandmother; grandfather)
Bachman, Bachmann	dweller at or near a brook or stream
Bacon	a swineherd or peasant, from the nickname Bacon; a bacon or lard dealer; dwellers at the sign of a pig, at a time when bacon meant the live pig
Bagger	one who made and sold bags; the peddler who carried his wares from place to place in a bag
Baggio	the toad, a nickname for a lean man

Surname	Meaning
Bailey	one charged with public administrative authority in a certain district by the king or a lord; one who acted as an agent for the lord in the management of the affairs of the manor; one who came from Bailey (clearing where berries grew), in Lancashire
Baker	one who made bread
Baldwin	one who was bald-headed; the fat or corpulent man; descendant of Bald, a short form of Baldwin (bold; friend)
Bancroft	dweller at an enclosure, or yard, where beans grew
Band	one who cut barrel hoops; a hooper
Banks, Bank, Banker	dweller near a mound or embankment
Barber	the hairdresser; one who practiced surgery, i.e., acted as a bloodletter
Baron, Barone	the landowner who held his land of the king; one who fomented strife; descendant of Baron (baron)
Barto	descendant of Bart, a pet form of Bartholomew (son of Talmai; furrow)
Baxter	one who made bread—although the name seems to be feminine, it is used chiefly for men
Beam	one who lived by a tree; dweller at a foot bridge; a tree trunk lying across a stream
Becker	one who made bread; a baker; dweller at a brook
Brooks, Brookes, Brook, Brookman, Brooke	dweller near spring or brook, or sometimes marsh
Brown	one with a dark complexion; descendant of Brun (brown)
Burns (Burnes)	dweller at a brook
Cabot	one with a small head; dweller at the sign of the miller's thumb; a freshwater fish
Cahill, Cahall	grandson of Cathal (battle; powerful)
Calhoun, Calhoon, Calhoune	grandson of Cathluan (battle hero; battle joyful)
Campbell	one with a wry mouth, or perhaps arched lips—it has been suggested that the epithet was applied by neighboring clans on account of moral, rather than physical, defects
Carson	dweller in or near a marsh; the garcon or servant; the son of Car; a pet form of names beginning with Car, such as Carmichael
Caruso	one with shorn or close-cut hair; one who worked in the sulphur pits

Surname	*Meaning*
Chambers	the officer in charge of the private household of a king or important nobleman; one who worked in the chamber, sometimes the reception room, of an important household
Charles	descendant of Charles (man); one who came from Charles (rock place), in Devonshire
Christopher	descendant of Christopher (Christ-bearer); dweller at the sign of St. Christopher
Cierniak, Cierny	the dark or swarthy man
Colegate, Colgate	dweller at a cool gap in a chain of hills
Connors, Connor	grandson of Concobair (meddlesome), or of Conchor (high will or desire)
Conti, Conte	a nobleman; the count; one in the service of a count
Cook, Cooke	one who prepared food
Cooper, Couper, Cowper	one who made and sold casks, buckets, and tubs
Dabrowski	one who came from Dabrowa (oak grove), the name of several places in Poland; dweller in or near an oak grove
D'Agostino, Dagostino	descendant of Agostino; Italian form of Augustine (exalted; majestic)
Dahl, Dahle	dweller in the valley
Dailey, Daily	grandson of Dalach (frequenting assemblies)
D'Amico, Damico	the son of Amico (friend)
Daugherty	grandson of Dochartact (unfortunate)
Dawson	the son of Daw; a pet form of David (commander; beloved; friend)
DeAngelis	descendant of Angel (messenger; angelic)
Decker, Dekker, Deckert	one who covered roofs with tile, straw, or slate; one who came from Deck or Decker, the names of places in Germany
Dempsey	grandson of Diomasach (proud)
Donato, Donati, Donat	descendant of Donato (given)
Donnelly, Donnelley, Donley	grandson of Donnghal (brown valor); descendant of the dark-complexioned, valiant man
Douglas, Douglass	dweller at the black water or stream; one who came from Douglas (dark stream), in Lanarkshire
Drell	dweller at the sign of the arrow
Duda	one who played a bagpipe
Dudzinski	one who played the shawm, a wind instrument in the oboe family
Durst	the bold or daring man
Dusenbery, Dusenberry, Dusenbury	one who came from Doesburg, in Holland; one who lived on the Dusen hill, in Germany

Surname	Meaning
Dvorak	one who belonged to the lord's estate; a vassal; a courtier or attendant at the court of a prince
Eagan	the son of little Aadk (fire)
Early, Earley	one who came from Earley (eagle wood), in Berkshire; dweller by the earl's meadow
Eberhardt, Eberhart, Eberhard	descendant of Eberhard (boar; strong)
Ecklund	oak river island
Ehrlich	the honest man
Eichelberger, Eichelberg	one who came from Eichelberg (mountain with oak trees), the name of several places in Germany; dweller on a hill where oak trees grew
Eide, Eiden, Eidson	descendant of Eden (rich)
Eisenhower, Eisenhauer	the iron cutter or iron miner; maker of eisenhauers, a saber or sword blade capable of shearing an iron nail
Elliot, Elliott	descendant of little Elijah or Elias
Elting	one who came from Eltingen, in Germany
Elton	one who came from Elton (Ella's homestead; village of Aethelheah's people), the name of eight villages in England
English	an Englishman—Possibly, the name was acquired while outside of England and brought back
Epstein, Eppstein	one who came from Eppstein (Eppo's stone), in Germany; one who came from Ebstein, a place no longer in existence in Austria
Etheridge, Ethridge, Etteridge	descendant of Aethelric (noble; reile)
Evangelicta	one who chants the gospels in church
Evanoff, Evanow	the son of Evan (gracious gift of Jehovah)
Evans, Evan	the son of Evan, Welsh form of John (gracious gift of Jehovah)
Everett, Everette, Everitt, Everard	descendant of Everard (boar; hark)
Faber, Fabre	the worker in metals; a smith
Fackler	one who gathers hemp or flax
Fairbanks, Fairbank	dweller on or near the ridge where bulls or sheep were confined, or by the beautiful banks or shore
Fairweather, Fayerweather	one who worked only in good weather; one with a happy disposition; one who came from Faweather (many-colored heather), in Yorkshire
Faraday	descendant of Feradach (illustrious man)
Fazro, Fazzi, Fazzio	one who acted as a watchman or sentinel; dweller by a beech tree

231

Surname	Meaning
Fee	grandson of Fraich (raven)
Feldman, Feldmann, Feltman, Feltmann	the worker in the field or open country
Feliciano	descendant of Feliciano, Spanish form of Felician (happiness); the happy, fortunate, lucky man
Filippi, Filippini	descendant of Filippo, Italian form of Philip (lover of horses)
Fisher	one who caught or sold fish
Fitzpatrick	the son of Patrick (noble; patrician)
Flood	dweller at or near the place where a stream often overflows; descendant of Floyd (gray)
Flynn, Flinn	the red-haired or ruddy-complexioned man
Fodor	one with curly hair; descendant of Feodor, Slavic form of Theodore (gift of God)
Fogarty, Fogerty	descendant of the exiled man
Foreman, Forman	one who tended pigs; one who supervises the work of others; an overseer; dweller by a ford
Fox, Foxx	dweller at the sign of the fox; one with some of the qualities of a fox
Fredrickson, Fredricksen, Fredriksen, Fredrikson	the son of Fredrik, Scandinavian form of Frederick (peace; rule)
Frost	descendant of Frost (one born at the time of frost); a contraction of Forrest, q.v. one cold in behavior or temperament
Fry, Frye	the free man, i.e., free of obligations to the lord of the manor
Gabler	one who collected taxes
Gabor	descendant of Gabor, Hungarian form of Gabriel (strong man of God)
Garfield	dweller on the grassy land or pasture
Gates	one who lived in or near the gate or gap in a chain of hills
Geiger	one who played a violin
Geraci, Gerace	one who came from Gerace, in Italy
Gibula	the mobile, active person
Gilbert, Gilbertson, Gilberts	descendant of Gilbert (pledge; bright)
Giovannetti, Giovannini	descendant of little Giovanni, Italian form of John (gracious gift of Jehovah)
Golembiecki	one with the qualities or characteristics of a dove
Gomez	the son of Gomo, a pet form of Gomesano (man; path)
Hacker	one who cultivates the soil with a hoe or hack, a maker of hacks

Surname	Meaning
Hand	dweller at the sign of the hand; one with a peculiar or misshapen hand
Heilman, Heilmann	the sound of a healthy man; descendant of Hailmann, a German Jewish synonym for Samuel (God hath heard); descendant of Heilman (salvation; man)
Helbraun	one who came from Heilbronn (safe spring; holy spring), in France
Henrici	descendant of little Henry (home; rule)
Hernandez	son of Hernando (journey; venture)
Hilton	one who came from Hilton (homestead on the hill), the name of several place in England
Hoffman, Hoffmann	one who worked a large farm either as owner or manager; the farm or manor servant
Hogstrom	high stream
Holliday, Holiday	descendant of Halliday or Holiday (name given to one born on Sunday or other holy day)
Horowitz, Horowicz	variant of Horwitz—one who came from Horice or Horitz (mountainous place), in Bohemia; the son of the mountaineer
Hussin, Hussain, Hussein	descendant of the good man
Ibarra	one who came from Ibarra (sandbank), in Spain
Ingels, Ingle	descendant of Ingulf (Ing's wolf), or of Ingald (Ing's tribute)
Ingersoll, Ingersol	one who came from Inkersall (the monk's field), in Derbyshire
Inlander	one who dwelt by, or worked on, the land belonging to the lord of the manor; one who came from the interior to dwell by the sea
Irwin	descendant of Erwine (sea friend); one who came from Irvine (green river), in Ayrshire
Jackson, Jaxon	the son of Jack, a pet form of John (gracious gift of Jehovah)
Jaime, Jaimes	variant of James, q.v. old French form of Jacob (may God protect; the supplanter)
Jaworski, Javorowski	one who came from Jaworow (maple tree), in Poland
Jorgensen, Jorgenson	the son of Jorgen; Norse form of George (farmer)
Jurkiewicz	the son of little Jur, a Polish pet form of George (farmer)
Justin, Justen, Justyn	descendant of Justin (the just)
Kabat	one who made and sold overcoats; one who wore an unusual overcoat
Kaczynski	one who came from Kaczyn (duck farm), in Poland
Kearney	grandson of Carney (victorious in battle)
Keim	one who raised plants from seeds

Surname	Meaning
Kennedy	one with an ugly or misshapen head; descendant of Cinnerdidh (helmet-head)
Kessler, Kestler, Kesseler	one who made kettles; one who came from Kessel (castle), the name of many places in Germany
Kielbasa	one who made and sold small sausages
Kirkegaard	one who dwelled near the church yard
Kitzman	one who tended young goats
Klein, Kleine	the small man; the neat, nice man
Kohler	one who burned charcoal; one who came from Koehlen or Koehler, in Germany
Kramer, Krammer	the shopkeeper or tradesman; one who traveled through the country buying butter, hens, and eggs
Kussman, Kussmann	one who made and sold cheese
Ladd, Ladds	common English lad of obscure origin, originally servant or man of low birth
Landon	one who came from Langdon (long hill), the name of several places in England; descendant of Lando (land)
LaPorta	dweller near the gate, probably the entrance to a walled town
Lavery	descendant of the speaker or spokesman
LaRue	dweller on an important street
Leventhal	an artificial name from Leven, a variant of the Hebrew Levi (united) plus suffix denoting "valley"
Lewis	descendant of Lewis (glory; battle; bear; fight; hale; wide)
Lindstrom	linden-tree river
Lippi, Lippo	descendant of Lippo, a pet form of Philip (lover of horses)
Locksmith	one who made and sold locks
Lodge	dweller in a cottage or hut
Lorengo, Lorenzi	descendant of Lorenzo, Spanish and Italian form of Lawrence (laurel, symbol of victory)
Lyons, Lyon	descendant of Leon (lion); dweller at the sign of the lion—Jacob's reference to Judah as a lion (Gen. 49:9) has led many Jews to adopt this name
McAdam	son of Adam
Macpherson	son of the parson
Makepeace, Makepiece	peacemaker
Mallard	wild drake
Mallory	the unfortunate; the unlucky
Manwood	dweller by the common wood
March	dweller by the boundary
Martinson	son of Martin
Michael, McMichael	who is like the Lord

Surname	Meaning
Moodey, Moody, Mudie	bold; impetuous; brave
Murphy	sea warrior
Neilson, Nielson, Nilson	son of Neil
Nessling, Neslin	"Nestling"
New	the newcomer
Newcomb, Newcombe, Newcombes, Newcome	newly arrived stranger
Newhall, Newall	dweller at the new hall
Niven, Neven, Nevin, MacNevin, MacNiven	little saint
Noake, Noakes, Noaks	oak
Noble, Nobles	well-known noble
Noel, Nowell, Nowill	Christmas; a name like the English *Christmas* and *Midwinter*, given to one born at that festival
Norris, Norriss, Norreys	northerner
Northcliffe, Nortcliffe, Norcliffe, Norclyffe	dweller by the north cliff
Northend	the man from the north end (of the village)
Northup	dweller north up (in the village)
Nugent	from one or another of the many French places called Nogent
Nutman, Nuttmann, Notman	dealer in nuts
Nutt	a man with a round head or brown complexion
Nutter	scribe; writer; derivative of the word *note*
Ny, Nie, Nay, Ney	from residence near some low-lying land by the stream
Oak, Oake, Oaks, Oke, Noak, Noake, Noakes, Noaks, Nock, Noke, Nokes	from residence by an oak or a group of oaks

Surname	*Meaning*
O'Brian, O'Brien, O'Bryan, O'Bryen	descendant of Brian
O'Connor	descendant of Conchobhor (high'will)
Odam, Odams, Odom, Odhams	son-in-law
O'Haire, O'Hare, O'Hear	hair
Oldershaw, Houldershaw	dweller by the alderwood
Oldham, Oldam	dweller by the long-cultivated river flat
O'Leary, Leary	descendant of Loaghaire (calfkeeper)
Olive, Ollive	olive—there were two saints named Oliva, one the patroness of olive trees
Oscroft	dweller by the ox-croft
O'Shea, O'Shee, Shea	descendant of Seaghdha (stately; majestic)
Osmond, Osmon, Osmund, Osmon, Osmont, Osment, Osmint	god protector
O'Sullivan, Sullivan	descendant of Suileabhan (black-eyed)
Oswald	god ruler
Outridge, Outteridge, Oughtright, Utteridge, Uttridge, Utridge	dawn; powerful
Packer	to pack; probably a wool packer
Painter, Paynter	painter
Paler, Paylr	maker or seller of pails
Pardner, Partner, Partener	the pardoner; a licensed seller of indulgences
Parkin, Parkins, Parkyn, Perken, Perkin, Perkins, Purkens	little Peter

Surname	Meaning
Parsons	one who lived or worked at the parson's house, at the parsonage
Patterson, Paterson	son of Patrick
Pease	metonymic for a seller of peas
Pickin, Picking	dweller on the hill
Pillman	dweller by the stake or the stream
Piper, Pyper	a player on the pipe; a piper
Platfoot	flat foot
Plummer, Plimmer	the pool by the plum tree
Portal	dweller by the town gate
Pothecary, Potticary	one who kept a store for spices, drugs, and preserves; later, one who prepared and sold drugs for medical purposes
Quant	cunning; crafty; wise; skilled; clever
Quarrie, Quarry	square; squarely built; stout
Quickly	nimbly; in a lively fashion
Quilter	a maker of quilts or mattresses
Reardon, Rearden	grandson of Rioghbhardon (royal poet)
Reece	the son of Rhys (ardor; a rush)
Reed	the red-haired or ruddy person; one who came from Reed (reedy or rough growth), in Hertfordshire
Ramos	descendant of Ramos (palms); a name given to one born during the religious fiesta of Palm Sunday; one who came from Ramos (branch), in Spain
Randolph	descendant of Randwulf (shield; wolf)
Revere	the robber; dweller on or near the bank or shore; one who came from Riviere, a village in Belgium
Ridenour	one who came from Rietenau (meadow with reeds growing), in Germany
Rimer, Rimerman, Rimes	one who produced rhymed verse; a poet
Ritter	a military servant; a knight
Rockey	dweller near a small rock
Sadowski	dweller at or near an orchard
Santana	one who came from Santana (Saint Ana), in Spain
Schlosser, Schloss	one who made locks; a locksmith; dweller in or near the manor house or castle; dweller at the sign of a castle
Schneider, Schnieder	one who made outer garments; a tailor
Schnell	the quick, lively person
Schoemaker	one who made and sold shoes

237

Surname	*Meaning*
Seidler	one who made and sold beer mugs and tankards; one who kept bees; a beekeeper
Serratino	one who came from Sorrento, in the province of Napoli in Italy
Sexauer, Sexaur	one who came from Sexau, in Germany
Siebert, Sibert, Seebert	descendant of Sigibert (victory; bright)
Simon	descendant of Simon (gracious hearing; hearkening; snub-nosed)
Smithe, Smith	the worker in metals
Stuyvesant	one who came from Stuvesant (quicksand), in Zeeland
Swift	one who was fleet of foot, probably a messenger
Taggart, Taggert	the son of a priest
Tanner	one who made or sold leather; one who came from Tann (fir trees), the name of several places in Germany
Taverna	dweller near the wine shop
Teacher	one who instructed others
Teller	one who made or sold linen cloth
Thacker, Thacher	variant of Thalther; one who covered roofs with straw, rushes, or reeds
Thomas	descendant of Thomas (a twin)
Tilden	one who came from Tillingdown (Tilmund's hill), in Surrey, or from Tilden (Tila's valley), in Kent
Tinker, Tinkler	one who mended pots and kettles
Tomasek	descendant of little Thomas (a twin)
Tunney, Tunny	grandson of Tonach (glittering)
Turk	one who came from Turkmen, now a Soviet Socialist Republic; one who came from Turkey; a Turk
Uhl, Uhle	descendant of Uhl, a pet form of Ulrich (wolf; rule)
Ulrich, Ullrich, Ulreich, Ulrick	descendant of Ulrich (wolf; rule)
Underwood	one who came from Underwood (within a forest), the name of places in Derbyshire and Nottinghamshire; dweller within a wood
Updyck, Updike	dweller on the dike
Urbanski	descendant of Urban (town dweller)
Usher	a doorkeeper; one who kept the door of the king's apartment

238

Surname	Meaning
Vaccaro, Vaccari, Vaccarello	one who tended cows
Vajda	one who acted as a military governor in Slavic countries
Vallee, Valley	dweller in a depression between ranges of hills or mountains; a valley
Van Buren	one who came from the neighborhood; or from Buren (neighborhood), the name of two places in Holland
Van Houten	one who came from Houten (wooden), in Holland; dweller in the woods
Velazquez, Valasquez	the sluggish, slow, or weak person; descendant of Bela (raven; crow)
Venezia, Veneziani, Veneziano	one who came from Venezia (Venice), in Italy
Vennell, Vennel, Vennall	dweller in a small street or alley
Vick, Vicks	one who came from Vicq (village), the name of various places in France; the small man
Villanova	one who came from Vilanova (village of the nobleman), in Spain
Vogelman	one who hunted or trapped birds
Vrooman, Vroman, Vromans, Vroom	the pious, devout man
Wachtel	one who caught and sold quail; dweller at the sign of the quail
Waite, Waet, Wayt	the watchman or lookout, especially in a castle or a fortified place
Walczak, Walczyk	descendant of little Wal, a pet form of Wolenty (valorous)
Wamback, Wambaugh	one who came from Wamback (marshy pool), the name of several places in Germany
Weaver	one who wove cloth; dweller near the Weaver (winding river), a river in Cheshire
Wechsler	one who changed money; a banker or money changer
Weisz	white; the light or fair complexioned man; one with white hair
Werner	descendant of Warinhare (protection; army)
Whitcomb	one who came from Whitcombe (wide valley), the name of places in Dorset and Wiltshire
Wilson, Willson	the son of Will, pet form of William (resolution; helmet)
Wojeck	one in military service; a soldier
Wrigley	dweller at the ridge meadow
Xander, Xanders	descendant of Xander, a shortened form of Alexander (helper of humankind)

239

Surname	Meaning
Xavier	one who came from Xaberri or Xaverri, abbreviated form of Etchaberri (new house), the name of numerous places in Spain
Yablon, Yablonski, Yablonsky	dweller near an apple tree
Yalman	modern name meaning "the highest summit of a mountain"
Yanaitis	variant of Jonaitis, the son of Jonas (gracious gift of Jehovah)
Yuengling	the willow tingling of gem pendants
Yurkovich	the son of Yurko, a Russian form of George (farmer)
Zabinski	dweller at the sign of the frog; one thought to resemble a frog
Zacharias, Zachary	descendant of Zacharias or Zachary (whom Jehovah remembers; pure)
Zaleski	dweller beyond the forest
Zalewski	dweller near a flooded place
Zapata	one who made and sold boots and shoes
Zaretsky, Zaritsky	dweller beyond the river
Zebrowski	dweller at the sign of the zebra
Zeidler	one engaged in bee culture; a beekeeper; dweller in a forest region where bees were raised
Zeigler	one who built with or made bricks or roof tiles
Zimmerman, Zimmer, Zimmermann	one who worked in wood; a carpenter
Zuckerman, Zucker	the robber; one who dealt in sugar
Zwicker	one who came from Zwickau (market town), a city and district in Saxony; one who made and sold nails; descendant of Swidiger (strong spear)

UNUSUAL NAMES IN AMERICA

Activities If you have ever thumbed through a postal zip-code directory, you must have given thought once or twice to how exactly a town came up with its name. This game was used by one of the authors to produce several student written-books. All that the children did was go through a directory, find names that intrigued them, and write the Postmaster of that town, asking how the name came to be. Most Postmasters responded, and the children (grades 4–12, all reluctant readers) showed an enthusiasm for reading and writing that they had never had before.

The children had to locate the towns (and be sure to use the zip code), compose the letters, enclose self-addressed, stamped envelopes, and decipher the writing of some of the Postmasters (no small task). After a student had written the report on a particular town, it was typed up and became a part of our "Americana" collection. Every student in the class read the books of other students, and names such as Uneeda and Left Hand, West Virginia, always generated laughter when it came to light how they got their names.

A small number of unusually named towns from each state are included here with zip codes. It is by no means exhaustive, as a quick perusal of any directory will confirm.

ALABAMA

Choccolocco	36254
Hatchechubbee	36858
Lower Peach Tree	36751
Opp	36467
Three Notch	36079

ALASKA

Clam Gulch	99568
Eek	99578
Flat	99584
Kake	99830
Tok	99780

ARIZONA

Blue	85922
Dinosaur City	86434
Eleven Mile Corner	85222
Happy Jack	86024
Surprise	85345

ARKANSAS

Bigflat	72617
Calamine	72418
Clifty	72720
Ink	71948
Old Joe	72659

CALIFORNIA

Big Bear City	92314
Birds Landing	94512
Petaluma	94952
Sheepranch	95250
Toms Place	93514

COLORADO

Cameo	81622
Climax	80429
Crook	80726
Divide	80814
Kit Carson	80825

CONNECTICUT

Cos Cob	06807
Hillside	06610
Moosup	06354

Naugatuck	06770
Rockfall	06481

DELAWARE

Bear	19701
Little Creek	19961
Saint Georges	19733
Winterthur	19735
Woodside	19980

FLORIDA

Bean City	33429
Bee Ridge	33581
Four Points	33406
Kissimme	32741
Okahumpka	32762

GEORGIA

Deepstep	31082
Doctortown	31306
Hephzibah	30815
Kite	31049
Plains	31780

HAWAII

Captain Cook	96704
Haiku	96708
Laupahoehoe	96764
Pawaa	96814
Volcano	96785

IDAHO

Culdesac	83524
Fish Haven	83261
Headquarters	83534
Lava Hot Springs	83246
Squirrel	83447

ILLINOIS

Bourbon	46504
Joy	61260
Moweaqua	62550
Ohio	61349
Oregon	60161

INDIANA

Chili	46926
Deputy	47230
Friendship	47021
Rising Sun	47040
Santa Claus	47579

IOWA

Diagonal	50845
Early	50535
Fertile	50434

Morning Sun	52640
What Cheer	50268

KANSAS

Argentine	66106
Bazaar	66837
Cuba	66940
Gas	66742
Home	66438

KENTUCKY

Democrat	41813
Dwarf	41739
Falls of Rough	40119
Hardshell	41348
Thousand Sticks	41766

LOUISIANA

Blanks	70717
Chef Menteur	70126
Cut Off	70345
Many	71449
Waterproof	71375

MAINE

Christmas Cove	04542
Limerick	04048
Lookout	04651
Mexico	04257
Wytopitlock	04497

MARYLAND

Accident	21520
Chewsville	21721
Cabin John	20731
Dames Quarter	21820
Detour	21725

MASSACHUSETTS

Assinippi	02321
Cuttyhunk	02713
Feeding Hills	01030
Hoosac Tunnel	01339
Sandwich	02563

MICHIGAN

Anvil Location	49902
Bad Axe	48413
Cement City	49233
Dollar Bay	49922
Owosso	48867

MINNESOTA

Ah Gwah Ching	56430
Dent	56528
Powder Horn	55407

243

Sleepy Eye	56085
Traffic	55403

MISSISSIPPI

Bourbon	38729
Chunky	39323
Darling	38623
D'Lo	39062
Egypt	38842

MISSOURI

Arab	63733
Blue Eye	65611
Bourbon	65441
Lone Jack	64070
Mexico	65265

MONTANA

Belt	59412
Box Elder	59521
Circle	59215
Fishtail	59028
Hungry Horse	59919
Savage	59262

NEBRASKA

Bee	68314
Flats	69136
Max	69037
Republican City	68971
Wahoo	68066

NEVADA

Beowave	89821
Contact	89836
Duckwater	89314
Jackass Flats	89023
Owyhee	89832

NEW HAMPSHIRE

Bath	03740
Guild	03754
Pike	03780
Rye	03870
Sandwich	03270

NEW JERSEY

Brainy Boro	08841
Circle	08638
Dividing Creek	08315
Green Pond	07435
Ho Ho Kus	07423
Tranquility	07879

NEW MEXICO

Coyote	87012

Cuba	87013
Elephant Butte	87935
House	88121
Pie Town	87827

NEW YORK

Ausuble Chasm	12911
Bliss	14024
Calcium	13616
Esopus	12429
Neversink	12765

NORTH CAROLINA

Advance	27006
Bee Log	28714
Cooleemee	27014
Kill Devil Hills	27948
Old Trap	27961

NORTH DAKOTA

Backoo	58215
Concrete	58221
Devils Lake	58301
Wild Rice	58080
Zap	58580

OHIO

Bath	44210
Felicity	45120
Kansas	44841
Put In Bay	43456
Wonderland	43020

OKLAHOMA

Bunch	74931
Disney	74340
Lookeba	73053
Okay	74446
Tom	74762

OREGON

Aloha	97006
Dairy	97625
Echo	97826
Riddle	97469
Sixes	97476

PENNSYLVANIA

Bird In Hand	17505
Cuddy	15031
Drums	18222
Egypt	18047
Manns Choice	15550

RHODE ISLAND

Escoheag	02821
Misquamicut	02891

245

Pilgrim	02888
Weekapaug	02891
Wyoso	02898

SOUTH CAROLINA

Ashepoo	29428
Fair Play	29643
Gooches	29720
Peedee	29586
Round O	29474

SOUTH DAKOTA

Box Elder	57719
Crooks	57020
Game Lodge	57730
Mud Butte	57758
Porcupine	57772

TENNESSEE

Bell Buckle	37020
Daisy	37319
Hornbeak	38232
Only	37140
Soddy	37379

TEXAS

Bangs	76823
Cee Vee	79223
Grit	76846
Pointblank	77364
Seven Sisters	78386

UTAH

Echo	84024
Ibapah	84034
Saltair	84101
Tad Park	84074
Zita	86761

VERMONT

Bread Loaf	05753
Mad River Glen	05673
North Hero	05474
Quechee	05059
South Hero	05486

VIRGINIA

Bee	24217
Cash	23028
Horsey	23396
Meadows of Dan	24120
Tiptop	24655

WASHINGTON

B and M	98258
Daisy	99120

Humptulips	98552
Pe Ell	98572
Startup	98293

WEST VIRGINIA

Bozoo	24923
Cucumber	24826
Droop	24933
Flower	26622
Uneeda	25205

WISCONSIN

Black Earth	53515
Combined Locks	54113
Humbird	54746
Land O Lakes	54540
Pound	54161

WYOMING

Bill	82631
Chugwater	82210
Hells Half Acre	82601
Old Faithful	83020
Thumb	83020

A variation on this game is to write only to cities and towns containing, for instance, the word *Bear*. Any word will do. It is very interesting to discover how they selected their respective *Bear* names. The reasons are often as varied as the occurrences.

On a limited scale, we also wrote to unusual names in England, Australia, New Zealand and Canada. The results were gratifying, although a bit more expensive. The point here is that there are many, many variations on this technique to interest children in reading and writing. As stated before, if all other methods have failed, this one could do the trick. What have you to lose?

GOT YOUR EARS ON, GOOD BUDDY?

Activities The United States is a land of fads. From the "hula hoop" to "CB," we have eagerly jumped on the bandwagon of the current phase. Because Citizen-band (CB) radio occupies a special place in the hearts of many Americans, we were quick to utilize this "craze" in working with disabled readers. A new world of colorful language has been opened to us. When you see a three-year-old pick up a seat belt in the car and state that his "handle is Stinky" and "Got Your Ears On, Good Buddy?" you know that it is a motivating influence not to be overlooked. Students will put forth great effort when something is of interest to them. Witness this when the youth of the United States reach sixteen. How quickly, by one method or another, they learn the questions and answers to any driving man-

247

ual, no matter how complex. It is this kind of enthusiasm we must build for the disabled reader. Using CB jargon is one way of catching their interest.

One might start simply by teaching the CB number codes. Many are presented here:

10–1	Receiving poorly
10–2	Receiving well
10–3	Stop transmitting
10–4	Message received
10–5	Relay message
10–6	Busy; Stand by
10–7	Out of service; Leaving air
10–8	In service; Subject to call
10–9	Repeat message
10–10	Transmission completed; Standing by
10–11	Talking too rapidly
10–12	Visitors present (Smokey?)
10–13	Advise weather/road conditions
10–16	Make pickup at
10–17	Urgent business
10–18	Anything for us?
10–19	Nothing for you; Return to base
10–20	My location is
10–21	Call by telephone
10–22	Report in person to
10–23	Stand by
10–24	Completed last assignment
10–25	Can you contact?
10–26	Disregard last information
10–27	I am moving to channel
10–28	Identify your station
10–29	Time is up for contact
10–30	Does not conform to FCC rules
10–32	I will give you a radio check
10–33	Emergency traffic at this station
10–34	Trouble at this station; Help needed
10–35	Confidential information
10–36	Correct time is
10–37	Wrecker needed at
10–38	Ambulance needed at
10–39	Your message delivered
10–41	Please tune to channel
10–42	Traffic accident at
10–43	Traffic tieup at
10–44	I have a message for you
10–45	All units within range please report
10–50	Break channel
10–60	What is next message number?
10–62	Unable to copy; Use phone
10–63	Net directed to
10–64	Net clear
10–65	Awaiting your next message

10–67	All units comply
10–70	Fire at
10–71	Proceed with transmission in sequence
10–73	Speed trap at
10–75	You are causing interference
10–77	Negative contact
10–81	Reserve hotel room for
10–82	Reserve room for
10–84	My telephone number is
10–85	My address is
10–89	Radio repairman needed at
10–90	I have TV
10–91	Talk closer to mike
10–92	Your transmitter is out of adjustment
10–93	Check my frequency on this channel
10–94	Please give me a long count
10–95	Transmit dead carrier for five seconds
10–99	Mission completed; All units secure
10–200	Police needed at

Learning all these numbers and phrases would seem to be very difficult; however, during the last few years, we have seen numerous children with reading problems struggle with the information and gain control of it. This, of course, is just the start of the CB parade. There is much more to learn, and all of it legitimately leads to word recognition and comprehension. Consider the following CB slang terms and meanings:

Term	Meaning
Affirmative	Yes
Aviator	Speeding driver
Back off the hammer	Slow down
Bean store	Restaurant
Bear den	Police station
City kitty	Local police
Country Cadillac	Pickup truck
Double nickel	55 miles per hour speed limit
Draggin' wagon	Tow truck
Ears	CB radio
Eatem up stop	Truckstop
Flagwaver	Road-Construction crew member
Fluff stuff	Snow
Gear jammer	Truck driver
Get horizontal	Go to bed
Haircut palace	Low bridge
Hammer down	Speed
Keep on truckin'	Take it easy
Kiddie car	School bus
Mama bear	Female police officer
Meals on wheels	Truck hauling cattle
Nap trap	Motel
Negative	No
Outdoor TV	Drive-in movie

Picture taker	Radar
Piggy bank	Tollbooth
Rat race	Rush-hour traffic
Read	I understand
Shout	Call on the CB
Smile and comb your hair	Radar ahead
Thermos bottle	Tank truck
Tijuana taxi	Marked police car
We gone	No longer sending;
Where do you get your	Just listening
green stamps?	Where are you employed?

As you can see, CB slang can bring a richness to the reading language of children heretofore disinterested. Did you not find yourself interested in the terms and their definitions? If not, go back and read them again until you begin to see the light.

The CB language has led to other interesting changes in our language. Many cities and towns have been given special names by truckers, which we now hear in our everyday conversation. Some typical renamings include:

Our Talk	Trucker Talk
Boston, Mass.	Bean Town
Chattanooga, Tenn.	Choo Choo Town
Dallas, Tex.	Big D
Houston, Tex.	Astrodome City
Las Vegas, Nev.	Dice City
Miami, Fla.	Bikini City
Milwaukee, Wis.	Beer City
Nashville, Tenn.	Guitar Town
Phoenix, Ariz.	Cactus Patch
Tampa, Fla.	Cigar City
Washington, D.C.	Watergate Town
Georgia	Peach State
Illinois	Land of Lincoln
Iowa	Tall Corn State
Minnesota	Gopher State
Pennsylvania	Quaker State

The "how to" in CB becomes obvious. Allow the children to learn the "slanguage" and put it in print. From that, they can read into make-believe microphones (or real ones if you are fortunate enough to have them) and attempt to confuse a classmate. For example, a message might read as follows:

"Breaker one-one."

"Go Breaker."

"This is Stinky rolling the thermos bottle at milepost 18 on I-80. Got your ears on, good buddy?"

"This is Freight Train talkin' at you. You got a 10-2."

"There's a lot of fluff stuff ahead, and a kiddie car and country Cadillac are twisted together. This gear jammer is lookin' for a nap trap to get horizontal. We gone."

"10-4, Stinky. Keep on truckin'."

If the receiving student is able to translate the message into everyday English, then he has the opportunity to send a message of his own. (It would be a disservice to translate this message for you. Try it yourself and see how much fun it can be.)

It is important to emphasize that you may receive some criticism for allowing your students to work this CB approach, but you can answer your detractors with the results you expect. The majority of your reluctant readers will become interested. "10-4?"

NEWSPAPERS

The reading level of most newspaper articles is reputed to be at about the sixth grade. This is an admirable thing since it offers the opportunity for less-able readers to become informed; but therein can lie a most unique rub.

The headlines of newspapers defy reading, often by even the most educated. The following headline is an example. Read it rather quickly, and then reread at a slower pace.

MCKEAN AWARDS REFUSE CONTRACT, ACCEPTS COMPENSATION BID

Did you say "re-fuse" the first time, or "ref-use?" Confusing, is it not? Disabled readers have even greater difficulty with headlines like this than most of us. Using articles cut from local newspapers to work on understanding headlines has proved helpful.

The shortened form of information commonly found in headlines is not meaningful to a person with a sixth-grade reading ability; it almost requires a Ph.D. in Linguistics to understand. Some examples follow:

LADY SCOTS KNOCK OFF ROCK
BOBCATS CLAW BRAVES
CROP SKI TO FIGHT
REC. COUNCIL SPONS PARTY

Since we have the ability to read the article and figure out the meaning of the esoteric headlines, it is not much of a problem to us. However, it is very confusing to the disabled reader.

Activities The sports section of the newspaper can be an aid here. It interests most adolescents and adults, and sportswriters are perhaps the

251

greatest creators of their own language. Simply taking a few head-lines and explaining the terminology can be very helpful as well as interesting to those with reading difficulties. In many cases, the interest is there, and all you need do is provide the wherewithal. It is simple and it works.

WORDS THAT TALK

Activities   A decade ago, while perusing a copy of a spelling series (Silver-Burdett, 1968), we found funny-looking words. Using them seemed to us a clever way of getting children involved in words. In fact, we found to our delight that the children became totally engrossed and came up with creations far superior to those suggested by the spelling series. A few samples appear on the facing page. The impact that this type of activity has on children is rather obvious.

Other words that may lend themselves to "word-picture" cre-ations are:

amphibians	knot	monkey
chatter	fiesta	happy
shaggy	pry	fossils
compass	moon	reflect
train	cactus	flame
look	cup	nail
wobbly	eye	bounce
candle	ball	bed

BIBLIOGRAPHY

BENTHUL, HERMAN F.; ANDERSON, EDNA A.; UTECH, ARLYS M.; AND BIGGY, M. VIRGINIA. *Spell Correctly*. Morristown, N.J.: Silver Burdett Co., 1968.

Appendix

Sources of Word Histories

ASIMOV, ISAAC. *Words from History*. Boston: Houghton Mifflin Co., 1968a.

_____ . *Words from the Myths*. Boston: Houghton Mifflin Co., 1968b.

_____ . *Words on the Map*. Boston: Houghton Mifflin Co., 1962.

_____ . *Words of Science*. Boston: Houghton Mifflin Co., 1959.

BARNES, DUANE CLAYTON. *Word Lore (Etymology)*. New York: E.P. Dutton and Co., 1968.

BLUMBERG, DOROTHY R. *Whose What?* New York: Holt, Rinehart and Winston, 1973.

EVANS, BERGEN. *Dictionary of Mythology*. Lincoln, Nebr.: Centennial Press, 1970.

FUNK, CHARLES E. *A Hog on Ice*. New York: Paperback Library, 1973.

_____ . *Heavens to Betsy!* New York: Harper and Row, 1955.

_____ . *Thereby Hangs a Tale*. New York: Harper and Row, 1950.

FUNK, WILFRED J. *Word Origins and Their Romantic Stories*. New York: Funk and Wagnalls Co., Harper and Row, 1950.

GARRISON, WEBB. *What's in a Word?* New York: Harper and Row, 1965.

_____ . *Why You Say It*. New York: Abingdon Press, 1955.

GILMARTIN, JOHN G. *Word Study*. Englewood Cliffs, N.J.: Prentice-Hall, 1955.

JENNINGS, GARY. *Personalities of Language*. New York: Thomas Y. Crowell Co., 1965.

KILMOWICZ, BARBARA. *The Word Birds of Davey McFifer*. Nashville, Tenn.: Abingdon Press, 1970.

KURATH, HANS. *A Word Geography of the Eastern U.S.* Ann Arbor, Mich.: University of Michigan Press, 1966.

LAMBERT, ELOISE. *Our Language: The Story of the Words We Use*. New York: Lothrop, Lee and Shepard Co., 1955.

MATHEWS, MITFORD. *American Words*. New York: World Publishing Co., 1959.

MORRIS, WILLIAM, AND MORRIS, MARY. *Dictionary of Word and Phrase Origins*. New York: Harper and Row, vol. 1, 1962; vol. 2, 1967; vol. 3, 1971.

NORMAN, BARBARA. *Tales of the Table.* Englewood Cliffs, N.J.: Prentice-Hall, 1972.

O'NEILL, MARY. *Words, Words, Words.* New York: Doubleday and Co., 1966.

SAGE, MICHAEL. *Words inside Words.* Philadelphia, Pa.: J. B. Lippincott Co., 1961.

SHIPLEY, JOSEPH T. *Dictionary of Word Origins.* New York: The Philosophical Library, 1945.

SOREL, NANCEY. *Word People.* New York: American Heritage Publishing Co., McGraw-Hill Co., 1970.

SORENSEN, THOMAS. *The Word War: The Story of American Propaganda.* New York: Harper and Row, 1968.

Slang

BARREY, LESTER. *The American Thesarus of Slang.* New York: Thomas Y. Crowell, 1953.

FARMER, JOHN STEPHEN. *Slang and Its Analogues, Past and Present* (a dictionary). Kraus-Thompson, 1965.

FRANKLYN, JOHN. *A Dictionary of Rhyming Slang.* Routledge, Kegan and Paul, 1960.

FRASER, EDWARD. *Soldier and Sailor Words and Phrases.* Detroit, Mich.: Gale Research Co., 1968.

LELAND, GODFREY. *The English Gypsies and Their Language.* Detroit, Mich.: Gale Research Co., 1969.

RADFORD, EDWIN. *Unusual Words and How They Came About.* New York: The Philosophical Library, 1946.

SCHMIDT, JACOB EDWARD. *Narcotics: Lingo and Lore.* Charles C. Thomas, 1959.

Acronyms

GALE RESEARCH CO. *Acronyms and Initialism Dictionary.* Detroit, Mich.: 1970.

KAWAKAMI, TOYO. *Acronyms in Education and Behavioral Sciences.* Chicago: American Library Association, 1971.

Dialects

REED, CAROLL E. *Dialects of American English.* Cleveland, Ohio: World Publishing Co., 1967.

Communication

FOSTER, G. ALLEN. *Communication: From Primitive Tom-Toms to Telestar.* Criterion Music Corp., 1965.

Vocabulary

PICKERING, JOHN. *A Vocabulary; or, Collection of Words & Phrases, Which Have Been Supposed to Be Peculiar to the United States of America, to Which Is Prefixed an Essay on the Present State of the English Language in the United States.* Hilliard and Metcalf, 1816.

Word Games

EPSY, WILLARD. *The Game of Words.* New York: Grosset and Dunlap, 1972.
STEIG, WILLIAM. *CDB!* New York: Windmill Books, 1968.

Etymology

PALMER, ABRAHAM SMYTHE. *Folk Etymology: A Dictionary of Verbal Corruptions or Words Perverted in Form or Meaning by False Derivation or Mistaken Analogy.* New York: Greenwood Press, 1969.
WEEKLEY, ERNEST. *The Romance of Words.* London: J. Murray, 1912.

Sources of Acronyms and Blends

CRAWLEY, ELLEN T., AND THOMAS, ROBERT C., eds. *Acronyms and Initialisms Dictionary.* Detroit, Mich.: Gale Research Co., 1970.
KLEINER, RICHARD. *Index of Initials and Acronyms.* Princeton, N.J.: Averbach Publishing Co., 1971.
MOSER, RETA C. *Space-Age Acronyms.* New York: I F I/Plenum Press, 1969.
PUGH, ERIC. *A Dictionary of Acronyms and Abbreviations.* Hamden, Conn.: Archon Books, 1970.
SPILLNER, PAUL. *World Guide to Abbreviations.* New York: Bowker, 1970.

Index